Retreat to the Ghetto

Retreat to the Ghetto

The End of a Dream?

Thomas L. Blair

HILL AND WANG · NEW YORK
A division of Farrar, Straus and Giroux

Copyright © 1977 by Thomas L. Blair
All rights reserved
Published simultaneously in Canada
by McGraw-Hill Ryerson Ltd., Toronto
Printed in the United States of America

First printing, 1977

Designed by Nanette Stevenson

Library of Congress Cataloging in Publication Data

Blair, Thomas Lucien Vincent.
    Retreat to the ghetto.

    Bibliography: p.
    Includes index.
    1. Afro-Americans—Civil rights.   2. Black
power—United States.   3. Black nationalism—
United States.   4. United States—Race relations.
I. Title.
E185.61.B634   1977   301.45'19'6073   77-4723
ISBN 0-8090-8078-8

For Myrtle

Preface

Rebellious protest was the hallmark of the sixties in America, a time when, as Supreme Court Justice William O. Douglas recalls in *Points of Rebellion*, many people saw the establishment as the new King George III and the only redress as revolution. A distinctive feature was the vigorous rise of black protest against segregation and discrimination and for the recognition and respect granted to other Americans. The widespread racial confrontations, the riots, fiery speeches, and militancy of the period, and the links of blacks with the radicalism of student youth, the New Left, and anti-war movements, all gave the black struggle its volatile flavor and its appellation "Black Revolution."

In the forefront of the black man's journey to the barricades were two opposing themes, two banner-waving legions as much in conflict with each other as with a common foe. One was dedicated to the mainstream ideas of non-violent integration and reform associated with Reverend Martin Luther King. The other was committed to the minor, but powerfully emotive, tributary of revolutionary black separatism represented by Malcolm X, a Black Muslim spokesman and founder of the Organization of Afro-American Unity. As each movement vied for the attention of black people and skirmished with the symbols and institutional forms of group oppression—poverty and disenfranchisement—a new dynamic was released and there arose an unprecedented level of mass cultural, economic, and political awareness and a vociferous demand for militant opposition to racism in American society.

This much is history, but what is most important and worthy of the reader's interest is the way in which rebellious ideologies were formulated and expressed, and then tempered and transformed in the crucible of racial dialectics. The book begins with a brief historical review of the themes of integration and separatism, two opposing philosophies by which blacks have dealt with a hostile white society and in the process shaped images of themselves. The black nationalist separatism of Malcolm X is examined, and then follows a chronicle of the eclipse of integration and the rise of Black Power movements. Chapters are devoted to key contemporary ideologies—revolutionary black nationalism, cultural unity, economic equity, and the "new black politics." The trials of strength between differing ideologies and movements are highlighted to illustrate the main ideas and issues which concern and divide black leaders. Special attention is given to organizations and strategies formed in opposition or as alternatives to established structures of order and power, and note is taken of modifications in the realm of life style, morality, and culture. Answers are provided to important questions about the Black Revolution. What were its origins? What leaders, ideas, and social groups sustained it? What brought about its end? What were its relationships with other social forces? What is its legacy?

No judgment of the Black Revolution can rest, however, solely upon an analysis of ideologies and the attitudes of principal adherents. Therefore, critical questions are raised in the book about their relevance to the crisis of survival of the mass of black people located now, after a half century of rural to urban migration, in the labyrinthine slums of the abandoned inner cities, the graveyards of American metropolises.

It seems apparent, though, now that the sound and fury has abated, that blacks have faded from their central place in the superego of America. After all, it is said, the Nixon-Ford Republican Administration has finally toppled, the ignominy of Vietnam is forgotten, the stench of Watergate has cleared, and there are promises of economic stability and progress. The social system has defused, coopted, or eliminated those black elements that too vociferously opposed it. A new class of black civic and political elites serve as intermediaries between black and white society. The protest style of the sixties has given way to the new black politics of today, a reformist strategy of political mobilization which helped catapult a white Southerner, Governor Jimmy Carter, into the presidency. The overwhelming majority of black voting opinion is apparently integrationist in outlook, aiming not at the destruction of American values but at their fulfillment.

From this point of view, it would not be too difficult for Americans, with their indefatigable sense of wonder and belief in national renewal, to sit back and say, "Thank God, the past is done with; let's get on with the future." But, surely, sighs of blessed relief are premature and assumptions that "things are all right" grossly ignore the elementary truths about black protest. Black dissidence in the sixties was aimed at the severe disabilities caused by physical and social segregation. These continue, and the increasingly larger and poorer black urban settlements are in more difficult straits than ever before. One third of all black incomes, compared with 10 percent for whites, are well below official government poverty levels, according to recent survey reports in *The Washington Post*, and 40 percent of all black children live in dire poverty. Though it is arguable that some material progress has been made, nevertheless, the structural supports of racial oppression and the intractable problems facing black people are still very much in evidence. American apartheid, called "ethnic pluralism" or "black separate development," remains, in all respects, the same. For these reasons, among others, the apparent decline and transformation of the sixties Black Revolution does not signal the demise of black dissidence, only the blunting for a time of its cutting edge.

Note by the Author

It is a rare author indeed who owes no debt of gratitude and appreciation. Personally, I do. I am indebted to library staffs for access to historical evidence, authentic sources, bibliographical information, and news clippings of significant events and activities of key individuals. The Schomburg Collection and Center for Research in Black Culture in Harlem, New York, and the library of the Johnson Publishing Company of Chicago deserve special mention. Documentary materials and tape recordings of Malcolm X's speeches were freely made available by George Breitman, and Henri Michaux, proprietor of the Black National Memorial Bookstore in Harlem, now sadly defunct, contributed greatly to my queries.

Two national tours of major American cities with large black populations were a rich source of current information on the changing urban scene and the social and city planning problems facing communities and their leaders. In the course of my travels I met many prominent advocates of civil rights and black political power. I recall, especially, in Atlanta, dinner with Rev. and Mrs. Ralph David Abernathy of the Southern Christian Leadership Conference and a midnight visit to the fire-lit memorial to Martin Luther King, Jr., a breakfast meeting at Paschal's with Georgia State Senator Julian Bond, an interview with Maynard Jackson during his mayoralty campaign, and informal talks with the interracial staff of Congressman Andrew Young, now U.S. ambassador to the United Nations. I remember vividly informative conversations in Washington, D.C., with California Congressman Ronald Dellums and his family, and my trip to Newark's city hall to see Mayor Kenneth Gibson and to visit the Temple of Kawaida headquarters of Imamu Amiri Baraka's Congress of Afrikan Peoples.

One recognizes, too, the insights gained on street corners and in parks and playgrounds "rappin" with Black Panthers and Black Muslims hawking their papers, with West Indian black nationalists at "Garvey Day" and Caribbean festivals, and with youth leaders at "Harambee" and "Africa Day" celebrations. There were hundreds of encounters, many of them all too brief, like that one summer evening in New York with Mrs. Betty Shabazz, widow of Malcolm X. All of them were miniature cameos in sound, color, and feeling of people's lives. I was privileged to meet and talk with people from many different walks of life—a city garbage-disposal worker in Memphis, a retired auto mechanic in St. Louis, the wife of a farmer and school-bus driver in the rural South, a mechanical engineer in Boston, a policeman in Brooklyn, the wife of a commercial pilot in Denver, a linoleum layer in New Jersey, a Catholic nun in New York City, a medical technologist who emigrated from Haiti, the daughter of a railroad foreman in Pittsburgh, a Muslim minister, a woman college professor in a small New England town, an eighty-five-year-old retired farmer and devout Baptist, a cable splicer for a public-utility company in Baltimore, city-planning students in Ann Arbor, Michigan, a real-estate broker in eastern Long Island, a Newark mother with three children living on welfare, an unemployed automobile worker in Detroit, and laborers, domestic servants, and service personnel in cafés, bars, hotels, offices, and factories in many states.

Participation in conferences and symposia helped me to assess the ebb and flow of opinion, especially among the middle classes. *The New York Times* seminar "A Decade of Black Revolution: Illusion and Reality," convened under the sponsorship of A. M. Rosenthal, managing editor, and chaired by Ernest Holsendolph, financial correspondent, gave me insights into key civil-rights issues as seen in retrospect a decade after the March on Washington. The Phelps-Stokes Fund Conference on Black Research Priorities, organized by Professor Charles V. Hamilton of Columbia University's Department of Government and Dr. Mabel Smythe, the fund's vice-president for research and publications, helped to illuminate the state of mind of the nation's eminent black academics. A seminar convened by the directors of the Metropolitan Applied Research Center, Professors Kenneth B. Clark and Hylan Lewis of the City University of New York, offered an opportunity to discuss views about alternative futures for America's "Black Cities" with an invited audience of professionals and practitioners in the field of housing and urban renewal.

My research was enriched by reference to the art and culture of black people, and by many long discussions over the years with university academics, among whom I would like to mention particularly Harold Cruse, Professor of History, Center for Afro-American and African Studies, University of Michigan; Elliott P. Skinner, Franz Boas Professor of Anthropology at Columbia University and former U.S. ambassador to Upper Volta; Hollis R. Lynch, Professor of History and Director of the Institute of African Studies at Columbia University; and John Henrik Clarke, Professor of Black Studies, Hunter College.

Thanks are due to C. Gerald Fraser, doyen of metropolitan journalism, for his advice and unfailing readiness to be of help, and to his colleague on *The New York Times* Charlayne Hunter, for many kindnesses; one notes as well the friendly supportive role of a wider circle of journalists—Ed Cumberbatch, Ernest Dunbar, Tom Johnson, Paul Delaney, Ron Smothers, Nancy Hicks, and George Goodman.

The writer is also deeply conscious of the degree to which his efforts were stimulated to fruition by the love of family and many old friends, among whom I value highly Rosa Guy, Paule Marshall, Maya Angelou, and Abbey Lincoln.

Contents

Perspectives

"1964 will see the Negro revolt evolve and merge into the worldwide black revolution that has been taking place on this earth since 1945. The so-called revolt will become a real black revolution . . . Revolution is always based on land. Revolution is never based on begging somebody for an integrated cup of coffee. Revolutions are never fought by turning the other cheek. Revolutions are never based upon love-your-enemy and pray-for-those-who-spitefully-use-you. And revolutions are never waged singing "We Shall Overcome." Revolutions are based upon bloodshed. Revolutions are never compromising. Revolutions are never based upon negotiations. Revolutions are never based upon any kind of tokenism whatsoever. Revolutions are never even based upon that which is begging a corrupt society or a corrupt system to accept us into it. Revolutions overturn systems. And there is no system on this earth which has proven itself more corrupt, more criminal, than this system that in 1964 still colonizes 22 million African-Americans, still enslaves 22 million Afro-Americans."

Malcolm X, "The Black Revolution"

"The White Man's Heaven Is the Black Man's Hell."

> Title of a popular song inspired
> by the Nation of Islam.

"We took a trip on a Greyhound bus
To fight segregation where we must.
Freedom, freedom, give us freedom."

> Refrain sung by integrationist
> Freedom Riders to the calypso beat
> of "Banana Boat," 1961

"For the revolutionary black youth of today, time starts with the coming of Malcolm X. Before Malcolm, time stands still, going down in frozen steps into the depths and the stagnation of slavery . . . Malcolm prophesied the coming of the gun to the black liberation struggle. Huey P. Newton picked up the gun and pulled the trigger, freeing the genie of black revolutionary violence in Babylon."

> Eldridge Cleaver,
> *Post-Prison Writings and Speeches*

"We believe we can end police brutality in our black community by organizing black self-defense groups that are dedicated to defending our black community from racist police oppression and brutality."

> Founding principle of the
> Black Panther Party, 1966

"There is more power in socially organized masses on the march than there is in guns in the hands of a few desperate men. Our enemies would prefer to deal with a small armed group rather than a huge, unarmed but resolute mass of people."

> Reverend Martin Luther King, Jr., 1962

"You can be up to your boobies in white satin, with gardenias in your hair and no sugar cane for miles, but you can still be working on a plantation."

Billie Holiday

"We armed ourselves solely to defend ourselves. And if we hadn't been armed we would have been the victims of one of the first modern pogroms against the Afro-American. Let the newspapers wail and bemoan about our rifles with the Communist insignia. I don't care what kind of insignias the rifles had on them. They were a godsend to us that Sunday, August 27, 1961."

Robert Williams, *Negroes with Guns*

"Don't protest against the puppet. Go work on the puppeteer. Go get the director of the show and take him off the scene, and then you can change the cast or you can change the script."

Malcolm X

"We must build pride among ourselves. We must think politically and get power because we are the only people in this country that are powerless. We are the only people who have to protect ourselves against our protectors . . . We have to get us some Black Power."

Stokely Carmichael, Chicago
July 28, 1966

"The whole NAACP program is about building group power . . . But not separate or black power . . . We must be for change, yes. Reform, yes. Sharp alteration in methods, yes. Acceleration, most certainly so. But separation, no."

Roy Wilkins, Annual Report of the
National Association for the
Advancement of Colored People, 1968

"Until the Harlems and racial ghettos of our nation are destroyed and the Negro is brought into the mainstream of American life, our beloved nation will be on the verge of being plunged into the abyss of social disruption. No greater tragedy can befall a nation than to leave millions of people with a feeling that they have no stake in their society."

Reverend Martin Luther King, Jr.,
during the summer riots of 1964

"We put America on notice: IF WHITE FOLKS WANT TO PLAY NAZIS, BLACK FOLKS AIN'T GOING TO PLAY JEWS."

H. Rap Brown,
Black Power activist, 1967
(The March on Washington, August 28, 1963)

"Personally, I marched that day, not with a black civil rights group but with the American Civil Liberties Union. I am delighted I did because I think it showed a perception of where the fight in the future was going to be for people like me—civil liberties, free speech, etc. I think now it would be very difficult for me to have credibility in the black community were I to so openly identify in the civil rights movement aspect of my life with a group whose leadership was so completely white, with the exception of one or two of us."

Mrs. Patricia R. Harris, lawyer and diplomat (appointed Secretary of Housing and Urban Development by President Carter), at *The New York Times* seminar, July 1973

"There's a growing awareness behind the walls; we're seeing through the madness of capitalism, class interest, surplus value and imperialism, which this Gestapo system perpetuates. It's this which we have to look at and understand in order to recognize the inhumanity inflicted upon the masses of the people here in America and abroad. As Brother Malcolm X once said, 'We as people, as human beings, have the basic human right to eliminate the conditions that have and are continuously destroying us.' "

Fleeta Drumgo,
in a letter from Soledad prison, 1970

"A black woman is a soldier. Revolution is a woman, a black woman in a blond wig and a docile face, sitting sweetly in the Pentagon mistyping or somehow delaying the orders directing the National Guards to Watts or Detroit. Revolution is a woman with a baby in a blanket—and a bomb. A black woman is a soldier, and, in the months and years ahead, she will stand side by side with her man in the escalation of our struggle to a new and necessary level."

> *Black Scholar*, special issue
> on the black soldier, November 1970

"Given the position of the Negro American population as a numerical minority of one-tenth and an economic, political and social minority of far less than one-tenth, the only tactical road for the black minority is integration into the general population."

> Roy Wilkins, Executive Director,
> National Association for the
> Advancement of Colored People, 1970

"Well now, a few years ago you so-called civil rights leaders told us that the most militant and progressive and meaningful thing that we could do was to integrate a lily-white suburb. Well, we took you at your word. My wife and I took the bull by the horns and we moved into Lovely Lane next door to Gorgeous Gardens. We bought a split-level house and we mowed the lawn. We faced all the gaff, all the rocks and garbage and the burning crosses and the isolation. Now, we have overcome. We are accepted by our neighbors. They invite us over for cocktails and we have them over for tea. But now we're called Uncle Toms for living out there with all those white folks."

> Comment of a middle-class black
> man to James Farmer, 1968

"I'll start by pleading guilty to a certain rigidity. I am, in terms of the goals in the civil rights movement. In 1973, I plead guilty that I see precisely the same goals I saw when I was an undergraduate in 1933, when I was a graduate student in the forties and when I entered the struggle in the early fifties—namely, freedom, the right of individual blacks to the same choices that other Americans have."

> Professor Kenneth B. Clark,
> *The New York Times* seminar,
> July 1973

"Political power and public office have been the keys which opened the doors of opportunity for various groups in America since the founding of our country. What is new in our day, however, is the use of political power and public office in pursuing the hopes and aspirations of black people."

> Edward Brooke of Massachusetts,
> lone black U.S. senator

"They ain't dead. No sir. Martin Luther King, the Kennedys and all the other civil rights figures are not dead. They're still in business, just moved upstairs."

Reverend Martin Luther King, Sr., prayer in support of nomination of Governor Jimmy Carter for President, 1976 Democratic Party Convention, New York

"How'm I doing? I'm just livin', man, livin' by the Grace of God."

> Elderly elevator operator
> in a downtown
> Chicago office building, 1976

"This electoral contest, taking place in an arena which is, presently, at the very center of the troubled world, seems to have invested the black vote with a power, and exhibits toward it a respect, which the black vote has never, in the memory of the living, had before . . . No matter how diversely, and with what contradictions, the black vote is cast in the 24 years left of this century's life, the impact of the visible, overt, black pres-

ence on the political machinery of this country alters, forever, the weight
and meaning of the black presence in the world."

James Baldwin,
The New York Times Book Review
September 26, 1976

Retreat to the Ghetto

1 Consciousness: Two Modes of Action

America in the seventies entered her third century of independence. The nation had passed through the traumas of colonial revolution and fratricidal civil war, the tumult and rewards of immigration, westward expansion, and rapid urban and industrial growth, the misery of depression and recurring national crises, two devastating world wars and the awesome responsibilities of unparalleled global power, but in the process—whatever happened to Black America?

Black communities in America are more than three hundred years old and with few exceptions remain segregated, powerless, and at a marginal level of existence. The historical pattern is one of forced emigration from Africa to the New World, plantation slavery, rural feudalism, and debt bondage, and in modern times racial co-existence on the basis of inequality. Black history must be seen, therefore, as a response to these incontrovertible facts. In this perspective, the black man's revolts, his prophetic religions, cultural negritude, and long periods of despair, the tactics of civil rights and civil disobedience, and the contradictory longings for integration or separatism are clearly revealed as adaptations and reactions to the not inconsequential impact of American society on transplanted African peoples.

America established the first successful republic of the modern era, and its democratic apparatus—its federalism and written constitution and bill of rights—has been copied around the world. Yet its rise to greatness is based in large part on a special blend of materialism and imperfect idealism, low cunning and high-mindedness. Its political history is as much a combination of demagogues as of democrats, and many episodes in its economic history provide sordid examples of the pillage of the earth's human and natural resources as fodder for its voracious productive system.

America is a unique testament to ethnic, religious, and linguistic pluralism—a "Nation of Nations," to use Walt Whitman's phrase—but it is also an example of the often heavy-handed use of state and private power to control fractious minorities and suppress opposition to the dominant ideology. At many stages of recent history there have been dangerous signs of American fascism, as evident on Wall Street, Main Street, and Tobacco Road as along the Potomac, and of gentlemen of piety, property, and standing who fanned the flames of hatred and conflict to protect their dominance and profit.

While it is true that America has created a distinctive mode of production, material benefits, and styles of life and institutional forms which have assimilated millions of Europe's poor into an unparalleled industrial democracy, it is also true that there is an unacceptable face of this democracy whose past is as dark as its complexion, and whose future seems darker still. There is an air of pious fraudulence in a nation that still remains the beloved community of white Anglo-Saxon Protestants, of Emerson, Thoreau, Melville, Twain, James, and others, and where the essential social levers of opportunity—education, jobs, housing, and political power—are kept out of the reach of the masses of black citizens. Upstairs in the bourgeois, suburban, materialistic House of America there is splendor, downstairs a crowded cellar of squalid confusion.

The ethos of American culture stresses competition; yet there exists a caste-like stratification which relegates blacks to a largely disadvantaged lower-class position. This racially based oppression, different from that of class or national origin, places upon them a special stigma. Immigrants from Europe, no matter how traduced, can still rejoice with Goethe: "Amerika, du hast es besser," no monarchy, no Jacobins, no restrictions, a land of opportunity; and even the poorest white man is infected with the grandeur of his race. But blacks have been forced to accept, and whites have condoned and forcefully encouraged, a pattern of adaptation which does not threaten the economic system, duly constituted government, and white supremacy.

Today, the existence of a large, disaffected black and poor subject population haunts America in its headlong quest for supremacy of the world and nature. The periodic spasms of black dissent relate and respond to all matters which concern Americans: the management of the economy, the use of governmental power in periods of crisis, the impact of industrialization on society, the monolithic industry and labor unions, the conflict of opinions about capitalism versus socialism, and the struggles between party and non-party liberals, conservatives, and radicals over the role of the state. Yet, for blacks, the issue, above all others, is exploitation and racism, the basic causes of conflict and disorder in society.

From the colonial period to this day there are two identifiable modes of action which blacks have used to assault the barriers that violate their rights as Americans and as human beings. One is to submerge their African heritage and despised traits of character, and by political and legal mechanisms and cultural imitation become integrated into the society as a whole. The other is to restructure black groups in order to resist white-imposed social deformations and to adapt to new circumstances with a revived sense of pride in their black heritage.

These two modes of action, one of integration and the other of separatism, were evident as long ago as the anti-slavery debates early in America's history. It was obvious in 1827 to educated free Negroes like Samuel Cornish, a Presbyterian minister and editor of *Freedom's Journal*, the first black newspaper, that one's color and previous condition of servitude were not sufficient reasons for withholding constitutional rights of freedom and equality. "You are COLORED AMERICANS; the Indians are RED AMERICANS, and the white people are WHITE AMERICANS," he used to say to his congregation, "and *You are as good as they, and they are no better than you.*" It was equally obvious to the rich black Massachusetts merchant and shipowner Paul Cuffe that "Africa, not America, is your country and your home," and immediate steps should be taken to emigrate and establish colonies in Africa. By mid-century these differing points of view were hotly debated. The colored peoples' conventions of the period, first convened in 1830 in Philadelphia, declared an implacable struggle for equal rights but also seriously discussed the necessity for racial unity and separatism. Key strategies included violence and rebellion to end slavery, economic cooperation for racial progress, independent political party activity, and emigration to Africa.

The conflict between integrationist and separatist tendencies was sharply evident in the contrasting efforts of two black leaders, Frederick Douglass and Martin Robison Delany. Douglass, son of a plantation owner and a slave woman, was perhaps the most famous agitator for desegregation, equal rights, and assimilation. He was the editor of *North Star*, the foremost black abolitionist journal launched in 1847, and an exponent of close collaboration with white anti-slavery societies. Douglass achieved lasting fame in the 1840's as a peripatetic propagandist recounting the tales of his flight from slavery, later recorded in his autobiography *My Bondage and My Freedom* (1855). The eloquence and resourcefulness of Douglass and his fellow abolitionist propagandists, William Wells Brown, Henry Bibb, Harriet Tubman, and Sojourner Truth, moved Northern white liberal audiences to tears, and kindled their belief that slaves were worthy of emancipation.

Martin Robison Delany, a highly esteemed, Harvard-educated physician and medical officer in the Union Army, was a leading advocate of emigration back to Africa. In his view he would rather have "Heathenism and Liberty before Christianity and Slavery." He vociferously opposed Frederick Douglass and the paternalism of white anti-slavery societies who presumed to speak for the Afro-American. As a testimony of his beliefs, Delany wrote an impressive book, *The Condition, Elevation, Emigration and Destiny of the Colored People of the United States, Politically Considered* (1852). In it he set down what is now the traditional schema of black nationalist separatist discourse: an exposition of the dire condition of blacks, a list of past racial accomplishments, a critique of wasteful efforts to change equal-rights movements from sterile debating societies into activist groups, and finally recognition of the African heritage and a project for a homeland in Africa. Delany believed the ultimate power of the black cause lay in the fact that whites were a world minority and that blacks everywhere should be prepared to fight hard against white domination to win respect and acknowledgment as equals.

The warring tendencies—integration and separatism—were not at this early stage concepts which rallied different people into diametrically opposite camps. They were two hostile tendencies within the same minds, each brought forward at different times to serve different purposes. Douglass, after his disillusionment with the anti-slavery societies, when speaking to black audiences often called for racial unity and solidarity. He urged that black people take the lead in the struggle for their own freedom and acceptance in American society. Yet, he was moved to say in a moment of candor, while speaking to a white audience on Independence Day, 1852, "This Fourth of July is *yours*, not *mine*. You may rejoice, I must mourn." Delany had a long and distinguished U.S. Army career in which he saw himself as a model of how, if given the chance, the Afro-American could demonstrate his sterling qualities and readiness for freedom and integration into American society. On the one hand, he could say, "We are Americans with natural claims upon this country"; on the other hand, rather than wait till Doomsday for equal rights, Delany sometimes felt it was wiser to emigrate and establish a "national position for ourselves."

This dream of self-determination and, if necessary, emigration from the harsh conditions prevalent in the South found its fruition at the end of the Reconstruction period 1865–75, when the gains of slave emancipation and federal protection were retracted and officially sanctioned second-class citizenship hung like a millstone around the masses of Afro-Americans. Educational opportunities were severely limited. Blacks were barred from white schools, and the few schools provided for them by white authorities were inferior. Jobs other than sharecropping were scarce. Crops failed. Many families faced starvation and thousands left their homelands to seek work in other parts of the country. The threat of racial decimation cast an ominous shadow on a beleaguered race and strengthened the resolve of the black middle and lower classes to build a community life around their own schools, small businesses, churches, and fraternal and mutual-aid societies.

Eminent spokesmen like Francis J. Grimké argued consistently for black control of their own schools and colleges. Religious leaders like Bishop Henry M. Turner of the African Methodist Episcopal Church reckoned that "the Negro race has as much chance of being a man in the United States as a frog has in a snake den." Turner preached that God is black and would wreak vengeance against the black man's enemies. In this opinion he was joined by several notable clergymen who denounced whites as ugly, primitive, amoral beasts whose ancestors were uncivilized by comparison with those in the great black kingdoms of antiquity. The only way blacks could achieve racial dignity, Turner often said, was by rejecting American society and either founding a separate nation in America or emigrating back to Africa. Arthur Anderson, another black leader, emphasized the growing interest in territorial separation by calling for the creation of a black nation in America subsidized by a $600 million indemnity from the government in repayment for the period of slavery, the loss of human lives, and the loss of country. He proposed that if the government did not heed this request, then the International Court of Justice at The Hague should be asked to endorse the Afro-American's case for nationhood as if black Americans comprised a modern nation in every respect, yet without protection, a flag, or a country.

Mass emigration from the Deep South to the West in the late 1870's was a characteristic response of black people during this desolate period. Their leaders, avowed separatists like Henry Adams of Louisiana and Benjamin "Pap" Singleton of Tennessee, petitioned Congress and President Rutherford B. Hayes for help and protection. If this was not possible, they asked the government to set aside a territory in the United States where blacks could settle in peace. Furthermore, if this plea was rejected, they asked for money and transport to Liberia, a free African state. Finally, they were determined to seek help from foreign governments should Congress refuse their requests. Though mass resettlement, especially in the North, was eventually aborted in 1880 by the grim hardship in the bleak climate and barren lands of the new territories and by the hostility of property owners, employers, and white settlers, nevertheless scores of all-black towns were established, particularly in the southwestern regions. Langston and Boley, Oklahoma, and Tennessee Town in Kansas, for example, had their own black governments, businesses, schools, and churches. And when the vision of an all-black state in the Oklahoma Territory failed, black colonists followed "Chief" Alfred Sam, an alleged Ashanti ruler, in an ill-fated attempt to settle in West Africa.

At the turn of the century, two men, Booker T. Washington and Dr. W. E. B. Du Bois, again reflected the differing attitudes toward integration and separatism. Washington, an outstanding educator and public speaker, accepted the "separate-but-equal" segregationist doctrine of his day and counseled members of his race to raise their own standards of living through hard work, self-help, and mutual solidarity. Opportunities abound if we would only grasp them, he said, and in one famous speech at the Atlanta Exposition in 1895 he urged the race to "cast down your buckets where you are" and cultivate the virtues of thrift, industry, Christian character, and the acquisition of property. Washington favored industrial and vocational training as the means of building prosperous communities and creating a capitalist employer class and "black captains of industry." To achieve these goals of self-development Washington's strategy was to bargain for the South's tolerance and the North's philanthropy with a promise of non-engagement in the field of civil rights. He assured whites that they had nothing to fear from his philosophy. "In all things purely social, we can be separate as the fingers, yet one as the hand in all things essential to mutual progress."

Washington's philosophy was one of appeasement and accommodation. He deprecated political activity, minimized the extent of racial prejudice, and often described Southern whites as the black man's best friend. In retrospect, accommodation was a form of conservative economic policy deftly used to gain time and financial resources to build schools and businesses. Washington founded a world-renowned vocational and technical school, Tuskegee Institute in Alabama, and organized rural credit and supply programs to aid black farmers and sharecroppers. He and his followers launched scores of small businesses in major cities and towns, and through the National Negro Business League encouraged the growth of marketing, retail, and real-estate activities in black communities, and trading relations with Africa. Washington laid the foundations of an economic theory for black development and his ideas infused all subsequent arguments for self-determination and economic advancement.

The major opponent of Washington's accommodationist ideas was W. E. B. Du Bois, an outstanding Harvard-educated social scientist, and a small interracial group of middle-class intellectuals and liberals. Du Bois and his associates placed full responsibility for the race problem squarely on the shoulders of racist whites. He denounced the inequities of the separate-but-equal doctrine, which barely masked the racism evident in segregation and the disenfranchisement laws. "Citizenship rights must be the same for all Americans," Du Bois said, "and the right to vote is essential for the economic progress of Negroes." Du Bois argued for immediate and complete integration, even assimilation, and created a national uproar because nearly all influential opinion at the turn of the century, on both sides of the color line, endorsed accommodation and segregation as the appropriate solution to the race problem.

Du Bois took issue with Washington on several counts. He favored intellectual not vocational training. He fought for civil rights rather than accept the pernicious implications of second-class status. He was an avowed integrationist and, following the bloody anti-black Springfield riots of 1908, founded with substantial white support the National Association for the Advancement of Colored People (NAACP), dedicated to litigation, legislation, and education on behalf of his race. But Du Bois also believed in the value of "race organizations" and collective racial endeavor in all fields, a belief expressed in his seminal publication *The Conservation of Races*, written in 1897. The salvation of the race lay, he believed, in forging a sound economic base. He encouraged a program of "cooperative economics" managed by black entrepreneurs operating within a "group economy." The black man's destiny, he said, was to be at the forefront of "Pan-Negroism"; his goal was not absorption by whites or a servile imitation of Anglo-Saxon culture but rather to preserve and develop a separate culture based on Negro ideals.

Cooperative black economics, Du Bois believed, was a healthy goal in a racist society, a goal he stressed to his black readers after he became editor of the NAACP's *Crisis* magazine in 1910. Pursued openly and implacably, and guided by a broader vision of changing world political and industrial forces, it would provide the basis of a revolutionary program for black development. At the heart of his program, which drew heavily upon the ideas of the utopian socialists, Robert Owen and Charles Fourier, was the necessity for economic planning to ensure adequate incomes for all members of the black community. Black-owned factories, farms, and merchandising operations would be run on a cooperative basis to eliminate private gain and thus place surplus capital at the service of the community. Black-controlled educational institutions, hospitals, socialized medicine, and cooperative organizations of black professionals would serve needy persons without regard to personal profit. Through cooperative economics a considerable store of white capital and resources in the black community could be released and transferred to the people. Du Bois foresaw the possibility that these demands could lead to a climactic rupture with what he considered archaic forms of laissez-faire capitalism, but blacks and the ascendant laboring classes would win concrete gains in the course of the struggle.

Though caught up in the political pursuit of integration, his major objective, Du Bois nevertheless staunchly defended his idea of a "New Negro" led by a corps of militant intellectuals, the "Talented Tenth." What was required was not dependence on the help of whites but organization for self-help, the encouragement of "manliness without defiance, conciliation without servility." The essential planks in the political platform of renascent Afro-Americans should be, Du Bois said, no less than full advancement through self-directed social change. The minimum program of demands he fashioned as early as 1903 expressed the goals of many later black organizations, both integrationist and separatist. Its four essentials were: full civil and political rights and the formation of legal aid and defense funds; universal education, industrial job training for the working masses, and higher education for selected youth; self-pride and self-knowledge through periodicals and scholarly studies; and an effective federation of voluntary societies and economic activities.

For the distant future, which Du Bois hoped would see the end of world colonialism, he sought common cause with the colonial peoples of Africa, Latin America, and the Caribbean, Egypt, China, and India. He examined the plight of non-whites under colonial rule and concluded that science denies the existence of super-races or of those naturally, inevitably, and eternally inferior. "The problem of the Twentieth Century," he declared in *The Souls of Black Folk* (1903), "is the problem of the color line," a theme he saw as increasingly international in scope. Its roots are economic and not racial, he advised delegates to the Second Pan-African Congress in Paris, 1919, and the main division in the world is not between "civilized Europeans and pagans" but between "exploiters and toilers." The wars of national liberation and armed and indignant protests of subject peoples are not racial in origin; they are the result of man's common urge to regain his own land, dignity, labor, and freedom. Du Bois's prophetic view of the black man in the twentieth century, and his poetic intuition about the value of historical black experience, tradition, and links with Africa gave him a position of centrality in all discussions of black unity and Pan-Africanism, of which he was a most important advocate.

Dreams of racial uplift and Pan-Africanism propounded by middle-class black intellectuals took second place to the scramble for employment in the first quarter of the twentieth century. The lure of booming wartime factories and cash wages attracted blacks to major Northern cities. Work was at hand, at the lowest levels of unskilled labor, but when the jobs reserved for blacks were filled, the new migrants were the hardest hit casualties of the urban economy. Jobless blacks joined the army of unemployed reserves; they were used occasionally as strikebreakers, and they became a supply of cheap labor and targets for the hostility of the new white immigrant working classes. There was a hardening of segregation and racial injustice. Anti-black violence took its toll in many cities. It seemed as if all the efforts of middle-class blacks were in vain and the black masses had naught for their comfort.

This grim setting marked the emergence, in the war years and immediately thereafter, of the first authentic and the largest separatist Black Nationalist mass movement. Marcus Moziah Garvey, a Jamaican, fresh from his travels in Latin America, Europe, and England, seized the opportunity in 1917 to try to organize slum-shocked urban blacks into a proud and productive community. Garvey was a stockily built, dark-skinned man descended from the black Maroons of Jamaica, whose fierce resistance against slavery won for them a treaty of independence from Britain in 1739. He was filled with profound dissatisfaction over the social and economic plight of the Negro; speaking to his earliest audiences in Harlem, he told them that a black skin was not a badge of shame but a symbol of racial greatness. At first, Garvey's organizational efforts were directed at the small, isolated West Indian community in Harlem. By 1919, according to Garvey's calculations, there were two million members and thirty branches in America of the Universal Negro Improvement Association and the African Communities League with the dual purpose of strengthening black communities and spearheading the liberation of Africa.

In America, Garvey, an admirer of Booker T. Washington's ideas of racial betterment and self-sufficiency, dreamed of black metropolises emerging as self-contained communities with their own political leaders, capitalists, professionals, technicians, and working class. His supporters established hundreds of small businesses, a chain of grocery shops, restaurants, laundries, hotels, a doll factory, and a printing plant and newspaper—*Negro World*. Garvey created the unique characteristics of the movement—a love of Africa; a black, green, and red flag; an anthem, "Ethiopia, Thou Land of Our Fathers"; and the African Orthodox Church, whose archbishop, Reverend George Alexander McGuire, preached of a black God, a black Christ, and a black Madonna.

"Up, you mighty race, you can accomplish what you will," Garvey roared, and his words, recorded in a noteworthy collection, *The Philosophy and Opinions of Marcus Garvey* (1923), captured the spirit of all blacks who listened to his speeches at Liberty Hall in Harlem or heard of Garvey by word of mouth. Garvey advocated an end to colonialism and called for migration back to Africa. He reasoned that whites would always be racists and that the black man must develop a civilization of his own. "The Negro in America will never be safe and secure unless there is a free and independent Africa," he said; "Africa for the Africans, at home and abroad" was his oft-quoted slogan.

No other black organization in history had been able to reach and stir so many black people and receive from them the generous support that Garvey obtained. Within a few years, news of his UNIA movement and his programs and policies of race redemption had reached a national and worldwide audience and penetrated every corner of colonial Africa. Estimates of Garvey's popularity at its peak in the early 1920's vary enormously. Most observers reckon that his own figures are grossly exaggerated, but certainly 50,000 people marched in support of his UNIA convention in Harlem in 1920, and in the ten years of the movement's heyday Garvey may have received dues from 250,000 enthusiastic members and had up to 2 million sympathizers in America and around the world. The beginning of the end came, however, in 1925, when Garvey was accused of, and sentenced to prison for, using the mails to defraud shareholders in his ill-fated enterprise, the Black Star Steamship Line. Toward the end of his career, Garvey urged his followers to "consolidate the political forces of the Negro through which the race will express its political opinion." He formed the Universal Negro Political Union and in the 1924 presidential election issued a nationwide list of candidates for his followers to support. Three years later, he was deported to Jamaica and after working there to form a Jamaican People's Party he left for London, where he died in 1940.

The twenties and thirties were difficult decades for most black people. The fervor of black separatism gave way before the necessity of securing jobs and cooperating with Roosevelt's New Deal, government bureaucrats, industrial and trade-union leaders, liberals, socialist militants, and intellectuals. There were mixed responses in black communities, however. Sufi Abdul Hamid organized the Negro Industrial and Clerical Alliance in the early 1930's as a means of providing jobs for unemployed blacks in Chicago's South Side and New York's Harlem. Many would-be entrepreneurs eschewed theoretical discussion and launched strikes and boycotts against white-owned businesses in black areas. Their motto was "Don't Buy Where You Can't Work" and "Support the 'Double Duty Dollar' "—that is, by purchasing household goods from local black businessmen and thereby advancing the race. Associations of skilled technical and clerical job seekers were organized in major cities to penetrate middle-class job markets, a notable example being the New Negro Alliance of Washington, D.C., whose motto was "Buy Where You Work—Buy Where You Clerk."

At the same time, during the twenties and thirties, there was an influx into black communities of trade unionists, socialists, and Communists advocating interracial equality and brotherhood. The Communists urged that Negroes be given the same political and industrial rights as whites, including the right to work, equal wages, admission into all workers' parties and trade unions, and the abolition of discrimination in all public places. Benjamin J. Davis, the foremost black Communist Party member, affirmed that the Negro struggle was not only part of the revolutionary movement of the whole American working class but was connected with the struggles of national minorities and colonial peoples throughout the world. Negro victories in the United States were therefore contributions to the cause of the world socialist revolution and the eventual triumph of the dictatorship of the proletariat.

Nevertheless, Davis put forward in his book *The Path of Negro Liberation* (1947) a controversial argument, first proposed by Communists in the thirties, for the right of self-determination in the heavily populated "Black Belt" of the South. In his view, blacks had been oppressed and molded into nationhood by a common struggle against American racism. The components of black nationhood were clearly visible, he said, and included a historically evolved stable community of language, territory, economic life, and psychological make-up manifested by a community of culture. Furthermore, they had a class structure which included a proletariat, a petit bourgeoisie, professionals, a middle class, and a distinct but weak capitalist class. He supported the right of self-determination as a step toward black-controlled, collectively run communities on the style of Russian soviets; but he stressed the need to leave open the possibility of black-white cooperation, particularly with white workers and poor farmers, against the common enemy, the big trusts and semi-feudal landlords. Equality of blacks and whites in the black Southern soviets, once established, would represent the highest expression of proletarian unity. It would represent the final triumph of class over race.

Black Communists like Ben Davis were skilled at propagating a theory of the two stages of development toward proletarian unity across the color line. Black unity, at certain stages of the socialist confrontation with capitalism, was a correct position insofar as it led to the withering away of racial chauvinism and the formation of a broad movement of unity among all workers regardless of color or ethnic background. The Communist Party during the years from 1930 to 1945 became the leading militant advocate of a black struggle for equal rights; at the same time it proclaimed "Black and White, Unite and Fight." In the vanguard of these activities was an emergent cadre of black Marxists, men like Ben Davis, William L. Patterson, James W. Ford, Louis Burnham, James E. Jackson, Pettis Perry, Hosea Hudson, Henry Winston, and Claude M. Lightfoot.

Perhaps the most notable non-Communist organizer of black working-class movements was A. Philip Randolph, who rose to prominence after World War I as editor of a radical socialist magazine, *The Messenger*. Randolph was deeply committed to the view that the causes of prejudice and discrimination are essentially economic. Only the united action of black and white workers against capitalism would achieve lasting social justice. And in this struggle for justice, he said, the black man must defend his rights as a member of the working class, and where necessary must put up physical resistance to white lynch mobs. In the course of his trade-union activities, he organized black workers on the railroads into the Brotherhood of Sleeping Car Porters, and in 1936 he was made president of the National Negro Congress, a federation of organizations created by blacks to advance the race and especially the interests of black workers. Five years later, as America geared for war, Randolph launched an appeal for a march on Washington of fifty to one hundred thousand blacks to petition for equal opportunities in wartime defense employment. The threat of the march, which was never held, led to President Roosevelt's Executive Order 8802 of June 1941 forbidding racial discrimination in the employment of workers in defense industries or government, and creating a federal Fair Employment Practices Committee with investigative powers. Though Congress effectively killed the FEPC in 1945 by refusing to vote funds for it, many states and cities, particularly in the North, enacted legislation with varying degrees of effectiveness.

Randolph's proposals of the early 1940's, though short-lived, represented the most significant attempt at an all-black mass movement to arise after Marcus Garvey. Somewhat embarrassed by the accusations of white allies and friends that the movement was anti-white, Randolph hastened to say that cooperation with white and interracial groups would be initiated but that the movement would remain all-black for several cogent reasons. Each ethnic or racial group must organize to fight the prejudice against it. Blacks must fight against color discrimination, and in doing so gain solidarity among themselves. In his view, when blacks formed their own organizations, they helped break down the slave psychology and the inevitable inferiority complex which is nourished when blacks rely on white people for direction and support. Nevertheless, Randolph assured whites that the movement was not black nationalist; it would use tested American techniques of pressure and militant action to achieve its goal—full integration of Negro citizens into all phases of American life on a par with other citizens.

Faced with recurrent economic crises and joblessness in the thirties, many black working-class urban dwellers gravitated toward separatist churches and prophetic sects. Two examples are Father Divine's Peace Movement and the Moorish-American Science Temple.

Father Divine's Peace Movement was a social response to poverty and deprivation; it was also a religious expression, somewhat outside the established black churches, of a hope for a heaven on earth. The Peace Movement was founded in 1919 on Long Island by George Baker, who called himself "Father Divine" and provided food, clothing, work, and shelter for thousands of his followers and unemployed people in major cities. By the 1930's, the heyday of Divine's popularity, peace missions called "Heavens" were open to the community, and Divine's staunch followers, once initiated by baptism, worshipped him as God, renounced their worldly goods, and practiced a strict regime of celibacy and puritan abstinence. Divine did not confront the power of the dominant society on behalf of blacks. On the contrary, the movement's slogan "Peace, It's Truly Wonderful" attracted some wealthy whites to the fold. With their support, Divine was able to finance his welfare programs and meet the needs of his black worshippers, many of whom were aspiring but frustrated working-class people.

The Moorish-American Science Temple was, like Divine's movement, a mission to the urban poor and downhearted. And it too bore the special personalized religious orientation of its creator. The temple was founded by Noble Drew Ali in Newark, New Jersey, in 1913. He preached that blacks were the descendants of the Moors of Northern Africa and were Asiatic in origin. By the mid-twenties Ali had also established temples in Pittsburgh and Detroit, but he died in 1929 and the movement splintered. One of his followers was an itinerant peddler named W. D. Fard, who founded the Nation of Islam in Detroit in 1930. Three years later he had built up a following of eight thousand and was preaching an unorthodox version of Islam in which he claimed whites were devils and the "Asiatic Black Man" was the original and rightful inhabitant of the earth. To further his ideas, Fard organized the Fruit of Islam, an all-male group of proselytizers and defenders of the faith, and the University of Islam, where children of his followers could be educated.

Fard disappeared mysteriously around 1934 and leadership of the Nation of Islam passed to Elijah Poole, a slightly built automobile worker who had migrated from rural Georgia. He soon changed his name to Elijah Muhammad and declared himself to be the "Messenger of Allah" and leader of the "Lost-Found Nation of Islam in the Wilderness of North America." Muhammad believed that it was just a matter of time before the black man would be restored to his original role as "the first and the last, the maker and owner of the Universe." In the meantime, through faith in Islam and hard work, black people could create better conditions for themselves, particularly through the organization of small business enterprises.

Without doubt these separatist churches and prophetic sects provided urban blacks with a haven during a stormy period of migration and economic hardship and helped them salvage their self-respect. That they offered only "pie in the sky" and did not challenge the powerful forces arrayed against black people did not seem to matter. Ecstasy was better than grim reality and the congregations were assured that they would be saved when the final holocaust burst upon the iniquitous world around them. More important, the missions and temples kept alive the idea of "blacks working for blacks." They provided an organizational base for segments of the black urban masses which contrasted sharply with the integrationist activities of middle-class professionals and community leaders beholden to the external power structure. In effect, separatist churches and sects served as a safety net under the poorest segment of black society and thus saved large numbers of people from impoverished oblivion. Along with the religious and welfare activities of the large traditional black churches, the Baptists and Methodists, for example, the urban missions were an important cornerstone of the black community and nourished its fragile sense of black consciousness.

With the advent of World War II, blacks found a new role in the industrial and military mobilization of America. One million black men and women served in the armed forces and millions more joined the industrial armies manning the home front. But wartime life was fraught with racial tension. In the military establishment segregation and assignment to low-grade jobs were standard practice. "Unnatural social relations," such as blacks socializing in places frequented by whites, were taboo, and black servicemen and women were beaten if they stepped across "the color line." The Red Cross separated the blood of black and white donors. Books on black history and culture were conveniently left off the shelves of service clubs. Daily annoyances like these, and more fundamental grievances over discriminatory job assignments and ranking systems and frequent courts-martial and bad-conduct discharges, led to protests and pitched battles between blacks and whites in military camps and on city streets all over America, Europe, and many other parts of the world.

On the home front, blacks moved into Oakland, Detroit, Cleveland, and Chicago and other wartime job centers to fill low-paid jobs left by white workers seeking higher wages in defense industries. Inevitably, as blacks sought entry into better employment and job-training programs, racial tensions increased. In Detroit, in June 1943, the most serious civilian race riot of the war period occurred. Twenty-five blacks and nine whites were killed and several hundred thousand dollars' worth of property was destroyed in a day and a half of rioting. In scores of other localities, racial clashes on a smaller scale highlighted the problems of jobs and housing and the inability of local authorities to protect blacks from hostile white mobs. Protests against racism came from many quarters, most vociferously from black nationalist leaders and supporters of the Garveyite movement. If color was their phobia and race their creed, it was an understandable response to the grave events of this period. Black popular opinion was bitterly critical of a war against fascism abroad which did not bring democracy at home, a view succinctly summarized by Ralph J. Bunche as early as 1939 in the *Journal of Negro Education* when he noted that "the white American may recoil with horror at the German barbarisms against the Jew. But the American Negro cries, 'Hitler be damned, and the Jew too; what about Jim Crow here?' "

When the war ended there was a wave of optimism as the nation set about the task of constructing a peacetime economy. Securing full citizenship and voting rights became a political issue of capital importance. The black vote assumed increased importance in closely fought national elections and helped elect Harry S. Truman President in 1948 after his assurances that freedom and equality of opportunity for all was a sacred and essential American principle which should not be legally denied black people. Nevertheless, words did not erase the very real barriers to freedom all too apparently connected with a deeply rooted pattern of institutional racism. As Gunnar Myrdal, the Swedish social scientist, pointed out in his widely read book, *An American Dilemma* (1940), there was something startlingly aberrant about America's pretensions to democracy while practicing racial discrimination which denied black people a chance for advancement.

In this climate the modern civil-rights movement was born. The National Association for the Advancement of Colored People was well established and well known for its legal and legislative battles against racially restrictive practices in housing, public facilities, and interstate travel. Though the NAACP much earlier under the leadership of Dr. Du Bois had been considered radical, it was in the forties a moderate organization seeking no changes in the power structure and asking only that the Negro be allowed to enter the mainstream of American life. Its tactics were to seek support of power elites while at the same time denouncing "extremist and anti-democratic tendencies," a label which it applied equally to Communists, black nationalists, and racist organizations like the Ku Klux Klan.

NAACP leaders and their executive officers, first Walter White and later Roy Wilkins, believed that American racism could be destroyed or rendered impotent only through a peaceful, nonviolent, and interracial civil-rights movement. The NAACP strategy aimed to collaborate with reformist elements in the political arena. Alliances were established with the major trade unions, reform Democrats, and liberal Republicans, civil-rights moderates, important business leaders and big-city bosses, middle-class liberals, intellectuals, and students. While the NAACP was nominally a Negro organization (it had several hundred thousand members) many whites in key policy-making positions gave it an interracial character and outlook in which whites played an influential role.

In the forties white organizations seeking to ameliorate race relations were steadily opening their ranks to Negroes. One small group which symbolized this change was the Fellowship of Reconciliation (FOR), a Christian pacifist group formed during World War I. Between the wars it attracted supporters from pacifist Quakers and the Protestant Youth Movement of the white Methodist Church, and appealed to middle-class liberals and intellectuals. In 1942 leaders of FOR created the Congress of Racial Equality (CORE), an interracial, non-violent, direct-action movement to resolve racial and industrial conflict. Prominent figures in the first CORE unit in Chicago were a white draft resister, George Houser, and James Farmer, the son of a black college professor, and their first followers were drawn from a small group of pacifists, young ministers, and University of Chicago divinity students. Their method of direct action combined the techniques of passive resistance and non-violent action or *Satyagraha*, introduced by Mahatma Gandhi in his fight against British colonialism in India, with that of the sit-down strike used successfully by militant factory workers in the 1930's period of the American labor movement. The major targets were discrimination in public eating places, housing, theaters, employment, and transportation. As early as 1947, for example, CORE and FOR activists, including George Houser and Homer Jack, both white, and Negroes Bayard Rustin, William Worthy, and Nathan Wright, conducted an interracial Journey of Reconciliation into the South to test compliance with the 1946 Supreme Court decision against segregation in interstate travel.

By the mid-fifties the stage was set for two events which captured the nation's attention and won the applause of Afro-Americans. The first was the famous U.S. Supreme Court ruling, in the case of *Brown v. Board of Education*, Topeka, Kansas, May 17, 1954, that school segregation was unconstitutional since "separate educational facilities are inherently unequal." The legal case for desegregation was launched in 1950 by a team of NAACP lawyers and strategists, including Thurgood Marshall and the social scientists Kenneth and Mamie Clark. The team stressed the social and educational value of desegregation for black and white Americans, and their plea for urgency was a crucial factor in the Supreme Court's later ruling that school integration should begin "with all deliberate speed." Sporadic and partial attempts at implementation took place in the District of Columbia and Southern border states, but there was a massive resistance in the Deep South, and in 1957 President Dwight Eisenhower ordered federal troops to Little Rock, Arkansas, to prevent segregationists and state officials, including Governor Orval Faubus, from interfering with school integration.

The second major event was the Montgomery, Alabama, bus boycott of 1955–56. It began when a black woman, Rosa Parks, refused to move from a seat in the "whites only" section of a city bus and was arrested. Later, her supporters mobilized a massive 381-day-long bus boycott in which Montgomery Negroes chose to "Walk to Freedom" rather than ride in segregated buses. The first circulars announcing the boycott carried a clear and forthright message:

> Don't ride bus to work, to town, to school, or any other place Monday, December 5th. Another Negro woman has been arrested and put in jail because she refused to give up her bus seat. Come to a mass meeting, Monday at 7:00 p.m. at the Holt Street Baptist Church for further instruction.

One of Mrs. Park's staunch supporters was Reverend Martin Luther King, Jr., a well-educated Baptist clergyman who held a Gandhian belief in the principles of non-violence. For him love was more powerful than hate, and the undeserved suffering heaped upon black protesters by hostile philistines contained the promise of heavenly redemption. Reverend King became in time the most prominent spokesman for non-violent, direct-action civil disobedience and in 1957 organized the Southern Christian Leadership Conference to coordinate demonstrations for civil rights, school desegregation, and voter-registration campaigns in the South.

These two events profoundly influenced the actions of middle-class Negro leadership for the rest of the decade. The success of the NAACP strategy of legal battles and reformist coalitions with power elites gave the organization's leaders prestige within the black community and grudging acceptance among many whites. At the same time, black preachers inveighed against the hypocrisy of white Christians on racial matters and Martin Luther King, Jr., led Southern blacks and liberal white churchmen in a national campaign of civil disobedience.

In the Deep South, however, the steady advance of the civil-rights movement did not go unchallenged. There was a rising tide of white hostility and the first White Citizens Council unit was formed at Indianola, Mississippi, in 1954 to combat desegregation. Emmett Till, a black youth of fourteen, was kidnapped and lynched in Money, Mississippi, in 1955; the homes of Reverend King and a colleague, Reverend Fred L. Shuttlesworth, were bombed in 1956; and Mack Parker was lynched at Poplarville, Mississippi, in 1959. It was in this climate of turmoil and fear that the first modern exponent of armed self-defense and the right to maximum retaliation by blacks emerged. He was Robert Williams of Monroe, North Carolina.

When Williams, an ex-U.S. Marine, returned home from the war, he found that little had changed. There were still high rates of black unemployment, illiteracy, and poverty. Those few who dared challenge the color line were severely beaten and driven out of town by hooded Ku Klux Klansmen. Williams first came to public attention in 1957, when, after his election as president of the small Monroe chapter of the NAACP, he challenged local segregation practices. He found supporters among town laborers, sharecroppers, and impoverished small farmers and organized them into a cohesive, well-disciplined group. Their immediate goals were equal rights and integration through organized peaceful action. Monroe whites responded with a sustained campaign of terror and the black community decided to arm in self-defense. A key figure in this decision was Williams, and on several occasions members of his citizens' militia fired upon attacking Klansmen.

Tensions in Monroe exploded in 1958 over the infamous "Kissing Case," a travesty of Southern justice in which two black boys, ages seven and nine, were arrested and charged with attempted rape for allegedly kissing a seven-year-old white playmate and sentenced to fourteen years in the reformatory. Shortly thereafter, Williams, angered at the continued attacks by whites and biased judicial decisions, declared that blacks must defend themselves and if necessary "stop lynching with lynching." "Negroes cannot receive justice from the courts," he said, "they must convict their attackers on the spot. They must meet violence with violence." These remarks and his subsequent suspension from the NAACP for advocating violence proved to be the turning point in Williams's career.

In the following two years, during a period of heightened Klan activity, Williams and his armed supporters helped protect Monroe blacks as they vainly tried to integrate the town's job market and social facilities. On one occasion, Williams rescued several civil-rights workers from a white mob. In the course of events he was accused of kidnapping and the attempted murder of a white couple who wandered into the fray. Faced with a warrant for his arrest, Williams fled to Canada, and later lived in exile in Cuba, China, and Tanzania.

Integration and separatism, two modes of consciousness and action, have at times been two warring ideas. Indeed, they reflect conflicting tendencies in the minds of black folk that must be recognized and acknowledged before proceeding to the focal point of our attention, Malcolm X, the eclipse of integration, and the ideological conflicts of today. The problem was eloquently expressed at the turn of the century by W. E. B. Du Bois, writing of the strivings of Negro people in *The Atlantic Monthly*, August 1897:

> One ever feels his two-ness—an American, a Negro; two souls, two thoughts, two unreconciled strivings; two warring ideals in one dark body, whose dogged strength alone keeps it from being torn asunder. The history of the American Negro is the history of this strife—this longing to attain self-conscious manhood to merge his double self into a better and truer self. In this merging he wishes neither of the older selves to be lost. He does not wish to Africanize America, for America has too much to teach the world and Africa. He does not wish to bleach his Negro blood in a flood of White

Americanism, for he believes . . . that Negro blood has yet a message for the world. He simply wishes to make it possible for a man to be both a Negro and an American without being cursed and spit upon . . .

Both themes, whether expressed pacifically or belligerently, tend in the same direction—namely, freedom from discrimination and segregation and the achievement of full equality of opportunity. But they differ in several crucial respects. The integrationist vocabulary is filled with phrases like collaboration, assimilation, equal rights, and peaceful non-violence. Appeals are made for loyalty to the two-party political system, alliances with power elites, and the brotherhood of all Americans. The language of separatism emphasizes the defense of community institutions, racial unity, self-determination, and independent economic and political activity. Separatists speak of land, territorial separation, and emigration, nationhood and reparations, Pan-Africanism and a universal brotherhood of men of color.

The integrationist position is based largely on a strategy of political alliances with white liberal and labor forces to put pressure on power elites in the ruling classes. The method seeks legal and judicial changes in the black man's status to allow for more effective participation and integration into the society. This often leads to being coopted into the power structure, small incremental gains, and only marginal improvements for the poor and laboring classes. The separatist strategy is one of power based on building a movement within the black community capable of remaining autonomous and free of external manipulation and control by whites. It stresses the formation and consolidation of a countercommunity with separate needs, values, structures, and life styles. It accepts the black community as the focal point of collective advancement in which alternative solutions to problems can be developed and possible challenges to the status quo kept alive. Pursuance of separatism often founders for a lack of financial resources and is associated with a highly inflated sense of power severely lacking in substance.

Each goal poses painful choices about self, race, whites, and the nation. Integration, in American society, tends to mean acceptance of the principle that blacks genuinely absorb and assimilate patterns of culture and enterprise determined by whites. It also means and requires the loss, as a black man becomes more successful, of his own distinctive characteristics. Separatism requires the mobilization of the race toward the construction of a new group status and identity, and the clear recognition that survival in the face of white racism must be predicated on group cohesion around group-led institutions.

In the day-to-day struggle for survival and progress, however, and in the context of changes in public opinion, governmental policies, legal and judicial precedents, it becomes increasingly difficult to maintain a social movement dedicated to one goal alone or to live one's life totally according to one ideal or the other. The difficulty with the integrationist mode is that, as racism beats him back, the black man is drawn toward separatism as an alternative mode of adaptation and action. With separatism, as blacks gain more opportunity, solidarity declines. The two themes—integration and separatism—are therefore in constant interaction, each vying at different times or stages of history for the all-consuming interest of black people.

2 Separatism: The Legacy of Malcolm X

Malcolm X, pre-eminent separatist leader of the turbulent sixties, was a man of apostolic and tormented temperament whose life was a many-faceted reflection of black life and discontent. His meteoric rise to national and international prominence was not without historic roots, however. He was, and felt himself to be, the inheritor of a dominant ebony mood reaching back to colonial times which claimed that fraternal solidarity and unity within a self-assertive, separate, and more powerful black existence was the answer to the black man's problems. This conviction was kept alive in the black ghettos early in this century by rebel-prophets whose mission, expressed with pentecostal vigor, sought to transform the malaise of recurrent failure and despair into the instruments of final, apocalyptic salvation. Marcus Garvey, Noble Drew Ali, W. D. Fard, Elijah Muhammad and countless itinerant street-messiahs were of this vein, sent, they said, from heaven itself to curb white racism and rescue their people from the bottomless pit of society. They were black gods of the metropolis calling the faithful and the faithless back to the fold, and their message of "black folks working for black folks" came from the depths of the black urban experience.

Malcolm's message was Black Unity and Separation, Armed Self-Defense, Freedom Now by Any Means Necessary. In time it became a searing indictment of American society and the basis for a powerful countervalent to integration—a veritable new theolatry of black nationalism. Malcolm challenged the academic notions of a perfect and multiracial democracy and the absurdity of the white man's pretensions to superior wisdom. He called for warfare every day against the injustices of every day. Integration was, he said, a fraud based on the myth of civil-rights progress and black-white unity. The supreme facts of life for black people were poverty, disenfranchisement, and racism perpetrated by whites, and they would never get their rights unless they fought for them. Arguing his case on the national media, in meeting halls, and from soapboxes on crowded avenues, Malcolm hammered home the main points of his philosophy—complete self-determination and autonomy for black people, and the right to defend themselves by any means necessary to achieve these goals. It was either the "Ballot or the Bullet," he said; either "total liberty for black people or total destruction for white America."

Malcolm X was born Malcolm Little in the black quarter of Omaha, Nebraska, May 19, 1925. He was the fourth of five children born to Louise, a West Indian from Grenada, and Earl Little, a Georgia-born, itinerant Baptist preacher. Malcolm's childhood was one of severe trauma, of deprivation, fire, hysteria, and death by violence. His father was a devoted disciple of Marcus Garvey and a zealous organizer for the Universal Negro Improvement Association. As a consequence, in the conservative Midwest, where belief in white superiority was backed by law, Earl Little was constantly harassed for "spreading trouble" among the town's black folk with his preaching about black redemption and emigration back to Africa. When Louise was pregnant with Malcolm, the family home was attacked by marauders and the Littles were forced to leave town. When Malcolm was four, tragedy struck again. The family

home in Lansing, Michigan, was burned down by masked vigi-
lantes, and two years later his father was badly beaten and thrown
to his death under a tram car by suspected Klansmen. Shortly
thereafter his mother went insane, the children were scattered in
state-run foster homes and detention centers, and the family was
destroyed.

Malcolm tried to fend for himself but was in constant conflict
with his guardians and the law. He attained excellent marks in
school, was a gifted debater, and had hopes of going to law school.
But he was defenseless against the prejudices of teachers and welfare workers who assigned all black people to a station in life well
below that of whites. Finally, in disgust, he quit school and in the
summer of 1940 went to join his sister in Boston. In the Boston–
New York area, Malcolm held a variety of dead-end, low-paid jobs
available to black teenagers: hotel busboy, shoeshine boy, soda jerk,
railway porter, and nightclub waiter. He drifted into the criminal
underworld and became a small-time crook, numbers runner, drug
pusher, pimp, and armed robber known as "Detroit Red." "I was a
true hustler—" says Malcolm in his autobiography, "uneducated,
unskilled at anything honorable, and I considered myself nervy and
cunning enough to live by my wits, exploiting any prey that presented itself." His criminal career was abruptly ended, however,
when he was arrested for burglary and theft in Boston and sentenced in 1946 to eight to ten years in prison. He was then just
twenty-one years of age.

In prison, Malcolm felt he had sunk to the lowest depths of
degradation—but why? Why was he doomed to so much suffering?
Why, indeed, were ignorance, poverty, and suffering the common
lot of black folks in America? Nothing in the books he read in the
prison library gave him a clue to the elusive and mysterious answer.

In the midst of his search he was introduced by his brother to
the ideas of the Honorable Elijah Muhammad, leader of a small
religious sect, the Lost-Found Nation of Islam. Muhammad
preached that the black man's hell in America was due to white
oppression, and that salvation would come only when blacks gave
up the white man's ways and adopted the true religion, Islam, as
revealed to him by Allah or God. The essence of Muhammad's

message was black redemption and his followers were called Black Muslims. Blacks, though degraded in America, could be redeemed, he said, but they must rediscover their glorious heritage. They must unite and maintain strict separation from the white race. Progress would come only through thrift, business enterprise, and economic independence. The motivating force behind these beliefs was the certainty that blacks were superior to whites and that one day, with God's intervention, the lost Black Nation would be restored to its rightful place of predominance in the world.

Malcolm studied these ideas, and by the time he left prison in 1952 he was converted and pledged to serve Muhammad. As was customary, he replaced his surname with an "X" to mark the abandonment of his "slave name" Little and the renunciation of his former way of life. Malcolm quickly rose to leadership in the Black Muslim hierarchy and in December 1954 was given ministry of the movement's Temple No. 7 at Lenox Avenue and 116th Street in Harlem, a teeming crossroads of New York's large black ghetto. It soon was the leading temple in the country, and Malcolm became a trusted minister, organizer, and disciple of Elijah Muhammad.

Taking his text from the teachings of Muhammad, and an obscure Black Muslim myth called "Yacub's History," Malcolm proclaimed that the "so-called Negroes of America" are part of an original Black Nation which comprises the "black, brown, red, and yellow races" of the world. They are totally different from, and superior to, the Caucasian race, who by trickery and force of arms had conquered the Black Nation and transported its people to America as slaves. There followed a profound material and moral impoverishment made all the worse by the treachery of false leaders and the corrupting influences of the Christian religion. Nevertheless, black people could reap the benefits of their suffering if they followed the teachings of Elijah Muhammad, God's Chosen Messenger. By exacting retribution, land, and reparations from America, they could start a new life under the divine leadership of Elijah Muhammad.

Malcolm preached that blacks in America are "lost sheep" who have been oppressed and seduced by the slavemaster. They were "lost" but could be "found" if they gave up the Bible and swore allegiance to the Koran and Islam, "the black man's religion." White people, he said, are devils incarnate whom Allah had decreed will be destroyed by fire, pestilence, disease, sin, and cosmic upheaval. Blacks, to be saved, must separate themselves from the white devils before the day of Armageddon. Moderate leaders like the Reverend Martin Luther King, Jr., who proposed integration and non-violence, must be totally opposed. Blacks must close ranks and run their own communities and businesses. They must give up evil ways learned from white people: unhealthy foods, including pork, fornication, drinking, smoking, carrying weapons, drugs, gambling, and race mixing, and prepare themselves through prayer, hard work, and supplication to Allah for a new day of freedom.

Malcolm was a tireless worker. He gave weekly lectures at the temple, wrote regular columns for black newspapers and the movement's journal, *Muhammad Speaks*. He scoured the main streets and back alleys of the ghetto looking for converts. And he was as well known in the sleazy underworld of juice joints, cafés, gambling dens, and bordellos as he was on the street corners of crowded working-class tenement areas. Malcolm's broad appeal was to the dissatisfied but striving masses, many of whom were migrant ex-Southerners. He "fished" for converts on the fringes of Saturday-night crowds and Sunday-morning church congregations. His message was simple and promised total relief from all ills: "Come, brothers and sisters, hear how the white man kidnapped and robbed and raped our black race. Hear how the Honorable Elijah Muhammad teaches us to cure the black man's spiritual, mental, moral, economic, and political sicknesses."

Malcolm's message attracted large numbers of talented, aspiring, lower-middle-class people: tradesmen, self-employed artisans, clerical workers, nurses, and service employees. Many of his earliest recruits were also urban outsiders like himself: ex-convicts, hustlers, thugs, storefront preachers, blues singers, pimps, con-men, and tricksters. Under his tutelage these disparate elements became dedicated converts, organizers, and operators of small Muslim-owned business enterprises. And to maintain discipline Malcolm helped train the Fruit of Islam, a corps of Black Muslim persuaders skilled in the techniques of self-defense and unarmed combat.

Despite his supreme self-confidence and considerable skill as a speaker, Malcolm might have remained in obscurity, isolated from popular opinion by conservative leaders in Harlem. But one night in 1957 Malcolm's vociferous protest against police brutality aroused Harlem citizens and won him a place in popular folklore. He and a squad of the Fruit of Islam, angered at the beating of a Black Muslim brother by the police, surrounded a Harlem police station and demanded his release and hospitalization. This dramatic and successful act of defiance, and the $70,000 suit for damages against the New York City police which followed, captured the imagination of black people all over the country. National recruitment began in earnest and Malcolm's influence steadily mounted. Through Malcolm's efforts, the membership of the Lost-Found Nation of Islam increased dramatically. He took what was a small, ailing sect with mainly middle-aged members and built it into a vibrant, youth-oriented organization with more than forty thousand adherents, and twice that many sympathizers in more than twenty cities. Membership fees, weekly tithes, and receipts from Muslim-owned small businesses contributed over $100,000 annually to the movement. Malcolm lived at first on a share of the collection at congregational meetings, but soon had a tax-free $150-a-week salary and a rent-free, seven-room suburban house in Queens, New York.

Malcolm was a powerful spokesman for the Black Muslim cause. He was tall and ruggedly handsome, with a verbal style filled with charismatic fervor. He had the ability to play with words and ideas, to abuse, amuse, and reach his audience at their level of understanding. He delighted crowds with his visual imagery, his hustler machismo, his ritualistic style, and his vision of salvation and redemption amid the violent upheaval of the white man's world.

Speaking at a "Black Forum" organized at Reverend Adam Clayton Powell's Abyssinian Baptist Church in Harlem in 1963, Malcolm challenged his audience to deny that the major question in America today is "Will these awakened black masses demand integration or separation from the cruel white society that has enslaved them?" As far as the Muslims are concerned, he said, it is crucial to understand one essential point in their doctrine: "We don't want to be segregated by the white man, we don't want to be integrated with the white man, we want to be separated from the white man . . . The Honorable Elijah Muhammad teaches us that this is the only intelligent and lasting solution to the present race problem."

To a chorus of amens from the devout congregation, Malcolm prophesied the end of "the wicked white man's Western world of Christianity" and the emergence of a divinely inspired black revolution destined to destroy the world of slavery and evil in order to establish a world based upon freedom, justice, and equality. Malcolm warned the congregation that America stands before the bar of God's judgment for her wickedness and her crimes against Negroes, and they would be foolish to accept her deceitful offers of integration. An integrated cup of coffee in a few desegregated luncheonettes, he said, was not sufficient pay for four hundred years of slave labor.

God's judgment, according to Malcolm, was total and final; there was only one way, one permanent solution, by which America could accomplish its salvation and that was to let blacks have a separate land base and a separate destiny financed adequately by the payment of reparations. This could be accomplished either by repatriation to an African homeland, where blacks could establish an independent nation, or, if this was too difficult a project, "America should set aside some separated territory right here in the Western Hemisphere where the two races can live apart from each other, since we certainly don't get along peacefully while we are together." The size of the territory should be judged by population: if one seventh of this country's population is black, then give us one seventh of the land, said Malcolm. Furthermore, the land should be fertile, with enough rain and minerals, and supplied for an initial period of twenty-five years from government sources. All this, Malcolm charged, the government owed blacks for their long years of enslavement. It was a bill that must be collected; a straightforward demand, not a servile request. When paid, America would be saved from destruction, but "if she doesn't pay off her debt God will collect and God won't take part payment. He will take the entire country . . . and give it to whom he pleases."

On many occasions in 1963 Malcolm elaborated on his remarks and expressed the conclusion that blacks have been asleep too long in the "American House of Bondage" and must end their subservience to whites by taking up the necessary and redemptive role of resistance against the violation of black rights. He rejected the "hate label" with which he had been branded, saying that the Muslim followers of Elijah Muhammad don't advocate violence but were taught that any human being who is intelligent has the right to defend himself. It was ludicrous to accuse him of hatred and violence, he said. "You can't take a black man who is being bitten by dogs and accuse him of advocating violence because he tries to defend himself from being bitten by that dog." The real culprit was the "tricknology" of the white man, the science of divide and conquer by which whites destroyed the black man's African cultural traditions and dehumanized him, and even now, in the form of the devious ploy of integration, was attempting to lull blacks into thinking that white attitudes were changing.

Malcolm's message of separatism and black revolution gained him considerable national media exposure in the early sixties. It was a time of widespread despair at the inability of civil-rights leaders and the government to rapidly implement desegregation and improve the ghettos, a time when blacks were sickened and angered by daily reports of beatings and bombings of civil-rights workers and the vicious dispersal of peaceful assemblies. Seizing every opportunity to speak out on important issues of the day, Malcolm criticized black and white integrationists for their failure to confront racism directly. In his speeches and media interviews he reserved a special place of scorn for what he called token black bourgeois leadership, especially that of Reverend Dr. Martin Luther King. He made this clear when he told an interviewer:

> Any Negro who teaches other Negroes to turn the other cheek is disarming that Negro . . . And men like King, their job is to go among Negroes and teach Negroes "Don't fight back" . . . But

King's philosophy falls upon the ears of only a small minority. The majority or masses of black people in this country are more inclined in the direction of the Honorable Elijah Muhammad than Martin Luther King . . . White people follow King. White people pay King. White people subsidize King. White people support King. But the masses of black people don't support Martin Luther King.

With an eye toward influencing public opinion, Malcolm unleashed a verbal attack on the major problems afflicting black people: bad housing, high rents, unemployment, inadequate welfare and education, and political emasculation. At street-corner rallies he denounced the major political parties for their poor voting record and called for a coalition of black politicians dedicated to no party or any cause other than the interests of their own communities. Malcolm began to distinguish between the differing perspectives of the masses and their middle-class leaders. He used to great advantage illustrations drawn from the period of slavery. Malcolm said there were two kinds of groups in the old days, the "House Negro," who lived and worked in the mansion of the plantation owner, and the "Field Negro," who toiled in the cotton fields. The House Negro identified with and loved the master "better than he loved himself"; but the Field Negro hated both the master and the cruel regime of slavery. In Malcolm's view, House Negroes exist today in the form of "Uncle Toms," whose purpose is "to keep you and me in check, to keep us under control, keep us passive and peaceful and non-violent." The House Negro is the old-time Negro, said Malcolm, that is, they represent the old hat-in-hand, patient, wait-another-hundred-years approach. Today's version of the House Negro favors integration, resents the stigma of his color, and imitates whites, and is quite satisfied with being considered a minority called the American Negro. By contrast, he noted, the Field Negro is today's New Negro. He is for separation and calls himself a black man; he doesn't brag about being an American and is confidently aware of his identity with Africa and the world's colored majority.

Malcolm was often pitted against black and white liberals and civil-rights leaders. The favorite questions raised were: What does the Negro really want today? Is there a "New Negro" and is he dissatisfied with the leadership of organizations like the NAACP? Is he developing a new identity based on inner reactions and relations with Africa? Where is the American Negro heading?

On a memorable Sunday afternoon in October 1961 Malcolm appeared on a television panel, "Open Mind," and matched wits with Eric Goldman, professor of history at Princeton, Professor Morroe Berger, a Princeton University sociologist and expert on Middle East affairs, Kenneth B. Clark, a black professor of psychology, Richard Haley of the Congress of Racial Equality, and Constance B. Motley, a black civil-rights lawyer, later a federal judge. Professor Clark denied the existence of a New Negro and affirmed that today's Negro is the same in that he still wants full equality as an American. Malcolm disagreed, saying that there is a New Negro who is tired of waiting for freedom. He is angrier and wants to take action for himself—he does not believe it is possible to achieve equality in America through integration. Integration is only a method of getting human dignity and it has failed. New strategies are necessary because: "If you try and swim the Atlantic Ocean and after several attempts you find you don't make it, well, if your objective is the other side, what are you going to do? It's not a case of having utter despair. You have to go back to shore and try and find another method of getting across if that's where you want to go."

But surely the Negro has made some progress? asked Mrs. Motley. To which Malcolm replied: "As a lawyer, I'm sure you'll agree that if you put a man in prison illegally and unjustly, one who has not committed a crime, and after putting him there you keep him in solitary confinement, it's doubly cruel. Now, if you let him out of solitary into the regular prison yard, you can call that progress if you want, but the man was not supposed to be put in prison in the first place."

Professor Clark then suggested that Malcolm was wrong in referring to "white schools" and "white industries." The schools are not the white man's schools, said Clark, they are owned by the public, which includes Negroes. Furthermore, he argued, Negroes are an integral part of America's economy, which was built in part by black labor; hence, he implied, there is no such thing as white industry. Malcolm's reply was skeptical: a horse can pull the plow, he said, but it doesn't own the farm.

A final exchange revealed some fundamental differences between the two men and the ideals they stood for. Malcolm stressed the importance for Negroes of the experiences of ex-colonial peoples of Africa, Asia, and Latin America. To which Clark retorted that the impact of the legal staff of the NAACP and the votes that Negroes in large urban centers use to elect congressmen and senators and to influence national politics are more likely to have a direct effect upon the rapidity of changes in their status than what happens in Africa. And after a moment's hesitation, Clark added, "Now, it may be that I am speaking only in terms of a personal idiosyncratic inability to identify with Africa. I confess, I identify with America. I'm American and I want my rights as an American."

Through his travels and speeches, and the outraged responses of his powerful opponents in interracial civil-rights organizations, Malcolm was thrust into national prominence. He became a debater with a national reputation. He matched wits on television, radio, and the public platform with politicians, college professors, and journalists. He was feared by the white public and dubbed a racist, black supremist, and "the Hate That Hate Produced." To the press he was a primeval *bête noire*, the horrible alternative to responsible black leadership and a peaceful America. Yet he was revered by many members of his race as the shining black prince sent to rescue and redeem them.

Malcolm was at the apex of his popularity when a sudden, and irrevocable, split occurred with Elijah Muhammad. He was suspended from his ministry in December 1963 for ninety days, allegedly for his intemperate remarks about the death of President John F. Kennedy. Malcolm had spoken out, against orders, and attributed Kennedy's assassination to the climate of hate and violence that white people had created and tolerated in America. "It is a case of chickens come home to roost," he had said; and "being an old farm boy myself, chickens coming home to roost never make me sad; they've made me glad."

Undoubtedly there were irreconcilable and growing differences between the leader and his disciple. Malcolm's popularity was a cause for jealousy, and there was the suspicion that he was a vain publicity seeker acting far above his station in Muhammad's organization. On the other hand, Malcolm was angered at the conservatism of Muhammad and his failure to let Malcolm bring the Nation of Islam directly into the black-freedom struggle. "The rest of us don't have Mr. Muhammad's patience with the devil," said Malcolm. "The younger Black Muslims want to see some action."

Perhaps Malcolm sensed that the success of the Black Muslims had led to a massive bureaucracy. Muhammad, his sons and faithful retainers, were at the top and a flock of unquestioning followers at the bottom. In the middle were the successful ministers and entrepreneurs aided by a large corps of Fruit of Islam enforcers. The Nation of Islam, whose success, he felt, was due largely to his own efforts, had become a powerful and effective economic as well as religious enterprise, firmly in the control of the aging and increasingly irritable and self-indulgent Elijah Muhammad.

What seems reasonably clear, from statements in his autobiography, is that Malcolm felt constrained by what he realized were the conservative doctrines of the Black Muslim hierarchy. The Nation's slogan of black unity appeared to be revolutionary when there were no other active groups in the field—no student protests, no riots, and no mass civil disobedience. But these and other new pressures for independent black political action had taken place, and blacks close to the civil-rights front lines were pressing the Muslims to join the fight. But Muhammad had not given the signal to join the fray; he was searching for converts, not for a confrontation with white society. For Malcolm's part, he wanted action, and felt the younger Muslims were restless too, and above all he wanted a relaxation of the movement's policy of nonengagement. He was forced to the conclusion that a movement whose program stressed moral reformation and didn't join the political battle was bankrupt. For these reasons, Malcolm was led inexorably to a split with the movement on the grounds of irreconcilable policy and tactical differences.

When, at the end of his period of suspension in March 1964, Malcolm was not reinstated, he was humiliated and in a dilemma. He wanted to remain in the Nation of Islam because it offered him a living wage, a parsonage, a car, a bodyguard, and a position of authority; it gave him material security and a powerful political base. But it seemed clear that he was no longer trusted and might even be in danger of elimination by jealous rivals. At the same time he wanted a leadership role in the radical wing of the civil-rights movement, but he needed the backing of a strong organization which he would now have to build himself.

Malcolm took the first step toward reorganizing his political and religious life at a crowded press conference early in March. Asserting that 1964 threatened to be an explosive year, he intended to be active in every phase of the Negro struggle for human rights. He announced his resignation from the Nation of Islam and his intention to create a new religious organization, the Muslim Mosque Incorporated. It would provide a spiritual base for the moral reformation of black communities and have a black nationalist, direct-action approach to economic, social, political, and cultural affairs. Its purpose was to organize millions of non-Muslim blacks into a militant movement and to seek cooperation with leaders of all religious persuasions and from all walks of life. Concerning the issue of violence and non-violence, Malcolm reiterated his belief that blacks should retaliate in self-defense whenever and wherever they are unjustly or unlawfully attacked. This held true particularly in densely populated areas in the rural South or urban North where blacks were constant victims of brutality and where the government was unable or unwilling to protect them. Finally, Malcolm said, he believed in black unity before any consideration of black-white cooperation. The new organization would remain open to ideas and financial aid from all quarters; whites could lend support but couldn't become members because "there can be no black-white unity until there is at first some black unity."

Malcolm's first recruits to his new venture were few in number, mainly fellow defectors from the Black Muslims and dissidents from Harlem black-nationalist groups. From the outset, the Muslim Mosque Incorporated was weak and ill-structured, but in the pursuit of his political and religious interests Malcolm forged an opportunity to explore the ideology of black nationalism and the world of Islam in a wider context than he ever had before.

In a seminal speech before a largely white audience gathered at the socialist Militant Labor Forum in New York, April 8, 1964, Malcolm spoke of the growing impatience with the "white nationalism" of America masquerading as democracy, and of the emergence of its implacable foe, a militant, uncompromising policy of black nationalism. He predicted the merging of an embryonic black American revolution with the worldwide revolution of black and colonized peoples which, he said, had been taking place since the end of World War II. It was a revolution for land and power that would not be without casualties on both sides, white as well as black.

Malcolm's Forum speech was especially important because two notable statements of conciliation were emphasized. First of all, there was a recognized mutuality of objectives between integration and separation, two forces which had hitherto been in opposition because of the divide-and-rule tactics of the white power structure. He now believed that:

> All of our people have the same goals, the same objectives. That objective is freedom, justice, equality. All of us want recognition and respect as human beings. We don't want to be integrationists. Nor do we want to be separationists. We want to be human beings. Integration is only a method that is used by some groups to obtain freedom, justice, equality and respect as human beings. Separation is only a method that is used by other groups to obtain freedom, justice, equality and human dignity.
>
> Our people have made the mistake of confusing the methods with the objectives. As long as we agree on objectives, we should never fall out with each other just because we believe in different methods or tactics or strategy to reach a common objective.

Second, it was extremely important for blacks, while making ready for battle, to recognize the possibility of a "bloodless revolution." American society was in a unique position to undergo a bloodless revolution because the Negro holds the balance of power, he said, and the added power of his vote could change the whole political structure, especially the Southern segregationism-controlled foreign and domestic policy. It was, as he had said many times, a question of obtaining the ballot and the freedom to use it, or resorting to the bullet.

In mid-April Malcolm left for an extensive tour of the Middle East and Africa, where he was received enthusiastically by heads of state, ambassadors, political leaders, students, and expatriate black Americans. He made a pilgrimage to Mecca, the shrine of orthodox Islam, and the fraternal relations that existed among the multiracial pilgrims were in marked contrast to the conscious racism of white Americans he had experienced. In Ghana, Malcolm met with President Kwame Nkrumah, leader of the first modern African state to win its independence, and they discussed the historical community of interests of Africans and Afro-Americans. Malcolm was now persuaded that it was time for all Afro-Americans to become an integral part of the world's Pan-Africanists, and even though they might remain in America physically while fighting for the benefits guaranteed by the Constitution, they must return to Africa philosophically and culturally to develop a working unity within the framework of Pan-Africanism. By the end of his trip, Malcolm had established a network of contacts in Egypt, Lebanon, Saudi Arabia, Nigeria, Ghana, Morocco, and Algeria. His pilgrimage and the honorific pilgrim's title "El Hadj" had given deep personal satisfaction, and he was impressed by the cordiality of Nigerian Muslim students who hailed him as "Omowale," the child who has come home. The Malcolm who returned from Africa as El-Hadj Malik El-Shabazz was far different from the one who had left. He returned with a sense of his African heritage and a broadened perspective on world forces affecting Afro-Americans.

Back home in New York, in the tense summer atmosphere of protest demonstrations and racial unrest, Malcolm reviewed his new experiences and formulated a plan to bring the problems of Afro-Americans to worldwide attention. His first objective was to win a place of leadership in the activist wing of the civil-rights movement. He assured his audiences that though he was now an orthodox Sunni Muslim he was prepared to work with black Christian leaders. He was not anti-white but anti-exploitation. He criticized Congress, particularly the Southern Dixiecrats, who were blocking civil-rights legislation. He called for the expansion of civil-rights activities to the level of human rights, and concluded, "We need new methods, new thinking, new direction, and new allies." In late June, Malcolm announced the formation of a secular black group, the Organization of Afro-American Unity (OAAU). It was to be modeled after the Organization of African Unity, an all-African confederation founded by heads of independent African states. The purpose of Malcolm's OAAU was to seek complete independence for peoples of African descent in the United States and in the Western Hemisphere, by any means necessary. To achieve this end, it would encourage the broadest possible cooperation between all groups seeking black freedom.

Malcolm's second objective was the formulation of a manifesto to the United Nations Human Rights Commission, calling for the prosecution of the United States government on the grounds that the deteriorating plight of Afro-Americans was a threat to world peace. In July, Malcolm returned to Africa to lobby heads of state gathered in Cairo for the second summit conference of the Organization of African Unity. He was given observer status and submitted a lengthy memorandum urging support for the black's struggle in America. Malcolm addressed the members as a representative of "your long-lost brothers and sisters" suffering from mounting acts of violence and a persistent pattern of racism and segregation. He then went on to declare that the brutal violation of the human rights of Afro-Americans can lead only to defensive retaliation by blacks and the escalation of racial conflict into a violent, worldwide, and bloody race war. Furthermore, he said, "the United States government is morally incapable of protecting the lives and property of 22 million Afro-Americans," and he beseeched the assembly to "recommend an immediate investigation into our problem by the United Nations Commission on Human Rights." Malcolm underscored his points by reference to the racially inspired murder of civil-rights workers in the South and attacks on African students and diplomats in Washington, D.C., and New York. He compared the open injustice of South Africa with the cunning dishonesty of America, and declared that both were equally guilty of heinous crimes against blacks. He urged the assembly: "Don't escape from European colonialism only to become more enslaved by deceitful, 'friendly' American dollarism."

Malcolm achieved a notable success at the meeting, which supported a moderately worded resolution acknowledging concern with racial problems in the United States. The OAU noted the recent enactment of the Civil Rights Act but was deeply disturbed by continuing manifestations of racial bigotry and racial oppression against American Negro citizens and urged the intensification of government efforts to ensure the total elimination of all forms of discrimination based on race, color, or ethnic origin. Malcolm's bold political moves won him many friends in Africa, and during the months after the conference he visited African capitals for talks with important heads of state: Nasser of Egypt, Nyerere of Tanzania, Nkrumah of Ghana, Kenyatta of Kenya, Obote of Uganda and Touré of Guinea. In all probability, Malcolm capitalized on a combination of factors to emphasize the urgency of his argument. Most important were the implications of the 1964 presidential elections for American policies of intervention in the former Belgian Congo and support of settler regimes in southern Africa.

When he returned to New York, November 24, 1964, Malcolm undertook an exhaustive speaking tour in major cities with black populations. His purpose was to educate and enlarge the consciousness of blacks, to reshape their sense of identity, and to prepare them for a revolutionary role. Malcolm told his audiences that America was a prison, a police state, and that the black ghettos were like colonies exploited by foreign businessmen and politicians.

In many speeches he gave during this period, his tone was vindictive, remorseless, and brutally frank. It was the tone of a man who was tiring under tremendous strain. The underlying theme was the Black Revolution, and he used it to give coherence to a wide range of topics that he was striving to understand. On a global level he noted that popular fears of the "population explosion" spread by ecologists was really the fear of whites being outnumbered by the colored races. At home, he said, the Dixiecrat Senators of the South manifestly feared any changes in the racial power structure. But what they did not realize was that racial tension in

America had finally arrived at a crisis point and could ignite a global powder keg. He warned white leaders against the delusion that because whites outnumber blacks in America there was no danger; they must bear in mind that in a largely non-white world it is they who are the minority. The days of waiting for freedom were over; blacks were learning new tricks and guerrilla tactics from observing other revolutionary conflicts. The catalysts of change would be black nationalist militants who, though small in number, would be the ingredient necessary to fuse and ignite the entire black community, he said, and added: "It was stones yesterday, Molotov cocktails today; and it will be grenades tomorrow and whatever else is available the next day."

The pendulum, he believed, was swinging in favor of the darker peoples, and therefore in favor of Afro-Americans, provided they had a correct understanding of the global balance of forces. It was absolutely vital to internationalize the struggle and to get power bases abroad, with the full support of African, Asian, and Latin American peoples. As for himself, he now clearly identified the cause of Afro-Americans with the anti-colonial revolutions of exploited peoples of the Third World. From his new perspective, and inspired by the socialist experiments he observed and discussed in Africa, Malcolm saw the coming battle as one against the triple evils of Western power groups: capitalism, colonialism, and racism—a battle which he felt must take place on two fronts: in the colonies and newly developing countries, and in the black ghettos of America, through the efforts of an Afro-American liberation movement dedicated to the goal of revolution and black liberation.

For the first time, Malcolm X began to express his views about socialism. It was plain that he was not a trained Marxist theoretician or a member of any Marxist party. But he had spoken with black and white socialists during his travels in America and abroad, and was particularly excited by his discovery that socialism in Africa and Asia offered another avenue for the development and progress of downtrodden people. Speaking at an OAAU meeting in the Audubon Ballroom in Harlem, December 20, 1964, Malcolm punctuated his lengthy remarks on the subject by saying: "Almost every one of the countries that has gotten independence has devised some kind of socialistic system, and this is no accident . . . You can't operate a capitalistic system unless you are vulturistic; you have to have someone else's blood to suck to be a capitalist. You show me a capitalist, I'll show you a blood-sucker."

There were, he found, obvious contradictions in American society which made socialism a desirable alternative for consideration by black people. For example:

> This is the richest country on earth and there's poverty, there's bad housing, there's slums, there's inferior education. And this is the richest country on earth. Now, you know, if those countries that are poor can come up with a solution to their problems so that there's no unemployment, then instead of you running downtown picketing city hall, you should stop and find out what they do over there to solve their problems. This is why the man doesn't want you and me to look beyond Harlem or beyond the shores of America. As long as you don't know what's happening on the outside, you'll be all messed up dealing with this man on the inside. I mean what they use to solve the problem is not capitalism. What they are using to solve their problem in Africa and Asia is not capitalism. So what you and I should do is find out what they are using to get rid of poverty and all the other negative characteristics of a rundown society.

Malcolm outlined his ideas at the homecoming rally held for him by his own group, at meetings sponsored by the socialist Militant Labor Forum in New York, and to students at Harvard University and Oxford University, England. But his reputation as a man of hate and violence continued to plague him. Black moderate civil-rights leaders thought him too militant. White liberals and the traditional Socialist and Communist Party leaders denounced his ideas as "racism in reverse" and as a danger to their hopes of forging a national alliance of whites, blacks, trade unions, and the Democratic Party. New radical groups in the ghetto thought he was losing contact with the "brothers in the streets" and abandoning black nationalism and separatism for Trotskyist socialism.

During this period Malcolm X found it difficult to adjust to his new and vulnerable situation and to maintain the interest and support of his small band of followers. At weekly meetings in January 1965, designed to educate and attract new members, Malcolm lectured on the relevance of Afro-American history, and explained the conditions and methods used to keep black people oppressed. At the February 7 meeting he planned to speak on the future of the Afro-American struggle and the goals and objectives of the OAAU program. However, Malcolm was away that week in Europe to fulfill a number of speaking engagements and the lecture was postponed. But Malcolm never had a chance to unveil his program. On his return from England the night of February 13, his house in East Elmhurst, Queens, was fire-bombed by unknown persons, and the next week, on Sunday, February 21, Malcolm X was shot down in a hail of bullets as he started to speak to an OAAU rally at the Audubon Ballroom in uptown Manhattan.

Three of his assassins were found, tried, and convicted. Two had known Black Muslim connections and may have acted in response to veiled suggestions from their leaders. Yet the legend has grown that Malcolm X was killed because he was a threat to the American establishment, on the instructions of the police and the Central Intelligence Agency. At his funeral in New York, thousands of mourners paid tribute to Malcolm X as the shining black prince, El-Hadj Malik El-Shabazz, who had challenged white power and paid for it with his life.

That Malcolm X attained a preeminent, controversial, though short-lived, position in the minds of black and white Americans at all is in itself remarkable; there were so many distortions in his personality, errors in his social analyses, and contradictions in his message, leadership style, and organizational tactics.

If childhood alone were the sole influence upon Malcolm X, then all the circumstantial conditions were at hand for a tormented adulthood. He was part hot-blooded, frustrated, alien Caribbean on his mother's side, and part puritan zealot on his father's. He hated the society that killed his father and filled his childhood home with tragedy; he was ashamed of the taint of white blood in his mother's family that bequeathed him a light skin with a reddish "rhiny" cast. As Malcolm Little, the ghetto charity child, he was severely traumatized, and as "Detroit Red," the parasitic criminal, he was alienated from black as well as white society. Malcolm the adolescent was a tragic victim of the ghetto slum, and in the prison of his mind he was an exile in his own country.

Malcolm X was a prophet-rebel produced from the grieving womb of the black masses. But he was too often manipulated by the media and the white power structure to make moderate black leadership more palatable as an alternative to black nationalism. Malcolm learned how to make whites jump when he roared "Black Revolution," and when he discovered how tantalizingly close the phantom-fear of black revenge lies to the surface of white consciousness, he could rarely resist the pleasure of artful masquerade. Though Malcolm spoke of revolution, and seemed the swaggering image of a hardened guerrilla leader—fierce, but charming and sexually attractive—he led no guerrilla campaigns. Malcolm was not, for example, the Che Guevara or Amilcar Cabral of black America, nor was his Organization of Afro-American Unity an Irish Republican Army, a German Baader-Mainhof group, or a Japanese Red Army. Malcolm's natural abode was the open city, not the pestilent swamps, shadowy forests, and craggy mountains. He was a media man, not a clandestine insurgent or maquisard.

Initiation into the Nation of Islam gave Malcolm a sense of identification, a set of religious doctrines to explain his personal failings, and an organization through which he could advance his own interests. He did not notice or seem to care that the millenarian creed he dutifully repeated contained a fatal flaw. The cries for retribution, land, and reparations from unjust rulers to start a new, separate life concealed an inordinate desire for material success here and now, while the Almighty Allah in his wisdom saw to the ultimate destiny of black power.

Malcolm the Black Muslim minister relied heavily on religious mysticism, denunciatory rhetoric, and a primordial Ethiopic alchemy. To reach people, Malcolm wove together bits of Garvey's black nationalism and race redemption with the demonology of the Black Muslims. He added fresh ingredients from his hustler background of violent confrontation, threat and counterthreat. He filled his speeches with visual images, with allusions to the blues, and with slogans and animal symbols. Whites were denizens of the jungle, vicious wolves, foxes, dogs, and snakes, preying upon the vulnerable blacks, who were lost sheep. When the break with Muhammad came, it was hard to adapt his style to meet the demands of secular political organization. To the end of his life, his speeches were delivered in the cadence and style of Bible-thumping Baptist and Pentecostal preachers and prophetic leaders of millenaristic sects. There was much in Malcolm like the early American Protestant exhorters of revelatory creeds, and his utterances were akin to that of political and religious nationalists in other lands whose verbal skills are nourished by cultural roots and dominated by a terrifying puritanism and incantatory power.

Violence for Malcolm seemed to take on a redemptive meaning in and of itself. Through armed struggle, he suggested, new recruits from the hard-core corrupted elements in the black community would be transformed into productive citizens in a restructured society. Surely, this was a grave political error. More often than not, such elements when recruited into political movements are conscienceless and in league with the same forces which oppress defenseless people. In the stormy passage from the underworld to the underground, even when useful as leaders of shock troops and attack gangs, the criminal mentality often reveals itself in brutal exploits and adventurism which must be curbed by the movement's political authority. Furthermore, it is historically true that though aggrieved, unorganized masses violently assert themselves against an oppressive society, such violence alone rarely leads to the overthrow of that society. To urge black people to violence as a broad fixed policy, as if they were crazed religious zealots in a holy war, without awareness of its implications and limitations, is to grossly misread Che Guevara's *Episodes of the Revolutionary War*, Fanon's *Wretched of the Earth*, and Chairman Mao's Little Red Book.

Malcolm was dedicated to the preservation of the ghetto and its transformation into a happier environment. This exemplifies a kind of simplistic black nationalism which literally means turning one's back on the wider society and saying, "What whites do to whites is their business. We have to solve our own problems." This view fails to recognize that the ghetto is dependent on the city and is affected by what whites think and how they act, and how the economy distributes resources. Surely blacks will remain inhabitants of obsolescent housing and environments, whether the ghetto is "liberated" or not, as long as the whites consider them a relatively insignificant and expendable part of modern urban industrial society.

Malcolm's failure, too, lay in his inability to create a sound organizational base for his post-Black Muslim activities. In the last year of his life he was unable to give the time required, and the necessary energy and effort. The black nationalist protest style he used so well on street corners and the media is not well suited to the long-term task of organization and institution-building. Although extremely popular as a device for attracting public attention, Malcolm's protest style did not forge permanent links; it only led to noisy demonstrations. Malcolm at the head of ill-disciplined ranks was a hapless political pariah, a far different man from Malcolm in the vanguard of a dedicated, single-minded, and well-trained corps of the Fruit of Islam.

Malcolm in building his quest for unity on the basis of color or some genetic *affinité naturelle* fell into the trap of the "skin myth." Historically, color defined the black American's experience, yet skin color itself does not explain the black man's slave status. Slavery and near-slavery have existed in one form or the other in many societies around the world at different stages in their formation. The black man's inferior status in the New World was mainly economic in its origins, and was subsequently epidermalized and internalized by black and whites alike. Furthermore, Malcolm's exhortations to unity based on the single issue of race protest ignores and does not dissolve the class interests and other factors which stratify black society. Deep-rooted class differences exist in terms of education, ownership, and income as well as in regional backgrounds and culture. Certainly, in the black community, the interests of the low-income tenantry are entirely different from those of the professionals, slum landlords, political elites, and vice bosses who gain their livelihood from the meager earnings of "the brothers." (Or, to be fair, does Malcolm mean that the birth of black awareness through the medium of skin-togetherness coincides with the birth of black proletarian consciousness? That direct action by blacks to smash white privileges is the first step toward attacking the system that creates and supports these privileges?)

In many ways Malcolm was naïve about the dynamics of the class structure of black society. He underestimated the willingness of the middle classes and enterprising individuals to adopt his program and use it to serve their own interests. Malcolm was not sure who would make and ensure the success of the Black Revolution. Was it the field Negro, as he exists today in the South and about whom Malcolm knew very little, or the ex-field Negro, now resident in Northern urban ghettos? Would it be the redeemed hustlers, the ghetto unemployed, college-educated youth, or workers in the trade-union movement? He could not distinguish the factors which would lead to a radical regrouping of the black poor and lower working class and their victory over the reformist opportunism of the affluent sections of black society.

On the international level, Malcolm's awareness of African political structures, despite his travels, was as superficial as the newspaper headlines. He was admittedly shocked at the murder of Patrice Lumumba, the Congo Prime Minister, and denounced Moise Tshombe for his criminal actions following the intervention of the major powers in the Congo. He referred on several occasions to Prime Minister Harold Macmillan's "Winds of Change" speech at the United Nations in 1962, citing it as a timely recognition of the changing colonial situation. He offered to send "some of the brothers" over to Kenya to help Jomo Kenyatta and Oginga Odinga wrest the reins of power from the British, and he applauded the efforts of Ahmed Ben Bella and the Algerian liberation movement to gain independence from French rule. But in many respects these gestures, though dangerous during a period when black free speech, especially on international affairs, was regarded with suspicion by the American government and white society, had no political substance beyond their immediate publicity value. Malcolm paid homage to nominally socialist leaders—Nasser, Touré, and Nkrumah—but was also dazzled by the opulence and hospitality of feudal monarchs like Prince Faisal of Saudi Arabia. He spoke out against "U.S. dollarism" but did not fully comprehend the subtler forms of neo-colonialism by which the great powers, multinational companies, reactionary military regimes, and the national bourgeoisie traduce the democratic goals of African independence. In his travels Malcolm did not really "see" rural Africa or understand its fundamental problems of habitat, land, and economy. He had limited knowledge of the complexities of highly stratified tribal societies and of the intense hatreds which divide the populations of some African nations into hostile groupings and often lead to civil war and a continual cycle of military coups d'état.

Malcolm's death brought mixed responses from people of varying political backgrounds. White liberals claimed he was becoming a black liberal. Marxists said he would have been a socialist had he lived. Applause came from Trotskyites, Maoists, Nkrumahists, Garveyites, and black nationalists; and the youth-led movements mourned the passing of a fallen warrior. However, Elijah Muhammad and Black Muslim leaders denounced Malcolm as an evil Angel of Death who had fallen from grace, and recognizable sighs of relief came from spokesmen of civil-rights organizations like the National Association for the Advancement of Colored People and the National Urban League.

Saviour or scoundrel? Alex Haley, the chronicler of Malcolm's memoirs, notes in the closing pages of *The Autobiography of Malcolm X* the range of opinions as the first shock waves of Malcolm's death hit Harlem and black communities across the nation. Peter Goldman, a white news reporter and author of *The Death and Life of Malcolm X*, describes him as a man pushed to the desperate edge of the nation's life and laments that "We are the smaller as a nation for having consigned him there. We are the less as a people for having lost him." A formidable and long-standing critic of Malcolm X, Bayard Rustin, a black social democrat and stalwart of the integrationist cause, could not accept his personal failings and lack of a strategy for social change; in a similar vein, the white liberal writer and essayist Irving Howe saw Malcolm as a "cop-out," an intransigent nihilist whose vehement rejection of American society turned him into a kind of apolitical spectator. C. Eric Lincoln, a black theologian, writing in *Malcolm X: The Man and His Times*, was charitable in his remarks, saying that, though Malcolm was an unacceptable participant in peaceful social change, he was a gifted charismatic leader whose spirit will rise again, not only because he is worthy of remembrance, but because the continued existence of the black ghetto in American society will not let him be forgotten.

Some observers are of the opinion that Malcolm died at a time when he was redefining his attitude to black-white relations. M. S. Handler, a white liberal *New York Times* reporter, says in the introduction to *The Autobiography of Malcolm X* that he had toned down his indiscriminate attacks on the whole society and all whites and begun to concentrate on countering the activities of white supremacists in the South and the North. Ossie Davis, a well-known black actor who eulogized Malcolm as an outstanding leader of his race, believes that after his trip to Mecca no one who had known Malcolm before could doubt that he had completely abandoned racism, separatism, and hatred. George Breitman of the Socialist Workers Party claims that when he had freed himself from the dominance of the Black Muslims, Malcolm was in the process of a great transformation. He was becoming a "black nationalist plus revolutionary." This means, says Breitman, a leading white Marxist theoretician, that he was beginning to question the pure and simple form of black nationalism which alienated people who were true revolutionaries, many of them whites, whose collaboration was needed if society was to be transformed.

But had Malcolm changed? Reverend Albert Cleage, a black nationalist preacher and one-time confidant of Malcolm X, holds the view that the "true Malcolm" has been submerged by stories arising from his last chaotic years. He hadn't changed; he was still a black nationalist and knew that the white man was the black man's enemy. "That is the message of Malcolm," says Cleage in *Malcolm X: The Man and His Times*, "and don't let anybody get you all mixed up. He never turned into an integrationist, never. He wasn't fooled in Mecca, he wasn't fooled in Africa. He told it like it was and he knew it like it was. That is our Malcolm. Some other folks may have another Malcolm—they are welcome to him. But, brothers, don't lose *our* Malcolm."

With these differing interpretations of Malcolm, as he was and

as he might have become, we are left with a large element of doubt
about the choices he would have made. Neither of his major biog-
raphers, Alex Haley and Peter Goldman, has fully grasped the political implications of Malcolm's life and death. George Breitman,
the socialist, appreciates Malcolm's political importance but is un-
questionably doctrinaire and severely handicapped by a heavy-
handed vindication of Malcolm's failings with reference to his
proto-revolutionary development in his last year. The writer John
Henrik Clarke and his black colleagues, many of whom were Harlem intimates of Malcolm, seem excessively laudatory in their
praise in *Malcolm X: The Man and His Times* and, like James
Baldwin's book *One Day, When I Was Lost*, too respectfully in awe
of Malcolm's meteoric rise and fall to bring their critical faculties to
bear. Scholars have tended to give Malcolm a wide berth and left
the field to journalists like Haley, Goldman, and Louis Lomax, author of *To Kill a Black Man*, who all too easily clothe Malcolm in
sensational and contrasting colors of black and white.

Would Malcolm have embarked on the last stages of a journey
from black nationalism through Pan-Africanism to revolutionary
socialism—for all these tendencies were encompassed within the
speeches of his final year? One will never know. Probably Malcolm, though maligned as high priest of the politics of violence,
thought of himself as a black man—a teacher—a minister—a
Muslim—a nationalist—a political revolutionary in the cause of
black America's other dominant and centuries-old mode of thought
and action, black nationalist separatism.

Whatever his failings, one cannot avoid the essentials of his
social thought. Through his travels around the country, Malcolm
gained a sense of the plight of the new urban black masses, many of
whom were aspiring but unwanted cast-offs from Dixieland. Their
wretched conditions appalled him, and he learned to identify with
the masses more than with the Nation of Islam. During the upsurge
of civil-rights protest in the sixties, Malcolm put the needs of black
people ahead of the Black Muslim hierarchy, and translated its cant
into a full-blown black nationalist ideology. His suspension com-
pelled him to see that blacks were in deep trouble. The Nation of
Islam had gone as far as it could—but he must go further. In addi-

tion to rejecting integration, there was the necessity to change American society, internally through resistance and rebellion, and externally through alignments with Africa and more powerful world forces. Malcolm believed that black liberation was a task that only blacks themselves could accomplish. This task required the mobilization of the ghetto masses and could not be successfully undertaken by a compromising approach acceptable to middle-class blacks and liberal whites. Alliances were needed, but they must follow not precede the organization of a militant black movement. Whatever facilitates mass mobilization, especially the language and methods of black nationalism, is good; whatever blocks it is bad; all else is irrelevant.

Malcolm recognized that in America there were basic shortcomings in the proposal: integrate or be rejected. It was palpably clear that though black men may want to prove to white men, at all costs, the richness of their heritage and the equal value of their intellect, white men consider themselves superior to black men and would ensure in every way possible that integration did not threaten their supremacy. Malcolm felt that the dream of integration was a false hope because of the nature of the society. America, he believed, is a pathologically Negrophobic society in which the slow and difficult rise of the black man is conditioned solely by the degree to which he conforms to white expectations or assimilates white patterns. Integration to the white man means "Be like me" and he believes that most if not all blacks can never be like him. Integration must therefore inevitably mean that the door of opportunity is only open to those "blacks who think white."

Integration should be opposed, said Malcolm, because it is a process by which white society exploits the talents of a few blacks and the best contributions of all Afro-Americans while the masses of people remain unequal and unbenefited. Under the present circumstances, integration only means racial coexistence on the basis of inequality. In the future it implies the inevitable whitening or Aryanization of blacks and their eventual assimilation out of existence—their cultural and physical demise.

There is a dire need, he concluded, to redefine the black self-image and to decolonize it. This decolonization process should include opposition to the label "Negro" because it is a dishonorable badge of slavery denoting stereotyped and debased traits of character, and helps to prolong and perpetuate oppression and discrimination. Blacks should also reject the so-called great documents of Negro progress, the Emancipation Proclamation and civil-rights legislation, and proclaim instead a Declaration of Condemnation of American Racism and a Proclamation of Restitution for the victims of group oppression.

In Malcolm's view, America owed its wretched blacks an immeasurable debt which had to be paid. He regarded the excessive materialism and affluence of America as an outrage, derived as it was from slavery and the robbery of black labor. ("America is as much a creation of blacks as Europe is a creation of the exploited resources of the Third World," he once said.) Government expenditure on foreign adventures, the Vietnam war, and the arms race should be used to solve domestic and urban ghetto problems. Failing this, he called for payment of indemnities. If the German government was paying reparations to Israel as compensation for Nazi brutalities against Jews, then why shouldn't the United States pay reparations to blacks on a scale sufficient to bring about their economic development?

Belatedly, Malcolm realized that decolonization required more than strong words and good intentions. What was necessary, especially for those who wished to place themselves in the vanguard of the struggle, was to help the black man to choose action to confront the real source of conflict—the unjust structures inherent in American society—and thereby discover a new possibility of existence. With these thoughts Malcolm had arrived in his own way at a view expressed by the black psychiatrist—maquisard of the Algerian revolution, Frantz Fanon, when he said in *Black Skin, White Masks:*

> My patient is suffering from an inferiority complex. His psychic structure is in danger of disintegration. What has to be done is to save him from this and, little by little, to rid him of this unconscious desire.
>
> If he is overwhelmed to such a degree by the wish to be white, it is because he lives in a society that makes his inferiority complex

possible, in a society that derives its stability from the perpetuation of this complex, in a society that proclaims the superiority of one race; to the identical degree to which that society creates difficulties for him, he will find himself thrust into a neurotic situation.

What emerges then is the need for combined action on the individual and the group. As a psychoanalyst, I should help my patient become *conscious* of his unconscious and abandon his attempts at a hallucinatory whitening, but also to act in the direction of a change in the social structure.

But the question was how to move toward decolonization—toward demystifying integration and cleansing black consciousness. How to propel blacks toward action against the structures affecting their destiny. Malcolm clearly wanted to use the conditions created by white racism, including the racial consciousness it fosters among its black victims, to bring about its abolition. He was convinced that black nationalism could contribute to the process of political mobilization in the same way as class consciousness and solidarity aids the formation of workers' movements. New focal points of power were necessary to confront old ones. Just as socialism confronts capitalism, so Pan-Africanism would consolidate the thrust of African independence movements against the white nationalism which lurks behind the hegemony of European states and settler colonies.

Malcolm's own bitter experiences had taught him the efficacy and appeal of some "basic truths." Unity and self-defense must be mobilized against the violence and terrorism used to maintain subordination, and against the integrationist policy of non-violence and black-white unity. Freedom must be fought for; it cannot be granted, it must be seized. The ghettos must be turned into focal points of liberation and of strategies for a grass-roots attack on specific problems. Blacks should orient themselves to other worlds of thought, including socialism, and internationalize their struggle in harmony with the anti-colonial battles raging in Africa and the rest of the Third World. They should seek alliances with friends of all colors and ideologies who share the same revolutionary goals. They must learn about their origins in order to build confidence and to understand present reality.

These basic points form the essential principles of Malcolm's black nationalist ideology. He felt that when they were organized into a program they could be systematically taught and, if practiced, could change the black man's status in America. It is clear that Malcolm did modify his earlier views. Separation was associated with ensuring the independence of black ghetto communities. His aggressive anti-white sentiments shifted toward the positive goal of freedom, justice, and equality, but with continued emphasis on liberating the black man in American society, not integrating him into that society.

Malcolm's black nationalism affirmed the desire of an oppressed minority to decide its own destiny by creating independent political, economic, and social institutions. It highlighted the themes of racial unity and pride, group consciousness, the hatred of white supremacy, a striving for independence from white control, and an international perspective. There were a range of options for survival and development. "Get ourselves together." Use the system to siphon off benefits to the black community. Oppose the system recognizing that racism in America cannot be finally erased without the replacement of capitalism.

In sum, the legacy of Malcolm X is the way he illuminated nine essential components of a black nationalist movement:

—Black unity: complete unity and advancement of peoples of African descent in America and the Western Hemisphere.
—Self-determination: the right of black communities to direct and control their lives, their history, and their future.
—Community politics and community control: strong all-black communities and organizations, and the voluntary preservation of black communities inside America; non-aligned political action and the organization of black independent voters, political clubs, and candidates responsible to the black community; an all-out attack on community problems—high rents, high prices, and lack of jobs.
—Education: original educational and cultural methods and black-led institutions which will liberate the minds of children and raise people to higher levels of excellence and self-respect.
—Economic security: end economic slavery by aiding the black

man to gain control of the economy of the black community and to develop technical and business expansion for the benefit of the people.

—Armed self-defense: black men should fight back in self-defense whenever and wherever they are unjustly and unlawfully attacked.

—Social and moral uplift: the community must rid itself of the effects of years of exploitation, neglect, and apathy, and wage an unrelenting battle against police brutality, organized crime, drug addiction, and delinquency.

—Rediscovery of the African heritage: communications with Africa should be reopened through the study of African history, travel, and the exploration of cultural and philosophical affinities.

—Internationalization of the black struggle: Pan-African perspective and increased awareness of the larger world of oppressed peoples should be developed through the study of their political ideologies, philosophies, and psychologies, cultures and languages, and the creation of alliances with new Third World power blocs in international organizations for common benefit.

What strikes one about Malcolm X and his black nationalist message to the grass roots is the way he restates in his own fashion so many of the voices of protest of the past. And how thoroughly American it is—for America in the course of its history has called forth a variety of religious, racial, ethnic, and secular nationalisms whose advocates have urged that a victory for their group is at once a major step forward to a more perfect democracy. What Malcolm will be remembered for, after all else is forgotten, is his definition of a way to deal with the system of racial politics and his efforts to redefine the relationships of blacks to the white power structure. He rejected the traditional model whereby black working people are led by the black middle class, who are in alliance with and dominated by the white power structure. He was moved to place the interests of all blacks against those of all whites; and much later, the interests of all revolutionary forces, both black and white, against all retrograde forces, black and white. If a compromise was necessary, it would be forged by the leaders of the mass of disadvantaged black people and their allies at the vanguard of a united front including at the rear a chastened and more socially responsible black middle class.

Malcolm's ideas foreshadowed the possibility of the evolution of black nationalism and black consciousness to a higher level of rational and objective discourse. In this respect, it is up to future generations to apply the crucial tests to his program. How can it be used to turn concrete problems and issues into ideological concepts for analysis, discussion, and action? How may it be used to transform ideas and goals into social levers to prize loose gains for blacks and change unjust structures? During Malcolm's life no black leader was free from the shadow of his thinking; in fact, he was singularly responsible for the demystification of the civil-rights movement and was a precursor of the rise of Black Power. In the decade after his death the main structure of his ideas, even if heavily attacked on a few exposed fronts, has not only endured but has informed all black expression from bourgeois to revolutionary.

3 The Eclipse of Integration

The civil-rights calendar of the sixties calls to mind black bodies straining under the impact of pistol butts, fire hoses, and cattle prods, and lives snuffed out in churches, swamplands, and jail houses. During these years an increasing number of moderate men and women, black and white, kept their faith in God and American justice and asked the nation to affirm its mandate: "No, to violence and racism; yes, to justice and civil rights for Negroes." The most dramatic of their experiences was the celebrated March on Washington in 1963, endorsed by the President of the United States, led by a coalition of civil-rights, trade-union, religious and political leaders, and powered by the dramatic eloquence of Dr. Martin Luther King, Jr.'s speech "I Have a Dream." But an examination of the events surrounding that sunny August day of interracial exuberance reveals much more illusion than reality. Was the march the beginning of a new era of imaginative interracial coalition politics, effective mass mobilization, and significant legislation? Or was it the final requiem of fifty years' non-violent civil-rights activity?

As the decade began, one major organization, the National Association for the Advancement of Colored People, and two minor ones, the Congress of Racial Equality and the Southern Christian Leadership Conference, were solidly entrenched in the integrationist civil-rights vanguard. Key leadership positions were held by priests-in-politics like Martin Luther King, Jr., and Ralph David Abernathy; the organizational apparatus was in the hands of the NAACP and its interracial allies. Legal and judicial maneuvers and sporadic non-violent protests in Southern towns and cities were the order of the day. With these limited goals, civil-rights protest might have remained becalmed in a windless sea of national indifference if it had not been for the college sit-ins of 1960, which turned isolated outbreaks of resistance into a vigorous mass movement.

On February 1, 1960, four black college students from the Agricultural and Technical College in Greensboro, North Carolina, entered Woolworth's and sat down at the lunch counter reserved exclusively for whites. They were refused service and sat quietly reading a Bible and philosophy books while the astonished patrons ate in indignant silence. "Sitting-in" for civil rights soon caught the imagination of black and white sympathizers and spread throughout the South and into many Northern cities. Within a year, more than fifty thousand people were drawn into peaceful direct-action protests. They sat in restaurants and hotel lobbies, and waded into the sea and into swimming pools in order to dramatize their goal of desegregation of public facilities. Demonstrations and violent clashes occurred in at least one hundred cities, and over 3,600 protesters went to jail. Their actions triggered the student-led "sit-in movement" and a new phase of modern civil-rights activity.

The key organization in this new thrust was the Student Nonviolent Coordinating Committee (SNCC), founded in 1960 to aid the protest activities of local youth and student groups, mainly in the South. SNCC was founded and financially supported by the Southern Christian Leadership Conference, and its members were heavily committed to a moral policy of non-violence and Christian purpose as preached by Reverend Martin Luther King, Jr. They sought, according to the SNCC founding statement, a "social order of justice permeated by love" and believed that "integration of human endeavor represents the crucial first step toward such a society."

SNCC's first taste of civil-rights combat began with support of sit-ins, protests, and marches to desegregate public facilities. Black student leaders like John Lewis believed that direct action could be a powerful weapon for change in its own right and was as important as the traditional tactics of integration by judicial process and agreements with the white establishment. By 1961 SNCC spearheaded the first voter-registration campaigns in Mississippi, using McComb County, a heavily populated black area, as the center of operations. SNCC also initiated with members of the Congress of Racial Equality (CORE) the first integrated "Freedom bus rides" through Southern states. Later, in 1961, SNCC became an integral part of a new Southern civil-rights coalition group, the Council of Federated Organizations, which coordinated the activities of NAACP, CORE, and the Southern Christian Leadership Conference (SCLC) led by Reverend King.

COFO, as the council was called, was a remarkable coalition. In it were student activists, religious and civil-rights groups. But SNCC's seemingly casual mode of organization and operation contrasted sharply with the more hierarchical and centrally controlled structure of the other groups. SNCC's structure, like that of many student movements of the period, was open and flexible, with no fixed bureaucracy. Local groups were encouraged to conduct their affairs within the general framework of integrationist objectives. But they were free to choose their own strategy and tactics to deal with local problems and grievances. The voter-registration campaigns were seen not as a means of delivering votes into one or the other national political parties but rather as a means of educating potential community leaders and organizing local communities to deal with broader issues of freedom and liberty.

Before long the SNCC-led campaigns, protests, marches, and boycotts became major instruments for challenging the Democratic Party-controlled Southern state political power. SNCC activists sought to consolidate short-term gains into permanent victories by making overtures for patronage on the national level. At first they found welcome support from the newly elected President, John F. Kennedy, but SNCC leaders resented the policies of gradualism suggested by Northern Democrats as a means of achieving peace in the South. The students concluded that the Kennedy Administration was interested only in black votes and not in black progress and would not voluntarily impose sanctions on the Southern segregationist wing of the Democratic Party.

Soon the students' mistrust of Kennedy's intentions tainted their respect and devotion to the SCLC leadership, and a major ideological rupture occurred during the March on Washington in 1963. In June of that year, President Kennedy became increasingly aware of the mounting atrocities against blacks and the widespread deterioration in race relations. He asked Congress to mark the one hundredth anniversary of the Emancipation Proclamation by completing the agenda of democracy with legislation desegregating schools, public facilities, and government programs. This brought enthusiastic liberal support and he endorsed the March on Washington organized by Bayard Rustin on behalf of A. Philip Randolph and other civil-rights leaders. In August, Washington was invaded by 250,000 civil-rights marchers, one third of them white, to emphasize the President's initiative and encourage the passage of the civil-rights bill then before Congress. Delegations met with the President and their congressional representatives and senators, and joined the multitudes at the Lincoln Memorial to hear speeches by clergymen, educators, trade-union officials, and other influential Americans. In the closing speech of the day, Martin Luther King, Jr., gave the most eloquent oration of his career, concluding with a soul-stirring prayer:

> I have a dream that my four little children will one day live in a nation where they will not be judged by the color of their skin but by the content of their character.
> I have a dream today.
> I have a dream that one day the state of Alabama, whose governor's lips are presently dripping with the words of interposition and nullification, will be transformed into a situation where little black boys and black girls will be able to join hands with little white boys and white girls and walk together as sisters and brothers.
> I have a dream today.
> I have a dream that one day every valley shall be exalted, every

hill and mountain shall be made low, the rough places will be made plain, and the crooked places will be made straight, and the glory of the Lord shall be revealed, and all flesh shall see it together.

This is our hope. This is the faith with which I return to the South. With this faith we will be able to hew out of the mountain of despair a stone of hope. With this faith we will be able to transform the jangling discords of our nation into a beautiful symphony of brotherhood. With this faith we will be able to work together, to pray together, to struggle together, to go to jail together, to stand up for freedom together, knowing that we will be free one day.

This will be the day when all of God's children will be able to sing with new meaning "My country 'tis of thee, sweet land of liberty, of thee I sing. Land where my fathers died, land of the pilgrims' pride, from every mountainside, let freedom ring." . . .

When we let freedom ring, when we let it ring from every village and every hamlet, from every state and every city, we will be able to speed up that day when all of God's children, black men and white men, Jews and Gentiles, Protestants and Catholics, will be able to join hands and sing in the words of that old Negro spiritual, "Free at last! Free at last! Thank God almighty, we are free at last!"

Ideologically, the conciliatory tone of King's speech was poles apart from that of young militants. While Reverend King extolled the virtues of non-violence and black-white unity, SNCC chairman John Lewis felt impelled to voice the radical opinions of young activists fighting for a social revolution in the South. In a written prepared statement, Lewis clearly intended to say that the proposed civil-rights bills were "too little, too late" and to denounce the Kennedy Administration for flagrantly violating democratic principles by appeasing Southern Democrats and their racist supporters. These direct accusations were stricken from the text finally delivered upon the advice of civil-rights leaders and presidential aides, and Lewis was forced to use indirect threats to indicate his anger and frustration. The new radicalism of black student youth was clearly evident in the uncensored version of John Lewis's speech, which read in part:

We are now involved in a serious revolution. This nation is still a place of cheap political leaders allying themselves with open forms of political, economic and social exploitation. . . .

The revolution is at hand, and we must free ourselves of the chains of political and economic slavery. The non-violent revolution is saying, "We will not wait for the courts to act, for we have been waiting hundreds of years. We will not wait for the President, nor the Justice Department, nor Congress, but we will take matters into our own hands, and create a great source of power, outside of any national structure that could and would assure us victory." We cannot be patient, we do not want to be free gradually, we want our freedom, and we want it now. We can not depend on any political party, for both the Democrats and the Republicans have betrayed the basic principles of the Declaration of Independence. . . .

Mr. Kennedy is trying to take the revolution out of the streets and put it in the courts. Listen, Mr. Kennedy, listen, Mr. Congressman, listen, fellow citizens—the black masses are on the march for jobs and freedom, and we must say to the politicians that there won't be a "cooling-off period."

We won't stop now. All of the forces of Eastland, Barnett and Wallace won't stop this revolution. The next time we march, we won't march on Washington, but we will march through the South, through the Heart of Dixie, the way Sherman did. We will make the action of the past few months look petty. And I say to you, WAKE UP AMERICA!!

Lewis was, of course, playing quite dangerously with the sources of finance and prestigious patronage supporting the Council of Federated Organizations and the whole civil-rights movement. Within COFO the radical and moderate wings of the movement were mutually interdependent. King, its nominal leader and head of the Southern Christian Leadership Conference, needed NAACP's aid and support for passage of the national civil-rights legislation it had promised to deliver as part of a program of black social uplift. NAACP, for its part, was committed to coalition tactics with wealthy and powerful whites and would disengage itself from COFO if uncontrolled civil disobedience by youth threatened its interests. Thus, while SNCC and CORE formed the basis of a left wing of the movement, with their emphasis on the fight against poverty and powerlessness through community organization, this left wing was almost totally dependent on a conservative establishment that reached all the way up into the national government, and the sources of philanthropy and political power. To these constraints, which youth found increasingly intolerable, one can add the conflicts inherent in the emerging ideology of the young activists themselves. Though Lewis called defiantly for the Kennedy Administration and America to wake up to the demands of Negroes, he was still at this stage an integrationist searching for a nonviolent dialogue with power elites. What Lewis did make clear, however, was that the task of leaders of direct action in the streets and communities must be to maintain the support of the mass base of the movement and oppose "selling out" to the political and legislative interests of Northern Democrats and liberals and their Southern Democratic allies.

Support for this view came from a new quarter, namely, young white students and activists in the New Left movement. In November 1963, SNCC field workers mounted a mass voter-registration campaign in Greenwood, Mississippi, and with the help of Yale students organized the Freedom Ballot, a mock election for a black governor in Mississippi. More than eighty thousand people voted in what was called the first free elections in the South. This was an electorate equivalent to four times the number of blacks actually registered to vote in the state—a colossal rebuke to Southern discriminatory electoral systems. In the following summer of 1964 a radical alliance of black and white student leaders took part in the COFO-sponsored Mississippi Summer Project, in which almost one thousand volunteers went into the South to work in areas of heavy black concentration. The young volunteers registered voters, opened Freedom Schools for voter education, and organized local communities to express their grievances. As a result of the intensive two-year registration efforts of black and white students and New Left activists, important steps were made toward educating disenfranchised blacks about the potential power of the ballot, and toward uniting them in a statewide political organization to challenge the state power structure.

One important result of the voter-registration campaigns was the demand for the formation of independent black political organizations free from the control of the Southern Democratic Party machine. In 1964, a presidential election year, local people and

SNCC workers formed the Mississippi Freedom Democratic Party (MFDP) to express the views of black communities. It was "open to all Democrats in Mississippi of voting age, regardless of race, creed or color." This was a remarkable innovation, and subsequent appeals for help launched by a local woman, Fannie Lou Hamer, gained respect and support among many Northern civil-rights groups. In August the MFDP sent a delegation to the national convention of the Democratic Party in Atlantic City, New Jersey, demanding to be seated instead of the regular Mississippi Democrats. They failed in this attempt but did receive an offer of two token seats as delegates-at-large with the state delegation, and this led to another policy conflict between SNCC and SCLC. Martin Luther King, Jr., and Bayard Rustin favored the Atlantic City compromise as a means of establishing an alliance at the national level with liberals and trade-union leaders capable of bringing about gradual improvements in the conditions of blacks and the poor. But the SNCC activists rejected the compromise, more convinced than ever of the great gap separating the intrigue of liberal-style race politics from their own experience with direct democracy.

The failure of the MFDP strategy had profound effects on the young leaders of SNCC. They began to call for totally independent action outside the established parties in all Southern areas of heavy black concentration. SNCC activists in Lowndes County, Alabama, helped form the Freedom Democratic Organization, a local militant group whose armed defenders were the first to use the Black Panther as a symbol and became known as the Black Panther Party in Alabama. Radical SNCC leaders openly questioned the value of alliances with other groups until blacks themselves built a substantial base of political power. Furthermore, the issue of free elections and civil rights in the South was raised continuously, and criticism extended to the government's failure to practice democracy at home while claiming to be fighting for freedom in Vietnam. In this context civil-rights work was deemed a valid alternative to the draft and any form of participation in an unjust war.

In the mid-sixties the center of gravity of the civil-rights movement shifted geographically and politically. Direct action appeared in the North in the form of school boycotts and demonstrations against discrimination by employers and trade unions. Spontaneous rent strikes by tenement dwellers coalesced into popular community movements. The frustrations of blacks erupted in ghetto riots in 1964 and 1965. Increasing militancy led to the steady erosion of non-violent principles among SNCC and CORE activists. Lower-class black youth from the streets, poolrooms, gangs, and reform schools struck back in anger against the hardening of racial oppression. Ghetto leaders expressed the view that racism was not just a moral failing of Southerners but a characteristic of the economic and social structure of the nation.

By 1966 SNCC and CORE leaders began to reflect the widespread disillusionment with the slow progress of the civil-rights movement. They were attracted by the rising militancy of blacks in Northern ghettos and regarded the wave of arson, looting, and riots as welcome expressions of rebellion against unjust authorities. It seemed to them that the powerlessness of poor and deprived people could be overcome only by a more violent claim to power. Stokely Carmichael noted the apathetic and frustrated spirit among his followers and indicated that the time had come for a bold new approach. In an interview in *The Movement*, a San Francisco-based journal published in February/March 1966, Carmichael said: "We recognize that people aren't impressed by demonstrations; they're impressed by political power . . . So what we're doing is something even Malcolm X was talking about. Political power has to lie within the community. And that's all: North, South, rural, industrial."

The new awareness was associated with a marked shift in SNCC policies from non-partisan non-violence toward militant black community political organization. Writing during this period of changing perceptions within the black student movement, Julius Lester, a former SNCC field secretary, said in "The Angry Children of Malcolm X" that at first students felt that if white America knew the wrongs that blacks suffered, these wrongs would be put right. Armed with this belief, and singing the movement's anthem, "We Shall Overcome," clean-shaven, well-dressed, middle-class Southern blacks gave themselves up to the fury of segregationist mobs and policemen—and all America watched the spectacle on television. Then white youth from all over the country joined in sympathy demonstrations. They went to jail with blacks, and were wounded, shot, or killed with blacks, because somehow they felt that freedom was their battle too and they could never be whole men and women in a segregated society. Some stayed in the South and moved into black communities to live and continue educational and welfare work. By this time, however, black students were beginning to see that the struggle was over power, not just about harmonizing race relations. They were angry at their white co-workers who were unwilling to go into white communities to deal with racism. There was a mounting anger, too, at the daily assaults upon black people. In 1963 the bombing by segregationists of the Sixteenth Street Baptist Church in Birmingham, Alabama, in which four little black girls died, was the final test of the students' moral endurance. When the messages of condolence came pouring in from white liberals, their statements seemed an immoral exercise.

James Forman, SNCC executive secretary during the crucial period 1961–66, gives some important clues to the transformation in his book *The Making of Black Revolutionaries.* He observes that SNCC was too reliant on whites for funds and it was becoming too difficult for blacks to maintain parity with whites in the leadership of interracial projects. Forman also notes that an overwhelming sense of racial solidarity and nationalism arose as students became more aware of the drive for African independence and the history of the black struggle. Black revolutionaries were born, he says, as youth turned to the writings and speeches of Elijah Muhammad, Malcolm X, and Frantz Fanon, and claimed that the structure of the Western world of white people was responsible for the conditions of black people in America and abroad.

These changing perceptions marked the end of the non-violent phase of SNCC's activity and a steady progression toward a more militant and black phase. Under Stokely Carmichael's leadership, and later through the fiery speeches of chairman H. Rap Brown, SNCC activists raised the cry of "Black Power" and affirmed that black solidarity was necessary for a black revolution. White members were removed from the ranks and SNCC became an all-black organization. The precipitating occasion was the angry response of Carmichael and Willie Ricks to the shooting of James Meredith during his protest "Freedom March" from Memphis to Jackson in the early summer of 1966. As the leaders of civil-rights organizations gathered to support Meredith, who only four years before had successfully entered the segregated University of Mississippi, divisive arguments broke out. Reverend King called for black and white to join together to finish Meredith's march, and Carmichael and Ricks said the time had come for blacks to go it alone behind the banner of Black Power. By the end of the year Black Power had become a popular rallying cry of racial pride and autonomy and generated much discussion about its real meaning and usefulness in the struggle for black freedom.

The CORE leadership and organizational structure was also undergoing dramatic changes as well. CORE like SNCC was actively engaged in Southern voter-registration campaigns in the summers of 1963 and 1964. Projects in Louisiana, South Carolina, and Mississippi were expanded and new ones added in the rural counties of north Florida. It was in these states that CORE personnel found themselves at the forefront of black strike action against discriminatory company policies and had to face up to the question of armed self-defense against white terrorism.

In Louisiana, CORE activists and workers challenged the management of the Olin-Mathieson chemical plant in Monroe, the paper-mill owners in Jonesboro, and the dominant Crown Zellerbach paper mill in Bogalusa. These factories maintained segregated lunchrooms and toilets and relegated blacks to low-paid, unskilled jobs. Furthermore, in all these localities there were active Klan cells launching attacks against black settlements and burning crosses to frighten prospective voters. In retaliation, black communities set up an armed guard called the Deacons for Defense and Justice to protect themselves and civil-rights groups. Local CORE activists were quick to note that after the Deacons were formed the attacks subsided. CORE national leaders were forced to accept the right of blacks to defend their homes and the need for local members to work very closely with the Deacons' defense group. "If violence is on the horizon," James Farmer said at the time, "I would certainly prefer to get it channeled into disciplined defense rather than random homicide and the suicide of rioting."

By the time of the CORE annual convention in Baltimore in 1966, it was clear that a turning point had been reached. CORE had begun as an interracial organization with a predominantly white leadership rooted in the pacifist movement. It was now under siege by militant blacks who wanted changes. And the militants won. The convention, dominated by speakers like Carmichael, Floyd McKissick, and Roy Innis of the powerful New York chapter, voted to endorse a Black Power slogan, to discard its commitment to non-partisan non-violence, and to condemn United States involvement in the Vietnam war.

Reflection on this period shows that the activities of SNCC and CORE and the youthful leaders of direct action had several crucial effects. They shook the power structure of Southern towns and cities and made direct action temporarily pre-eminent as a technique of non-violent social change. They encouraged the rise of autonomous black groups and challenged NAACP's domination of the civil-rights movement. They introduced new imperatives into the process of change in race relations and turned black-protest organizations toward a concern with economic and social problems of the masses. Their actions heralded the emergence of a new breed of Southern black youth, militants no longer fearful of lynch mobs and jails, and ready to act boldly and collectively. They called America a sick nation, and demanded basic changes in its structures. The stage was set for the Black Power phase of the civil-rights movement.

In the autumn of 1966 Carmichael spelled out the political dimensions of SNCC's Black Power policy. Now was the time for a political organization speaking directly for blacks and representing their needs and interests. There must be independent political action outside the established parties. The only effective instrument for black participation in the nation's political decision-making process was the exercise of power, and not moral judgments. Speaking more and more in the vein of Malcolm X's black nationalist ideology, Carmichael asserted the right of self-defense, because of the ineffectiveness of non-violence in situations where blacks were threatened. Furthermore, Carmichael recognized the need to build a strong all-black movement before creating any coalitions with whites, so as not to run the risk of being absorbed or betrayed. Whites should work in their own communities in order to free them of racism. The tasks of the Black Power movement should be the reconstruction of the black community and its identity, the rediscovery of its values, and the creation of independent political, social, economic, and cultural institutions.

The Black Power slogan, first loudly proclaimed by Carmichael in the "Freedom March" through Mississippi, was born of anger and resistance. It expressed an emotional post-Malcolmist mood of black consciousness and racial pride rather than a concrete program. Intellectually its immediate roots were in the writings of Richard Wright, whose book *Black Power* sought to unravel the problems of Ghana, the first West African nation to emerge from colonialism. The popular Harlem Baptist clergyman, Congressman Adam Clayton Powell, Chairman of the Education and Labor Committee, used the term in his baccalaureate address at Howard University, a Negro school, May 29, 1966. Congressman Powell distinguished between "God-given human rights" and "man-made civil rights" and urged the assembly to devote their lives to the implementation of human rights. Furthermore, he said, "to demand these God-given rights is to seek black power—the power to build black institutions of splendid achievement." It was only a week later that Stokely Carmichael, a former student at Howard, raised the cry "Black Power," and in the following year the newly born movement was endorsed by over a thousand delegates to the National Conference on Black Power held in Newark, New Jersey.

At first Black Power was a fervent hope expressed by a highly controversial political figure and charismatic Harlem minister, then a rebellious war chant of young bloods devoid of specific content. But later in the cut and thrust of urban racial politics it took on a meaning not too far removed from Malcolm's black nationalist program. Politically black power meant independent action to control the electoral power of black communities and improve conditions of life. This could be achieved by organizing a black political party, winning control of the Democratic and Republican Party machinery, mobilizing voter campaigns to elect black candidates, and restructuring electoral boundaries to ensure black voting majorities. In the economic sphere black power meant creating self-sufficient business enterprises, and on the cultural front young militants unashamedly called for black consciousness as the paramount goal of all endeavors of black people. SNCC was in the process of moving from being an integral part of the civil-rights movement and a founding member of the New Left in close cooperation with radical white student youth to trying to develop an autonomous organization of blacks. After 1966, SNCC was composed of blacks only and functioned mainly as a platform for black power with a decided orientation toward a Malcolmist ideology.

All the young leaders of the sixties point to Malcolm X as the inspiration for their actions. More than any other black ideologue, he was responsible for the explosive and strident militancy that entered the student and Black Power movements. Julius Lester, for example, recalls in "The Angry Children of Malcolm X" that "Malcolm X said aloud those things Negroes had been saying among themselves. He even said those things Negroes had been afraid to say to each other. His clear uncomplicated words cut through the chains on black minds like a giant blowtorch." In the Northern black areas, particularly, SNCC leaders took a Malcolmist line. A SNCC manifesto issued in Chicago during the summer riots of 1967 affirmed Black Power and declared that "What Brother Malcolm Taught Us about Ourselves Was Right"; it urged an alliance with peoples' movements of the Third World and extolled the need for organized urban guerrilla warfare and sabotage.

In a series of adroit maneuvers SNCC leaders disengaged from the civil-rights movement, abandoned their Southern bases, and took up the cause of the urban black revolt. There was a marked emphasis as well on a vision of total unity with Africa and the oppressed peoples of the world. James Forman traveled to Africa and later won nominal representation for SNCC at several United Nations meetings. He mounted an attack on American religious institutions and called for the payment of reparations for the long years of slavery and hardship. He took a Malcolmist line and called for "the final destruction of this mad octopus—the capitalistic system of the United States." Stokely Carmichael led the revival of black militancy in colleges and high schools. From 1966 to 1968 he and his SNCC colleagues converted middle-class students to a Black Power outlook and the demand for community control and curriculum changes in ghetto educational institutions. Carmichael had a brief relationship with the Black Panther Party, serving as their prime minister, and then went to Africa to study the methods and theories of African socialism expounded by Kwame Nkrumah of Ghana and Sekou Touré of Guinea. Carmichael's African excursion and his observations of two nations avowedly on "a socialist path to African independence" had a profound effect on him. It offered, he says, new images of black culture and history and attractive models of ideology and action in the international power struggle. SNCC leaders maintained this international perspective by visiting Puerto Rico in support of indigenous independence movements; and they also canvassed black communities in America as part of the anti-Vietnam war struggle, claiming that no Negroes should fight abroad until America guaranteed basic freedoms within its own borders.

In contrast to SNCC's insistence on independent political action by black people themselves, CORE leaders at first advocated working within the Democratic Party. CORE stressed a strategy of electoral politics with a view toward influencing the 1968 elections, and the formation of alliances with other groups to demand federal enforcement of civil-rights laws. Violence and urban riots were deplored, but accepted as a natural expression of oppressed people. CORE favored the formation of urban action centers and job-training programs backed by foundation grants, and the evolution of a black consumer and entrepreneurial class based on markets in the black community. In sum, CORE's Black Power message was: Reorganize the community through new leadership and political power within the two-party system, cultivate a more positive black self-image, and build up enough economic power to command a greater share of federal resources.

There was great diversity in individual approaches, however. Floyd McKissick rejected the view that Black Power meant violence and fascism, saying, "Black Power is not Black Supremacy; it is a unified Black Voice reflecting racial pride in the tradition of our heterogeneous nation." And he called for a strategy of "racial co-existence to replace integration." When Roy Innis took over leadership in mid-1968, he emphasized the development of community corporations and ownership of capital-producing wealth. Innis's first press release declared that CORE was now irrevocably a black nationalist organization with separation as its goal. He went on to endorse separatism as a system under which blacks could control their own destiny, saying, "When we have control of our own destiny, then we can talk about integration, for those Negroes who want it." In his opinion the traditional goal of integration of the civil-rights aristocracy, which they viewed not as a means to an end but as an end in itself, was passé. He demanded a new American constitution that would recognize blacks as a "Nation within a Nation"—and he envisaged nationlike structures created out of a collection of black enclaves woven together as a separate political entity. With these views Roy Innis's rise to leadership marked the emergence of separatist tendencies within the CORE organization.

James Farmer, a founding member of the early interracial CORE group, took yet another view. Farmer's goal was to bridge the gap between the integrationists and black nationalists. His strategy was to encourage "Freedom and Choice," unrestricted by race, in all crucial aspects of life. In housing, for example, he believed that blacks as well as whites should have the freedom to choose whether they wished to live in mixed or separate neighborhoods. He argued that CORE should pursue two aims at the same time. It should fight for integration and desegregation, and also encourage ghetto residents to build their own community life and spirit. The issue, he said, was not "separation versus integration" but "struggle against oppression."

The conflicts within CORE reflected the dilemma raging in black communities. Black nationalists and militant youth were calling for the use of the ghetto as a power base. Moderates, on the other hand, sought integration and the elimination of the disprivileged ghetto and its associated evils: slums, inadequate schools and police services, high crime rates, and family malaise. It was obvious that one organization could not encompass both tendencies at the same time without great difficulty. Building ghetto power bases requires one set of priorities; and integration requires another. In the end CORE's shift to Black Power politics brought about a great schism in the organization. Reformists like Dr. George Wiley, a chemistry professor and associate director of CORE, left to form a movement against poverty, the National Welfare Rights Organization, which stressed non-violent tactics, interracial cooperation, and community organization to achieve redistributive economic justice. James Farmer went into government service and held a high post in the Department of Health, Education and Welfare under the Nixon Administration. Innis and McKissick and others took up the cause of black ghetto economic development. CORE, like SNCC, made a number of contributions to the civil-rights movement, some of which stand out clearly. Through its technique of direct action, CORE played a major role in desegregating public accommodations. It significantly aided the passage of the Civil Rights Acts and, through its demonstrations, sensitized whites to the problems of the poor. Finally, CORE activities helped set the stage for the new wave of political activism that swept blacks into office in the South and into key positions in the national political party conventions of 1968 and 1972.

The civil-rights movement produced some of the most exciting and heroic moments in modern history, and more than enough stirring prose and anthems like "We Shall Overcome." One cannot easily forget the massive "Walks to Freedom," the "Prayer Pilgrimages," the "Freedom Rides," and the solidarity expressed in the manifestations at Albany, Georgia, Birmingham, Alabama, and Bogalusa, Louisiana. The strategy in those halcyon days was one of direct encounter with Southern racism, dramatizing flagrant injustices and involving blacks and whites as individuals in the civil-rights struggle. In the end, however, the thrust for freedom through interracial fellowship fell short of its goal. The civil-rights movement succeeded in abolishing the worst segregationist laws, alleviated the harassment of black voters, and speeded up the enactment of civil-rights legislation. But the movement failed to deliver broad economic gains or to hold white middle-class supporters who were appalled at the mounting radicalism and violence of black protest. Finally, black leadership fragmented as the movement, forged in response to the single issue of desegregation in the South, moved North and faced the complexity of urban ethnic politics.

I sought further opinions on these matters in July 1973 at a *New York Times* roundtable seminar of black Americans discussing what the decade of the sixties and the March on Washington meant to them ten years after, and what developments since then suggested about the future. The participants in what turned out to be a grueling four-hour session of spirited debate, flashes of anger, subtle yielding of deeply ingrained prejudices, and passionate soul-searching, were, in the main, a cross section of privileged, elite black Americans. Assembled at a long table laden with electronic recording apparatus were a psychology professor, an urban politician, a finance specialist, a legislator, a political scientist, a former U.S. ambassador, a Columbia University graduate, and a formidable team of expert black reporters from *The New York Times*. The question put to them was: "How important was the March on Washington, 1963—was it the start of something, or the culmination of developments and events that had transpired before?"

Three important observations emerged from the discussion. First of all, there was general agreement that the 1963 march was the culmination of the civil-rights movement as it had developed early in the century. According to Mrs. Patricia Harris, a prominent lawyer and former ambassador to Luxembourg, "It was the last time that, in a political way, the old leadership was able to call upon both the white and black community, upon persons without regard to political and ideological position, to come together without disagreement on a generic cause called civil rights." She recalled that Stokely Carmichael was a student at Howard University, where she herself was once Dean of the Law School, and that he was in her judgment a "very moderate young man with deep concern who later, out of frustration of the fight for effective civil rights, became more bitter and less convinced that the democratic, the coalition, approach was useful." The psychologist, Dr. Kenneth Clark, saw the march as a "gala festival of hope" which was premature; and the political scientist, Dr. Charles V. Hamilton, co-author with Carmichael of the controversial book *Black Power*, said, "When I look back at the march, I see it clearly as the beginning of the spread of the movement beyond the South. Civil rights mass activism became 'nationalized' rather than 'localized.' You began to get people marching in their home communities, chaining themselves to the barricades and so forth." What began with an emphasis on the moral and legal aspects of civil rights, Dr. Hamilton said, was followed by an emphasis on power and politics.

Second, there was a distinct difference in view about the contribution of previous events to the march. Dr. Clark and Mrs. Harris, both of whom were hardened veterans of civil-rights litigation, stressed the major importance of the Supreme Court's school desegregation decision, *Brown v. Board of Education*, Topeka, Kansas, May 17, 1954. By contrast, there was equal stress placed by other seminar participants on popular protest movements, such as the Montgomery bus boycott of 1956, as the crucial factor stimulating the rise and spread of civil-rights protest within the South and beyond to other regions of the country. This view was put by two participants who claimed a greater awareness of grass-roots opinion. One of them was George Forbes, president of the Cleveland City Council, and the other was Fred Gray, a lawyer who had the distinction of defending Reverend King and Rosa Parks in Montgomery, where he still practices, and of being the first black elected member of the Alabama legislature since Reconstruction.

Finally, there emerged a clear difference of opinion between the sole youth at the seminar, Roger Newell, and the arch-integrationists Clark and Harris on the question of the meaning of all these events for the masses of black people. Making up for what he lacked in years of experience by his avowed socialist views and the confident way he wore his dashiki and Afro haircut, Newell, a former youth activist in Washington, D.C., and a recent graduate of Columbia University in sociology, began his discussion by reference to the causes of urban rioting in the mid-sixties. In his view it was not the Brown case, congressional legislation, or Supreme Court decisions that really motivated black people to come out into the streets; rather, people felt that their actions would bring about changes in their material conditions; it was the only weapon available to them after all else had failed. Facing an increasingly restive and hostile audience, Newell stressed that little had changed since the March on Washington; the conditions of the majority of black people had not been radically affected by the court decisions. Furthermore, he said, the civil-rights movement is basically directed toward the up-and-coming black middle class; it was designed to create a larger and more stable buffer zone between white America and the volatile masses that took to the streets in urban insurrections to demand improvements. Then he began to sum up, and his voice broke as if to ease his contempt for the integrationist views of his fellow participants.

I think that in our discussions one of the primary shortcomings of a number of black academicians, black psychologists, and black historians has been primarily to focus the strength and the weaknesses of the movement on these so-called landmark legislations without really analyzing the conditions of the majority of black people. If we don't really begin to do an analysis of this society and see that the problem we are confronting is not just a problem or question of race and the elimination of the barriers to upward mobility, but a question of the economic infrastructure of the society which itself prevents black people from doing certain things, then we'll continue to go around in a circle. And we'll be in a position like right now where we cannot see in what direction we must go in the future.

An international perspective was extremely important, he said.

We must not look at the movement here inside the United States among black people in isolation, or outside the pattern of history. Because if you examine other movements in other countries around the world, you see patterns of development that fit quite closely to what's happening and what's happened here in the United States among black people. It is quite important, as we consider ourselves students of social change, that these things be examined so that we can see where we're progressing from here.

In his conclusion, Newell stressed: "What I am trying to say is not that other things, such as the legal decisions, Supreme Court decisions, do not matter. But that we have to have an understanding of the pattern and development of history. Those things are necessary to our understanding but they are not sufficient. They do not comprise the totality of the movement. And if sole reliance is placed on those type of tactics in the future there will be no movement. The emphasis now has to be placed on the development of a mass movement among the majority of black people to deal with the day-to-day problems of the masses."

Long after he had concluded, Newell's remarks hung suspended like a gigantic question mark over the remaining discussion. He had unleashed from a Pandora's Box grave elements of dissatisfaction, the Black Genie of Discontent which spurred the dynamic transformation of civil rights to Black Power. This was decidedly a post-Malcolm X phenomenon. With Malcolm's death the gauntlet of black nationalism fell to young student militants who radically reoriented moribund civil-rights protest into a Southern, and a national and international, issue. The immediate cause was disillusionment with the integrationists who had failed to secure black rights and protection from racist attacks. Ranged against the student and ghetto militants was a civil-rights establishment formed around the Democratic Party in 1964 by President Lyndon B. Johnson—it was a wide coalition of groups, interests, and forces encompassing Wall Street, Harvard, social democrats, city bosses, Senator James O. Eastland, and Martin Luther King, Jr. Black leaders supporting Johnson's Politics of Consensus fought back against the embryonic Black Power movement with their own brand of rhetoric and disdain. King and his SCLC colleagues spoke to white audiences of "a creative psalm of brotherhood, love and non-violence," and went into the ghettos to quell unrest and to contest the claims of Black Power militants to leadership. Roy Wilkins of NAACP rejected Black Power separatism and called for sweeping reforms, claiming that there was a "legitimate role of white liberals in the Fight for Freedom." Whitney Young, Executive Director of the National Urban League, and Professor Kenneth Clark denounced the "ambiguous concept of pseudo-power." And Bayard Rustin, organizer of the March on Washington, warned black people against the "Disease of Racism" and asked, "Are we becoming the thing we hate?"

But to no avail. The thrust of Black Power into national politics sounded the death knell of civil-rights alliances. It brought the black masses into what Frederick Douglass called the "awful roar of struggle." It revealed basic differences over ideology, methods, tactics, and strategy, and exposed the conflicts over power and status within the vaunted black-liberal-labor–Democratic Party civil-rights establishment. Fragmentation set in over the correct strategy to follow after the passage of the moderate Civil Rights Acts of 1964 and 1965. A civil-rights movement that had started with a burst of rising expectations ended with relatively few tangible gains and the outright failure of many campaigns. There were disagreements over the correct interpretation of the Vietnam war. SNCC and CORE youth saw the war as an extension abroad of domestic racism and colonialism. Reverend King joined with prominent national figures like the venerable child-guidance specialist Dr. Benjamin Spock in condemning it as an international tragedy, and NAACP took the view that the war was irrelevant to the attainment of civil rights for black Americans.

Finally, the civil-rights movement, no more than a marriage of convenience, split into four partisan groups unable to operate effectively together. SNCC held the "left wing" position, which called for independent political action based on the potential of the united vote of the black masses to wage a vigorous independent fight for social change in the Black Belt counties of the rural South and the black ghettos in Northern cities. CORE advocated challenging the Democratic and Republican Party political machines from within, and trying to elect officials that truly represented the interests of the poor and black people. NAACP held the "right wing" position. It was impressed by the new civil-rights legislation and the elevation of prominent protest leaders into high public office, and viewed the Democratic Party establishment and city machines not as enemies but as allies. NAACP leaders stressed the use of the courts, lobbying state and national legislatures, nonpartisan voter-registration campaigns, and reliance on executive action. The "centrists," like Reverend King and Bayard Rustin, sought to mend the tattered remains of a theory of coalition politics between white moderates, liberals, the clergy, labor leaders, and black people.

By the early seventies, the major civil-rights organizations which had held the commanding heights of popular esteem and national opinion had declined. The Student Nonviolent Coordinating Committee, no longer led by the quixotic Stokely Carmichael and the imprisoned Rap Brown, went out of business. The Congress of Racial Equality, under the leadership of Roy Innis, took on a black orientation and turned to voluntary service work financed by government and foundations, but has proven unable to harness the energies of the most aggrieved black populations. The Southern Christian Leadership Conference, whose major spokesman, Reverend King, was murdered, suffers from a lack of support and financial aid, despite the undoubted qualities of King's successors, Coretta King, his widow, and Reverend Ralph David Abernathy.

Only the old middle-class organizations—the National Urban League and the National Association for the Advancement of Colored People—remain powerful influences on a national level. And this is due, in large part, to the remaining store of good will and participation of whites, many of whom hold leadership positions, and to the continuing patronage of government, industry, labor, and philanthropic foundations.

The National Urban League, founded in 1901 and almost totally dependent on government-financed programs and non-black resources, is the wealthiest of the two organizations. Half of its $23 million annual budget comes from federal sources and the rest from corporations and foundations. Its director, Vernon Jordan, Jr., describes the League as an "advocacy agency" providing social welfare, job training, and health services, while maintaining almost daily contact with centers of policy-making on issues facing black people. NAACP, founded in 1909, and led until recently by its septuagenerian executive director Roy Wilkins, has returned to its traditional concerns: winning legislative and legal battles, and working with whites within the existing framework of free enterprise and constitutional democracy. Its leadership is aged and conservative and heavily criticized as being white-dominated and unrepresentative of black people. The Observations made at recent annual conferences of the League and NAACP indicate a waning unanimity and enthusiasm among members toward leaders who have no fresh ideas about combating rising black unemployment, especially among youth, about the widening income gap between the races, or about the growing isolation of black children in public schools. It is also evident that in a climate of economic stringency both organizations face severe financial difficulties which seriously curtail their ability to provide professional leadership to run local offices and service the needs of black communities.

While the Urban League and NAACP have survived the end of the civil-rights era, their credibility among the black masses has declined. There are signs of a drop in new members and a diminution of overall membership. More importantly, there has been a shift of black middle-class interest towards smaller groups with more narrowly defined purposes. For example, there is a proliferation of black caucuses among professionals, teachers, civil servants, and municipal workers, of city-renewal groups in major cities, and of anti-poverty groups like the National Welfare Rights Organization and the Movement for Economic Justice founded in 1966 by the late Dr. George Wiley. It is hardly likely that the League and NAACP will remain unaffected by the remarkable changes taking place on the community level. Interracial organizations are changing from white and upper-class black leadership to all-black and working-class leadership, and new groups are in formation with a greater concern for direct action and the mobilization of ghetto people along political and economic lines.

In sum, the recent history of integration and civil rights is simple to relate. A spate of laws and welfare programs, heralding a Second Black Reconstruction, momentarily stemmed the tide of black anger and eased the nation's conscience during the Kennedy-Johnson years. Since then, periodic recessions have diverted needed funds from beleaguered black communities. Governmental and business commitments to the welfare of needy low-income blacks faded away during the Nixon-Ford Administration, and white liberals, no longer confident masters of furtive interracial trysts, retired from the field of battle. By the early seventies the period of idyllic hope for racial harmony and justice, called integration, came to a grim, gradual, and inevitable end. The Age of Innocence was over.

4 Revolutionary Black Nationalism

Malcolmist ideology did not die as the youthful energies of Black Power-oriented students were dissipated in a maze of interracial politics; it found a troubled resting place among many black people engulfed by the pressures of survival. Hardened prisoners of the ghetto and the penitentiary were influenced by Malcolm's words. Leaders of black nationalist splinter groups called for armed belligerency. Aimless wanderers in the wastelands of crumbling tenements burst into the streets hailing Malcolm as the long-lost savior, and low-paid strivers and disillusioned students joined rebellious festivals of indignation against "Racism and Exploitation—the twin horns of the white bull that seeks to gore us."

Emergent leaders of these restive elements tossed up on the surface of black discontent rejected, as Malcolm did, the integrationist arguments of well-established bourgeois elites. They sought instead to exorcise the hypocrisy and racial injustice they saw in Western democracy, Christianity, and the capitalist state with revolutionary black nationalism. Their message to the deprived masses was for black liberation; they advocated armed self-defense, Black

Power, and community control, and unity and solidarity with
Africa and the oppressed peoples of the world. Some of their organizations, like the Black Panther Party and the Revolutionary Action Movement, espoused a cause of armed belligerency and attracted public attention in screaming headlines. Others, like the
Republic of New Africa, whose guerrilleros claim a black nation in
the heart of the South, had less impact on the nation's awareness.

What appealed most of all in Malcolm's words was his emphasis on the gun. "For the revolutionary youth of today, time starts
with the coming of Malcolm," wrote Eldridge Cleaver in *Post-
Prison Writings and Speeches*. "Before Malcolm, time stands still,
going down in frozen steps into the depths of the stagnation of slavery . . . Malcolm mastered language and used it as a sword to
slash his way through the veil of lies that for four hundred years
gave the white man the power of the word . . . Malcolm prophesied the coming of the gun to the black liberation struggle. Huey P.
Newton picked up the gun and pulled the trigger, freeing the genie
of black revolutionary violence in Babylon."

In October 1966, a year and a half after Malcolm's death,
twenty-four-year-old Huey P. Newton and his friend thirty-year-old
Bobby George Seale founded the Black Panther Party for Self-
Defense in Oakland, California. Newton was born in Monroe,
Louisiana, the son of a hard-working laborer and sometime Baptist
preacher, and grew up in Oakland, where he finished high school
and enrolled in 1959 at Oakland City College (now Merritt College). Seale was born in Dallas, Texas, the son of a poverty-stricken
carpenter, and after graduation from Oakland High School served a
stint in the U.S. Air Force. Both men were rebels in a town where
the blacks, Chicanos, and Chinese of East and West Oakland lived
apart from whites in neighborhoods of decaying, ramshackle
houses. Newton, who has a disarming baby face and personal
charm, had many tussles with the law. During the course of a wild,
disordered adolescence, says Newton in the autobiographical sections of his book *Revolutionary Suicide*, he stumbled along the
same tortuous road as his older brother, "Sonny Man," a hustler in

the lower-class community. He was a wino, gambler, street fighter, petty criminal, and casual pimp. Bobby Seale, who was to become his comrade, never got on well in the air force. He clashed with his commanding officer and was jailed, court-martialed, and released with a bad-conduct discharge. Returning to Oakland's ghetto streets as an unemployed sheet-metal mechanic, Seale lived an aimless life, relieved occasionally by his friends' applause at his comic impersonations and his hustler's bag of dirty tricks.

The two young men met in 1962 at Oakland City College, a bleak redoubt of urban education and a haven for aspiring youth of the surrounding North Oakland black community. Newton, inquisitive and daring, tilted at the windmills of collegiate education, and like a Don Quixote he led his friend Seale, a reluctant Sancho Panza, into a campaign for black-history courses and the hiring of black instructors. They worked together at a local anti-poverty center and joined a black-nationalist group, the Afro-American Association, whose leader preached a gospel of race pride. What seemed to affect them most were the heavy-handed actions of the police in black areas, and they began to raise the question Malcolm had posed: "What good is non-violence when the police and the white society they protect are determined to rule black communities by force?"

When Newton heard Malcolm X speak one time in Oakland, he was impressed by "his disciplined and dedicated mind." Here was a man who combined the wisdom of book learning with the world of the streets. He had the cool style of a strong prison man, and a program: armed defense when attacked. He knew how to reach people and identify the causes of their condition without blaming them. The slain black-nationalist leader was admired, says Newton in his book *To Die for the People*, because "Malcolm, implacable to the ultimate degree, held out to the Black masses the historical, stupendous victory of Black collective salvation and liberation from the chains of the oppressor" and from, he added, the treacherous embrace of black leaders endorsed by the white power structure. Only with the gun were the black masses denied this victory, says Newton, but "they learned from Malcolm that with the gun they can recapture their dreams and make them a reality."

It was clear to Newton and Seale that Malcolm X had been on the right road toward establishing a black organization, the Organization of Afro-American Unity, that would speak to "the brothers on the block" in words they understood. Malcolm had died, but someone had to take up the challenge of forging a successful political organization and a liberating cultural program. The paramount issue was survival, physical and mental, whether one was a poor worker or a college or high-school student. In the communities and on the campuses of Oakland, San Francisco, and Berkeley, the police and the white power structure left no other choice. Black people had to defend themselves against brutality and miseducation. With these thoughts, the two young men began to explore the ideological and organizational problems of building a militant black movement, and the gun, Malcolm's gun, and his slogan, "Freedom by any means necessary," became for them a defiant challenge to the power structure in defense of the survival of black people.

But Malcolm was only one of the many influences on the development of their ideas. Newton and Seale were full of praise for Fidel Castro and the Cuban revolution, the Deacons for Defense and Justice in Louisiana, and the freedom struggles of liberation movements in Vietnam and Southern Africa. There was a special place on their bookshelves for the works of Frantz Fanon on colonial violence, Chairman Mao on people's war, Che Guevara on guerrilla warfare, and Robert Williams on armed self-defense in Monroe, North Carolina. They argued against the strategy of legal and non-violent integration proposed by campus civil-rights groups and criticized the inactivity of the Muslims and radical groups like the interracial Progressive Labor Party and the black Revolutionary Action Movement.

From all these influences the idea of an organization was forming. One day, suddenly, almost by chance, a name was found. Newton had read a pamphlet about voter registration which described how black people in Lowndes County, Alabama, had armed themselves against Klan violence and created the Freedom Democratic Organization with a black panther as a symbol. "A few days later, while Bobby and I were rapping," says Newton in *Revo-*

lutionary Suicide, "I suggested that we use the panther as our symbol and call our political vehicle the Black Panther Party. The panther is a fierce animal, but he will not attack until he is backed into a corner; then he will strike out . . . At this point, we knew it was time to stop talking and begin organizing . . . The time had come for action."

The Black Panther Party for Self-Defense began as an armed community patrol dedicated to the defense of the Oakland black community against the brutality of the city police. Its members were recruited by Newton and Seale from among college students and "street brothers" in poolrooms and bars. The ten-point party program, written in twenty minutes in the back of a local anti-poverty center, began with the words "We want freedom. We want power to determine the destiny of our Black community." In a series of demands, underscored by reference to the Constitution and the "right of separation" contained in the Declaration of Independence, the October 1966 Black Panther Party platform and program called for:

—Full Employment for Our People
—An End to the Robbery by the White Man of Our Black Community; Payment in Currency As Restitution for Slave Labor and Mass Murder of Black People
—Decent Housing, Fit for Shelter of Human Beings
—Education for Our People That Exposes Decadent American Society
—Exemption of Black Men from Military Service for a Racist Government
—An End to Police Brutality and Murder of Black People by Organizing Armed Self-Defense Groups
—Freedom for All Black Prisoners Because They Haven't Had a Fair Impartial Trial
—Black Defendants Should Be Tried by a Jury of Their Peers
—Land, Bread, Housing, Education, Clothing, Justice, and Peace
—A United Nations Plebiscite in the Black Colony to Determine the Will of Black People as to Their National Destiny

The Black Panthers' message was simple and explosively direct—Black Power grows out of the barrel of a gun. Armed patrols emanating from the first Panther office at Fifty-eighth Street in Oakland spread to black communities in Richmond, Berkeley, and San Francisco. And when the Panthers mounted an armed guard for Malcolm's widow, Mrs. Betty Shabazz, at a memorial rally in San Francisco in February 1967, the group's attractiveness to ghetto youth was assured. It was, says Eldrige Cleaver, who was there, "the most beautiful sight I had ever seen." As the hall's front door opened, in walked four men wearing black berets, powder-blue shirts, black leather jackets, black trousers, shiny black shoes—and each with a gun. In front was Huey P. Newton with a riot pump shotgun. Beside him was Bobby Seale, a .45-caliber automatic in a holster on his right hip. A few steps behind him was Bobby Hutton with a shotgun, and next to him was Sherwin Forte cradling an M1 carbine.

Several months later, in May, the Panthers took advantage of a state law permitting citizens to carry unconcealed loaded guns and marched into a California state assembly debate on gun control armed with rifles to assert the constitutional rights of black people to bear arms against their oppressors. The impact of this brazen display on the national news media was instantaneous, and by the following year, 1968, the Panthers symbolized a major shift of events in national life. The Panthers burst out of their Oakland headquarters and opened up recruitment centers in lower-class black communities all over the nation. News of their exploits vied with headlines announcing the assassination of Robert Kennedy and Martin Luther King, Jr., the ghetto riots in Cleveland, Baltimore, and Washington, D.C., the police riot in Chicago, and Tommie Smith's Black Power salute at the Mexico City Olympic Games.

The Panthers were hailed by many blacks and radical whites as the first genuine American revolutionaries since 1776. They were also labeled irresponsible racialist gangsters by black and white establishment groups. These charges were formalized in 1968, when J. Edgar Hoover, head of the Federal Bureau of Investigation, called the Panthers a black extremist organization of hoodlum-type revolutionaries who stockpile weapons, espouse Marxist-Leninist doctrines, and terrorize black communities. They were, according to Hoover, "the No. 1 threat to the internal security of the nation," and in November 1968, he ordered agents in Oakland and thirteen other bureaus to exploit "gang warfare" between black groups and to employ "hard-hitting counterintelligence measures to cripple the Black Panthers."

Once cast into the limelight, Black Panther leaders tried to explain their views on all the major problems and goals outlined by Malcolm X and Black Power militants in SNCC and CORE. Speaking about their policy of armed self-defense, Panther Chairman Bobby Seale said, "The party realizes that the white power structure's real power is its military force . . . We have to face them how they come down on us. They come down with guns and force. We must organize ourselves and put a shotgun in every black man's home. Our political stand is that politics is war without bloodshed, and war is politics with bloodshed." Hunger and deprivation among blacks would be dealt with by a Panther community survival program providing free food and breakfast for needy families, and there would be free health clinics and "liberation schools" for political education. These were reformist measures but according to Seale they would help to "meet the needs of the people, strengthen their resolve, and weaken the camp of the capitalist power structure." In addition, the Panthers called for the withdrawal of police forces, large-scale economic aid, and black control of community institutions. These measures would enable the black community to gain time to think about solutions to their long-term problems.

Speaking to an interviewer from *The Movement*, an underground journal, on the question of black unity and black-white alliances, Panther Minister of Defense Huey Newton said: "The Black Panther Party is an all-black party because we feel as Malcolm felt that there can be no black-white unity until there is first black unity . . . We'll make the theory and we'll carry out the practice. It's the duty of the white revolutionary to aid us in this." He further stated: "We don't hate white people; we hate the oppressor. And if the oppressor happens to be white then we hate him. When he stops oppressing us then we no longer hate him." In the long term, the Panthers endorsed Malcolm's acceptance of alliance with whites once the black community was united and after white radicals had closed ranks in the struggle on the side of the oppressed. Yet, in the short term during the 1968 national elections, Panther leaders felt justified in forming an alliance with the Peace and Freedom Party, composed mainly of young white liberals, radicals, and socialists. Both groups were pledged to seek radical change in their respective communities. The Peace and Freedom Party would undertake grass-roots organization among whites and respect the autonomy of the Panthers in the black community.

Like Malcolm, the Black Panther leaders spoke warmly of socialism and in less than two years after its formation claimed that the Panthers are a "Marxist-Leninist party dedicated to a socialist revolution to free the oppressed people of America, regardless of race," and that this goal took precedence over the national libera-tion of Black America. Newton himself claimed to be a socialist and explains how this came about in *Revolutionary Suicide:* "It was my studying in college that led me to become a socialist. The transformation from a nationalist to a socialist was a slow one, although I was around a lot of Marxists. I even attended a few meetings of the Progressive Labor Party . . . I supported Castro all the way . . . My conversion was complete when I read four volumes of Mao Tse-tung to learn more about the Chinese revolution. It was my life plus independent reading that made me a socialist— nothing else." Bobby Seale expressed his own developing awareness in an article, "Revolutionary Action on Campus and Community," in the journal *Black Scholar,* in December 1969, written while in the San Francisco County Jail. "I am a political prisoner," he said, "a revolutionary who has been captured by the state because he challenges its crimes against his people—its wholesale robbery, rape and murder and oppression of the people."

Borrowing and adapting ideas and slogans from the Chinese experience, Newton and Seale attempted to apply them to the United States. In an interview with members of the Students for a Democratic Society in 1968, Newton spoke of the implacable differences between two forms of nationalism, revolutionary and reactionary. Revolutionary nationalism, he said, is for socialism and a people's revolution, while reactionary nationalism is conservative and its goal is oppression of the people. A specific example of the latter is cultural nationalism, which under the guise of a return to Africa oppresses people and supports conservative bourgeois interests and backward regimes such as François "Papa Doc" Duvalier's in Haiti. Newton concluded that "culture itself will not liberate us. We're going to need some stronger stuff . . . We have two evils to fight, capitalism and racism . . . if the black bourgeoisie cannot align itself with our complete program, then it sets itself up as our enemy. And they will be attacked as such."

This definition of cultural nationalism as reactionary set the Black Panther Party well outside the popular emphasis on black studies and "Black is beautiful," a tendency which Newton and Seale denounced as a new "trick bag" of racialist exploitation of black values. Referring with scorn to cultural nationalists like Ron Karenga and Imamu Amiri Baraka, the Panther leaders said that they had cloaked themselves in exotic Africanisms of dress, style, and language which alienated them from the majority of blacks, and whites, in the society. Cultural "blackism" is a retrograde concept, they said; it is more important to hold a correct race-class political line. A widely publicized statement in the party's journal, *The Black Panther*, in 1969 declared: "There is a need among Blacks for self-rule—and there's an equal need for these Blacks to work in very close working coalition and close communication with their class brothers, regardless of color, regardless of whether you're for or against intermarriage, whether you want to live in Beverly Hills, or Watts or Oakland or Washington, D.C., it doesn't make any difference. The need is for constant maintenance of a correct class line . . . because the main problem in the United States is not the race contradictions but the class contradictions."

The Panther "race-class line" stressed that many different peoples had similar experiences of oppression and should unite against their common oppressor, the exploitative capitalist system. The Panther Party had no illusions that black liberation could be achieved under capitalism. What was necessary was a socialist revolution in the whole society and this required building firm alliances with other oppressed minorities who share the ultimate aim of overthrowing the American establishment. As a symbol of their intentions, the Panther leaders gave support to radical ethnic-based political groups and called for unity across ethnic lines. Among blacks they encouraged the creation of student associations and worker caucuses. At the same time, they sought alliances with the Puerto Rican Young Lords, the Chicano Brown Berets, the white Young Patriots, and the Chinese-American Red Guards.

The Panther leaders were groping toward an international and world revolutionary perspective. They saw a commonality of interests of black Americans and the peoples of the Third World. Both suffered under colonialist and imperialist oppression. Blacks were a colony within imperialist America, while abroad the dependent colonial and ex-colonial peoples were beset by the imperialism of America and other powerful Western nations. In the struggle for liberation their tasks were complementary. Third World revolutions must cut off the tentacles of the imperialist octopus and the rebellions of the internal black colony must attack its body. By the early 1970's the Panthers proclaimed in a national statement "revolutionary solidarity with all people fighting against forces of imperialism, capitalism, racism and fascism . . . we will not fight capitalism with black capitalism; we will not fight imperialism with black imperialism; we will not fight racism with black racism. Rather we will take our stand against these evils with a solidarity derived from a proletarian internationalism born of socialist idealism."

That the Black Panthers were able to keep up a constant stream of ideological commentary was remarkable; it was made more so by the fact that both Newton and Seale spent long periods in jail. One of the key lieutenants manning the ideological barricades in their absence was Eldridge Cleaver, the Panther Minister of Information, recruited shortly after the confrontation with police at the Malcolm X memorial rally in San Francisco. Cleaver, born in Little Rock, Arkansas, in 1936, was the son of a peripatetic musician–dining-car waiter and a schoolteacher mother. Like Malcolm X and Huey Newton, Cleaver had a long record of youthful crime and delinquency, hustling marijuana, and petty theft; he also specialized in violent rapes of white women, which he called insurrectionary acts. While in prison he was converted to the Black Muslim religion and became a minister, but he resigned when Malcolm was expelled and turned to writing and teaching Afro-American history to his fellow inmates.

While he was on parole in the spring of 1968, a series of important events overwhelmed Cleaver and changed the course of his life and the Panther Party. Cleaver led major rallies to free his comrades and also ran for President of the United States on the Peace and Freedom–Black Panther coalition ticket. Widespread notoriety followed the publication of his book *Soul on Ice*, a collection of essays on race, sex, and black politics written while in a cell at Folsom State Prison, California. The turning point in Cleaver's life came, he says, with the assassination of Martin Luther King, Jr. It ended for him any thought that non-violence would work in America; it was as if the assassin's bullet that struck down King had closed the door of opportunity for blacks forever. "Now," he said, "there is only the gun and the bomb, dynamite and the knife, and they will be used liberally . . . . America will bleed. America will suffer . . . Action is all that counts now. And maybe America will understand that. I doubt it." Within a matter of hours of writing these angry words for publication in the journal *Ramparts*, as an article "Requiem for Non-Violence," Cleaver was wounded and another Panther, "Little Bobby" Hutton, was killed in a police raid. Later in the year, when Cleaver was ordered back to prison on a parole-violation charge, he fled into exile, first to Cuba and then Algeria.

Cleaver played a strategic role in the writing of all major Panther documents during the early period and edited *The Black Panther*. He contributed a number of basic position papers on the class nature of American society, the dual struggle against capitalism and racism, and the concept of national liberation for the black colony and socialist revolution in the mother country. Two vintage Cleaver essays, published separately as *On the Ideology of the Black Panther Party* and *On Lumpen Ideology*, excoriate outmoded Marxist parties and their naïve emphasis on the progressive tendencies of the working class. The real revolutionaries, he declared, are the Lumpen, i.e., those who have been left out or cast out of the productive system, especially colored minorities and the permanently unemployed. In his view, Lumpen consciousness is more advanced than "the accommodationist, job-seeking, fringe-benefit consciousness of the AFL-CIO/Communist Party/Working Class movement." By contrast, the basic demand of the Lumpen "to be cut in on Consumption in spite of being blocked out of Production" is the ultimate revolutionary demand. Cleaver concludes *On Lumpen Ideology* by suggesting to both black and white militants that aid to the Lumpen is more essential for revolutionary purposes than continued belief in the discredited notion of the proletarian revolution. "The basic task confronting revolutionaries today," he said, "is to further define the Lumpen condition, to refine Lumpen ideology, spread Lumpen consciousness, and lead the struggle, through righteous practice, to seize physical control of the machines, of technology, and destroy, forever, the hegemony of the usurpers over the social heritage of humanity."

These two seminal papers draw quite heavily on ideas developed during his brief flirtation with the hippies and Yippies of Haight-Ashbury and on Telegraph Avenue in Berkeley. Cleaver was also clearly impressed by movements for national liberation in various parts of the world and by the major work of Frantz Fanon, *The Wretched of the Earth*. He expressed real doubts about the Panthers' ability to expropriate "white" Marxism into the black-liberation struggle. It could not be done, he said, without fundamental adaptations of Marxist theory to the conditions of the black experience with racism and exploitation. At the same time he was also seeking to explore, without direct reference to color, the dimensions of a dynamic worldwide revolution of oppressed people, proposed by Fanon, of which the black struggle was an integral part. The result was an interesting but unhappy marriage of the Marxist concept of the "decadent" lumpenproletariat, the "scum-layer" beneath the proletariat, and the Fanonist view of the "progressive" struggles of the peoples of the Third World against the domination of imperialistic, technologically powerful nations.

But all this has changed now. In the late sixties the Black Panthers were hit hard by FBI agents, police infiltration, and arrests;

many were killed or given lengthy prison sentences. Violent confrontations with other black groups decimated their ranks. And the Panthers failed to build strong local organizations and consummate their proposed alliances with minority and disadvantaged urban groups. Imprisonment of Panther leaders and internal dissension took a severe toll. Bobby Seale and Huey Newton served long periods in jail, and in their absence the party split into warring factions. One faction lined up behind Cleaver and advocated continued violent confrontations with police, only to fall into disarray when Cleaver fled the country and was later expelled from the party by Newton. Another group turned to non-violent political and social work in the black community. Others shifted their allegiances to militant organizations like the Republic of New Africa, the Revolutionary Action Movement, and the Black Liberation Army. Moderate tendencies in the Panthers finally prevailed and were reinforced by fear of continued slaughter, which had robbed the party of some of its best young people, among them Alprentice "Bunchy" Carter and John Huggins, killed by black cultural nationalists at the University of California in Los Angeles, Fred Hampton and Mark Clark killed by police in Chicago, and the Panther sympathizer George Jackson, who was shot dead by guards in San Quentin Prison.

Newton and Seale reassumed full leadership of the Black Panthers in 1971, after charges against them were dropped when their juries failed to agree on a verdict. Back on the streets of Oakland, they identified with the moderates and steered the Panthers on a non-violent "survival course." Black store owners were urged, under threat of boycott, to contribute supplies to the free-food program. Community groups previously scorned were warmly encouraged to cooperate with the "new look" Panthers. The black church was praised as "a relevant force that needs to exist." Support from the black middle class was welcomed as "the source of skills which black folks need," and black capitalism was declared "an essential part of black control of community institutions and potentially of service to the survival of everyone." Acceptance of black business and black capitalism, surprising as it was, formed part of a wider appeal in black communities for funds to fill the party's empty coffers. In launching the appeal, Huey Newton admitted the party had made errors in the past by relying heavily on white support. In a revealing confession in *To Die for the People,* he said: "In order to carry out our programs we have always needed money. In the past we received money from wealthy White philanthropists, humanitarians, and heirs to the corporate monopolies. At the same time we were engaged in blanket condemnation of the small victimized Black capitalists found in our communities. This tactic was wrong since we receive the money for our survival programs from big White capitalists, and we freely admit that."

Changes were now evident across a broad spectrum of issues. The Panthers had swelled in numbers largely through the recruitment of ill-lettered, untrained, gun-crazy ghetto youth. It now embarked on a purge of the ranks to crush mindless vulgarity, senseless violence, and provocation of the police. Eldridge Cleaver was dismissed in absentia in 1971 for "violent adventurism" and "provocative tactics" and was denounced as the perpetrator of the "fantasy of spontaneous revolution." In dismissing Cleaver, Huey Newton, said, "The correct handling of a revolution is not to offer the people an 'either-or' ultimatum. Instead we must gain the support of the people through serving their needs. Then when the police or any other agency of repression tries to destroy the program, the people will move to a higher level of consciousness and action." This new line against "revolutionary cultism" coincided with a broad appeal to win acceptance by moderate black and white groups in order to solve ghetto ills. The original ten-point Panther program was toned down. Its anti-white and separatist statements were eliminated, and the demand for a United Nations-sponsored plebiscite on black nationhood and independence was deleted.

Ideological purification was clearly part of a new strategy to present a moderate image, but ideological consistency was never a trait of Panther leaders. There were always subtle shifts of orientation and hero-worship, twists and turns in anecdote and innuendo, and now and then a clumsy, opportunistic *volte face.* In the late sixties, for example, the Panthers basked in the glory of bourgeois Radical Chic and wooed silk-suited, wide-eyed debutantes with a special blend of sullen charm and funky insolence. As the Panther meteor flashed across the "Black Rage–White Guilt" firmament of America, it left a scattered trail of burned-out principles. The Panthers began as a youth-led black nationalist and Black Power group swearing eternal allegiance to principles enunciated by Malcolm X. Under the influence of white radical groups in 1967–68, the Panthers embraced "revolutionary nationalism," that is, nationalism with a socialist perspective, which suggested that to be a revolutionary nationalist one had to be a Marxist-Leninist socialist. (It should be noted, however, that this emphasis on Marxism-Leninism coming from a black organization with no Communist or socialist origins was unprecedented in black history.) Then in 1969–70 the Panther Party switched to "internationalism," stressing anti-capitalism and anti-imperialism; it also aimed to build alliances to crush the ruling classes, free the black colony, and unite with national liberation struggles throughout the world. By the mid-1970's, the position of the moderate Panther wing was "inter-communalism," which stressed the interdependence of poor and oppressed communities of the world and looked forward to the time when people gained control over the means of production and distributed wealth and technology in an egalitarian way to the world's needy.

By 1973 the Panthers had slipped out of the public eye and its future was in doubt without a resurgence of its old appeal to ghetto youth. The party still supported its newspaper, now called *The Black Panther: Intercommunal News Service*, and sponsored community survival programs—free food packages, a medical clinic, shopping assistance to old people, a prison visiting system, and a children's preschool group. Membership declined and there was only an estimated dozen chapters around the country in full operation, some twenty fewer than during the Panthers' heyday. The Panthers no longer maintained offices in Los Angeles, Denver, Seattle, and Baltimore. They were finding it very difficult to stay in operation in Washington, D.C., and in fact, their only real base was their Oakland birthplace.

But is the old leadership today in any position to push the struggle they proclaimed in 1966? It seems not. Gone are the days of the guns, the black berets and leather jackets, and the clenched-fist salute that symbolized the sixties. Gone also are the days when the Panthers declared themselves a revolutionary nationalist party in the vanguard of an "anti-fascist united front" in the struggle for a socialist society. The Panthers have stopped snarling, and "A chicken in every bag" has replaced "Off the pigs" as the Panther rallying cry.

Bobby Seale, the Panther Chairman, was acclaimed as a martyr by black and radical groups in 1969, when at the Chicago Seven trial Judge Julius Hoffman ordered him bound and gagged while he was charged with incitement to riot during the Democratic National Convention in Chicago. He stirred their attention again in 1971 when he was acquitted of murder charges in the death of a suspected police informer Alex Rackley in New Haven, Connecticut. But in a surprise switch to a sober middle-class image, Seale ran for mayor of Oakland in 1973, along with Elaine Brown, Panther Minister of Information, who sought election to the city council. Seale lost his bid to unseat the incumbent John Reading but successfully wooed an astonishing 44,000 votes (6,000 of them white) out of 120,000 votes cast. Now, according to reports, he is job hunting in Los Angeles and thinking about taking up an acting career.

The poster-photograph showing the stern visage of Huey Newton, Panther Minister of Defense, behind a shattered, bullet-ridden pane of glass no longer adorns the walls of adolescent bedrooms, college dormitories, coffee shops, and offices of radical groups. The days of advocating violence and "Off the pigs" are past, Newton told a crowd of one thousand students at the University of Colorado in Boulder in 1972; the Panthers had moved toward community work and registering black voters. By 1975–76 Huey Newton was reportedly in exile in Cuba contemplating the "contradictions and incorrect attitudes" which led to accusations against him of extorting business support for Panther community-survival programs by violence. He was also said to be facing charges, allegedly part of an FBI "dirty tricks" campaign, of murdering a seventeen-year-old prostitute who was shot on an Oakland street and of assaulting two black vice-squad officers.

David Hilliard, Panther national chief of staff and a long-time stalwart of the party, spent time in prison for involvement in the Oakland shoot-out of 1968 and has been penniless and unemployed following his release.

Warren Kimbro was one of fourteen Black Panthers, including Bobby Seale, charged in the killing of Alex Rackley; his twenty-year-to-life sentence, following a plea of guilty to second-degree murder, was later reduced to four years after he served as a prosecution witness against Seale. After his release he was unanimously approved for an assistant deanship at Eastern Connecticut State College. According to an Associated Press release in September 1975, Charles R. Webb, Jr., president of the college, praised Kimbro, who has a master's degree from Harvard, as the best qualified of the four top candidates for the job. "You just can't go on trying a person for something," Mr. Webb said, adding that "it's irrelevant that he pleaded guilty to second-degree murder and spent four years in jail."

As for Eldridge Cleaver, the former Panther Minister of Information and international publicist for armed black militancy allied with international socialism has now disavowed all his former views. In 1975, while languishing in a small Paris flat after fleeing Algeria, he became an outspoken anti-Communist, pro-American patriot mouthing tales of sinister forces betraying the Panther cause and African revolutionary governments, and pleading with American embassy officials for a government pardon so he could get home in time for the July 4, 1976, Bicentennial celebrations.

Cleaver no longer identifies with the rage he expressed in "Affidavit No. 2—Shoot-out in Oakland," April 19, 1968. Then he said:

> Eldridge Cleaver died in that house on 28th Street, with Little Bobby, and what's left is force: fuel for the fire that will rage across the face of this racist country and either purge it of its evil or turn it into ashes. I say this for Little Bobby, for Eldridge Cleaver who died that night, for every black man, woman and child who ever died here in Babylon, and I say it to racist America, that if every voice of dissent is silenced by your guns, by your courts, by your gas chambers, by your money, you will know, that as long as the ghost of Eldridge Cleaver is afoot, you have an ENEMY in your midst.

Like a self-confessed penitent sorrowing for sin, the "new Cleaver" said in a *New York Times* article, "Why I Left the U.S. and Why I Am Returning," published November 18, 1975: "With all its faults, the American political system is the freest and most democratic in the world. The system needs to be improved, with democracy spread to all areas of life, particularly the economic. All of these changes must be conducted through our established institutions, and the people with grievances must find political methods for obtaining redress." Furthermore, while in Paris Cleaver was reported in a lengthy interview in *Rolling Stone*, September 11, 1975, as saying: "If we are truly the force for democracy in the world, then we have an obligation to help in the total disintegration of the totalitarian Soviet regime. They have to go just like Nixon did; they are the same."

Now the repentant sinner has returned home. Ensconced in a plush high-rise federal prison block in San Diego in early 1976, Cleaver, sharing private rooms with Timothy Leary, a former exile with him in Algeria, pondered the "new perspective of black Americans" and claimed their status has "undergone a fundamental change for the better." America is the black man's home, not Africa or anywhere else, he now believes. Cleaver's return after a seven-year exile in Cuba, Algeria, Guinea, North Korea, and Russia leaves him facing charges arising from a gun battle in 1968 with Oakland police that could land him a jail sentence of fifteen years. There is some speculation that he has been promised a suspended sentence in return for fervent expressions of patriotism. Associates close to Cleaver say now that J. Edgar Hoover and Richard Nixon have passed from the scene, and Ronald Reagan is no longer the governor of California, he feels he can get a fair trial. Certainly the stage is set for a full-scale national performance as the prodigal son. His expected appearance before the Senate Judiciary Committee to testify on terrorist acts in the United States will undoubtedly give him a chance to recant publicly and in the process give his trial judge good reason for being lenient.

Prison has often been called the university of the revolution, and never has this adage been more true than it was of American

blacks in recent decades. One has only to think of the literary out-
pourings from ill-lettered black youth who found behind the gray
walls of prisons and detention centers a new lease on life: Malcolm
X's autobiography, Huey Newton's *Revolutionary Suicide* and *To
Die for the People*, Bobby Seale's *Seize the Time*, Eldridge Cleaver's
Soul on Ice, and George Jackson's *Soledad Brother* and *Blood in My
Eye*.

One of these men, George Jackson, an honorary member of
the Black Panther Party with the rank of general and field marshal,
is a unique example of a man who never had a chance to pursue a
political-activist career outside prison but inside prison underwent
the slow, painful transformation of a black prisoner into a black
revolutionary. Jackson was a school dropout and petty criminal,
ghetto-bred in Chicago and Los Angeles. His offense in 1960,
when eighteen years old, was driving the getaway car of a friend
who robbed a gas station of $70. Given an indeterminate sentence
of one year to life, Jackson spent the next eleven years in prison,
most of it in solitary confinement, allegedly for fostering racial
fights and assaulting prison guards. While in Soledad prison, California, Jackson developed his political consciousness through a
series of confrontations with the authorities. He broke all the rules
by which the prison system maintains control over the spread of
"radical views," including Black Muslim, black nationalist, and
left-wing opinions. He challenged prison officials to end cen-
sorship, restricted privileges of correspondence, reading, and visiting, and the curtailment of freedom of speech and assembly. He
identified himself with the ideas and exploits of Malcolm X and the
Panthers, and through them with the works of Marx, Lenin, Mao,
and Che Guevara. In an extraordinary burst of creativity he developed a powerful and eloquent style, writing essays and letters to his
parents, his friends, and his seventeen-year-old brother, Jonathan.

The prison letters of George Jackson are passionate testimony
to his ability to criticize the penal system and place the issue of
black prisoners firmly into black revolutionary consciousness. Jackson calls the prisons human warehouses and prison labor a form of
slavery. The penitentiaries are huge garbage dumps where the
peace of the staff is purchased at the exasperation of the inmates.
Punitive discipline, pettifogging rules and restrictions of mail and

visitors are common grievances. Psycho-drug therapy turns men into robots. Rehabilitation programs are shamefully inept and the brutalization of libidinal expression encourages homosexuality and rape. Above all, the indeterminate sentence places complete power in the hands of the parole board to keep some inmates in jail forever. Jackson bitterly complained about racially segregated facilities and the use of maximum-security cells as dentention camps for politically motivated actions by black prisoners. The conditions in these cells were so bad, he remarked, that "no black leaves Max Row walking. Either he leaves in the meat wagon or he leaves crawling, licking at the pig's feet."

Jackson rejected the criminal label placed on most black prisoners. Crime, in his view, is the response of victims of social and economic injustice, and official definitions of crime are simply attempts by the establishment to suppress the forces of progress. The issue for men like himself was to combat racism in prison and the socio-economic and political structures of the society which maintain it. Prisoners must be reached and made to understand that they are victims of social injustice, and are a mighty reservoir of revolutionary potential. What emerged from Jackson's experience was a determination to build a prison movement—a veritable convict army of liberation—which would transform the prisoners and link them with broader struggles waged by the Black Panthers and other political movements. Inside the prison there must be reform and unity among blacks and with white prisoners. "We have got to get together," Jackson wrote in *Blood in My Eye*. "We have got to be in a position to tell the pig that if he doesn't serve the food when it's warm and pass out the scouring powder on time, everybody on the tier is going to throw something at him, then things will change and life will be easier." Outside the prison it was necessary to combat all attempts to "isolate the black vanguard commune, the black colony, from the larger body of the class structure." It was essential that the black industrial worker be encouraged to carry out a valid workers' revolutionary policy, namely, the seizure of union leadership and the enforcement of demands against capital. In the end, as victory grew nearer, the new black communes in major urban centers would be "A BLADE AT THE THROAT OF FASCISM."

Jackson could not promise black prisoners in American society—those inside and outside the penal walls—more than unceasing struggle and eventually death in their cause. The purpose itself was clear enough for him: "bringing the U.S.A. to its knees." But in embarking on this task through organizing, mobilizing, and altering attitudes of people toward their class enemies, black and white, Jackson saw that urban guerrilla forces in the black colony must accept the consequences, "the closing off of critical sections of the city with barbed wire, armored pig carriers criss-crossing the city streets, soldiers everywhere, tommy guns pointed at stomach level, smoke curling black against the daylight sky, the smell of cordite, house-to-house searches, doors being kicked down, the commonness of death."

Concerning wider issues, a number of basic themes occur throughout George Jackson's letters. He speaks in praise of the revolutionary role of the prisoner/Negro/slave against the system. He says the forces of revolution in America lie in wait inside the black colony, and this is a potential inherent in all black social classes. He advocates urban guerrilla warfare linked with Third World liberation movements to halt American fascism and to destroy institutions that support existing property relations.

Repeated denial of parole hardened Jackson's resolve not to cooperate with prison authorities. In February 1970, Jackson and two other inmates of Soledad prison, Fleeta Drumgo and John Clutchette, were charged with the murder of a white guard and faced a mandatory death sentence. All three were known to be politically conscious militants, their case became a cause célèbre and they were referred to as "the Soledad Brothers." Jackson's life during this time was haunted by the grim hostility of his guards and by the death of his brother Jonathan in an ill-fated attempt in August 1970 to seize hostages at San Rafael county courthouse and dramatize the plight of the Soledad Brothers. Finally, a year later, Jackson himself was shot and killed under mysterious circumstances for allegedly trying to escape from detention in San Quentin prison.

One of the most passionate defenders of the Soledad Brothers was Angela Davis. Fresh from her organizational activities with Black Panther and SNCC groups in Los Angeles and her own struggles for "Free Speech" on California University campuses from 1968 to 1970, Miss Davis, a black college lecturer and member of the Communist Party, threw herself into support of the prisoners' movement. Her involvement began, she recalls in her autobiography, when she picked up the *Los Angeles Times* in mid-February 1970 and glanced at a photograph of three imposing black men—the Soledad Brothers. "Their faces were serene and strong," she says, "but their waists were draped in chains." This image was to haunt her during the next days; they were "three beautiful virile faces pulled out of the horrible anonymity of prison life." And before long she was convinced "there were impending explosions behind the walls, and that if we did not begin to build a support movement for our brothers and sisters in prison, we were no revolutionaries at all." On behalf of the Soledad Brothers and the mounting protests of black prisoners in all parts of the country, Miss Davis and her Marxist and liberal colleagues made a series of telling accusations against the legal, judicial, and penal system. The intensification of police control over black dissidents was seen as an abridgment of freedom under the guise of surveillance of "people likely to commit crimes." The use of the prison system as an instrument of mass intimidation was denounced, and it was charged that the whole body of law and justice when applied to working people and colored minorities serves to perpetuate second-class citizenship, to combat differing life styles, and to silence those who challenge the status quo.

Miss Davis in her many speeches on behalf of the Soledad Brothers, recorded in the book *If They Come in the Morning*, sought to aid them in the creation of centers of resistance against the unjust prison regime. She reminded her audiences that American history is filled with examples of inequitable justice. Have we forgotten, she asked, the story of the Scottsboro Boys—nine black youths arrested in Jackson County, Alabama, in March 1931 and charged with the rape of two white girls; the "murder frame-ups" of the trade unionist IWW organizer Joe Hill in 1914; and the execution of the anarchists Sacco and Vanzetti, accused of robbery and murder, as an excuse for silencing militant crusaders against oppression. Can we forget, Miss Davis asked, the attacks against black radicals and Marxists like Dr. W. E. B. Du Bois, who was indicted in 1951 by the federal government under the spurious charge of failing to register as an agent of a foreign principal? And she recalled that Du Bois himself had said:

> What turns me cold in all this experience is the certainty that thousands of innocent victims are in jail today because they had neither money nor friends to help them . . . They daily stagger out of prison doors embittered, vengeful, hopeless, ruined. And of this army of the wronged, the proportion of Negroes is frightful. We protect and defend sensational cases where Negroes are involved. But the great mass of arrested or accused Black folk have no defense. There is a desperate need of nationwide organizations to oppose this national racket of railroading to jails and chain gangs the poor, friendless and Black.

The prisoners' movement gained impetus in 1971 with the outbreak of rioting at Attica Prison, New York. Like many other penal institutions, Attica had become a non-white—black and Spanish-speaking—detention camp guarded by white correctional staff. Earlier in the year, a manifesto written by inmates made a series of moderate demands—legal representation before the parole boards, improvement of facilities, and an end to the segregation of political, black, and ethnic nationalist prisoners. Eight weeks of unsuccessful negotiations ended with a call by young black leaders at Attica for a day of prisoners' solidarity and protest over the killing of George Jackson in a California prison. Then an outburst of chaotic violence, sparked by a black prisoner's refusal to leave an exercise yard, led to a prison uprising in which hostages were taken. Finally, Attica prison was recaptured by a heavily armed State Police assault on September 13, 1971, in which thirty-nine prisoners and hostages died and more than eighty others were wounded. "With the exception of Indian massacres in the late 19th century," states the preface to *Attica: Official Report of the New York State Special Commission*, "the State Police assault which ended the four-day prison uprising was the bloodiest one-day encounter between Americans since the Civil War."

What happened at Attica symbolized the wretched situation in many prisons, and Miss Davis and a fellow Marxist Bettina

Aptheker issued a nationwide appeal on behalf of all prisoners. They expressed special concern for four classes of prisoner: political prisoners, which they defined to include political leaders in their own communities, such as the Black Panthers; leaders of civil disobedience and draft-resistance groups like the Berrigan brothers; victims of class, racial, and national oppression who are arrested and lack legal and political redress; and criminals who develop a political consciousness in jail and are victimized, for example, George Jackson. The initial efforts of Davis and Aptheker coincided with the activities of a wide range of penal-reform groups. Prisoners' solidarity committees were formed to protest the institutionalized racism of prison systems. Old and prestigious groups like the John Howard Association in Chicago sought redress of specific faults which deprive prisoners of their humanity and prospects of self-development and rehabilitation. Many civil-rights groups declared that the rapid increase of black populations in prisons was due to racialism in the police force and judiciary and was a blight on the nation's conscience. And in the summer of 1974 Miss Davis shared a speaking platform in Raleigh, North Carolina, with the integrationist leader Reverend Ralph David Abernathy to draw attention to the special problems of more than forty blacks on death row awaiting execution in the state's prisons.

Angela Davis, who was born in 1944, has had a long career as a fighter for militant black and left-wing causes. She is most notably remembered as a rangy, chain-smoking intellectual with a glorious Afro hairstyle who associated with the Panthers and the Communists. In 1969 she lost her position as assistant professor of philosophy at the University of California, Los Angeles, because of her affiliation with the Communist Party and the Che-Lumumba Club, a black cell of the party established in Los Angeles in 1967. Following her disappearance after the Jonathan Jackson courthouse drama in which four people died, she was declared a dangerous, most-wanted criminal in FBI bulletins. In 1970 she was arrested and charged with kidnapping, murder, and conspiracy in the Jonathan Jackson case, but was acquitted two years later. Now a well-known Marxist spokesman on black and international issues, she has told audiences in America and abroad: "I am a Communist because I am convinced that the centuries-old suffering of Black people cannot be alleviated under the present arrangement." Furthermore, she says, "Black people can never truly be free—economically, socially, politically—until the entire fabric of this society is first dissolved, then transformed and restructured in harmony with our needs, our interests and our dreams."

Despite her publicity, Miss Davis has never built up a large following among the black masses, who remain skeptical of her middle-class, intellectual background and white Communist connections. At one of her rallies in Los Angeles on behalf of the prisoners' solidarity campaign, the audience was mainly white, well-heeled, middle-aged veterans of the Communist movement. This does not deter her, however. She feels that her court victory has won for black people "the right to be a Communist and black." "What were people fighting for in the sixties," she asks, "if not the right of people to be in the revolutionary activity of their choice?" She has therefore stayed in the Communist Party, which is predominantly white, because, she says, "I believe it is the body that will lead the country to revolution." She has moved into a long-term program working with white and black Marxist-oriented youth, and resumed her academic career teaching weekend classes on "Black Women and the Development of the Black Community" at Claremont College in Southern California, a system of colleges with a conservative reputation.

Revolutionary black nationalism in the post-Malcolm X era attracted many other groups to its banner. In the wake of the Black Panther Party and the prison movement came two death-dealing revolutionary terrorist groups. One of these, the Black Liberation Army, was indicted in 1973 on charges including murder, robbery, grand larceny, and possession of guns. The army's guiding spirit and the leader of a closely knit band that reportedly broke from the Black Panther Party in 1971 is said to be Joanne D. Chesimard. The group's membership is small, estimated at one hundred, of whom twenty-five to forty live in the metropolitan New York area, and they are accused of ambushing policemen in New York, St. Louis, North Carolina, and California. Another group, Cinque's

Army, or the Symbionese Liberation Army, was the most bizarre and smallest revolutionary terrorist group to emerge from the black prison movement in California. While the twelve-to-twenty-member SLA was on the rampage, it sent shock waves of horror and outrage through the nation, not only because of the armed robberies and violent crimes attributed to it, but by obtaining as a most unlikely recruit the newspaper heiress Patricia Hearst, who was originally kidnapped by the SLA to dramatize their revolutionary goals.

The full history of the Symbionese Liberation Army is not known, but its founder was a black escaped convict, Donald Defreeze, who called himself Field Marshal Cinque after the leader of an 1839 slaveship revolt. Defreeze preached a message of "Death to the fascist insect that preys upon the life of the people." He also created the group's emblem, a seven-headed cobra, which stood for self-determination, cooperative production, creativity, unity, faith, purpose, and collective responsibility. Most of Defreeze's followers, unlike those of any group discussed so far, were white, college-educated, young people from middle- and upper-class homes. After very obscure beginnings in the early seventies, the Symbionese Liberation Army moved from talking about revolution to armed violence. Members were charged with the killing of Marcus A. Foster, a black superintendent of schools in Oakland who was ambushed and murdered with cyanide-coated bullets November 6, 1973. Following an audacious bank robbery in San Francisco, Defreeze and five others were wiped out in a police assault on a SLA hideout in Los Angeles in May 1974. Finally, the fugitive Patty Hearst, apparently an SLA convert, and the remaining known members of the group were captured, and she was brought to trial in 1976 on various charges of armed robbery. Under the fluorescent glaze of the courtroom, with constant attention from a large corps of media news reporters, Miss Hearst pleaded "brain washing" and misadventure with scoundrels as the cause of her errant ways. She was found guilty, but after a period of intense observation was released on $1 million bail in the care of her wealthy parents, pending further charges.

Revolutionary black nationalism is also marked by an emphasis on territorial separation, a vociferous claim for a geographical share of the country that black labor helped to make prosperous. Such groups believe in the formation of all-black towns and states, or an all-black nation encompassing several states. Particular attention is directed to the growth and development of existing communities in the central districts of major cities and in the rural South. In addition, specific demands are made for reparations, armed struggle, and community control.

Historically there are many dramatic examples of the attraction of national territorial separatism to the black masses and leading middle-class intellectuals and religious leaders. Uprooted slave communities searched for "some place of our own over yonder"; others sought to withdraw into "Heavens of racial salvation." The migrants of the mid-nineteenth century held utopian hopes that America would grant blacks land or money to buy their freedom. And in the mid-twentieth century the Black Muslims were the most strident group demanding the partitioning of America into two separate and independent states, one for whites and the other a homeland for blacks. The Muslims argued that integration can only lead to assimilation and the loss of black identity. Rather than continue to suffer injustice and alienation within America to gain the dubious privilege of assimilation, separation was the best way to minimize racial friction and ensure black development. To this end the Muslims' religious beliefs and economic and political activities were part of a broader strategy of disengagement from an oppressive society and eventual withdrawal into a separate black state. In the interim, as citizens of the United States, the Muslims claimed full rights to equality of religious freedom, legal treatment, and educational opportunity. On these grounds they defended their right to conscientiously resist participation in the "white man's wars," boldly dramatized by the draft protests of the Muslim prizefighter Muhammad Ali, and the right to lobby against integration and for the creation of their own schools.

Territorial separation is, therefore, not a new idea. But in the volatile atmosphere of the sixties, first in the fiery words of Malcolm X and later in the belligerent demands of the Revolutionary

Action Movement and the cry of "Land and Power" by the Republic of New Africa, territorial separatism took on a new and cogent meaning.

One of the first secular black nationalist organizations to wave the banner of territorial separatism was the Revolutionary Action Movement (RAM). It was a loosely structured group formed in the mid-sixties by college-trained and ghetto youth as a "third voice" alongside the Black Muslims and SNCC. RAM began in Philadelphia with a campaign against police brutality and the urban renewal that threatened the tenuous hold of black people on a meager and diminishing stock of bad housing. In an era of widespread suspicion of urban planning, RAM's emphasis on resistance and defense of black neighborhoods found fertile ground in many East and West Coast cities. The movement's life was brutally short, however. It was infiltrated and broken up by police, and its leaders arrested in 1967. Max Stanford, RAM's field director and leading spokesman, was charged with arson and conspiracy to commit criminal anarchy against the state of New York. Stanford's "Manifesto Toward a Revolutionary Action Movement" remains, however, the basic text and illustrative guide to the movement's philosophy.

At the outset the RAM manifesto defines its philosophy in the Malcolmist tradition. It is "revolutionary nationalism, black nationalism, or just plain blackism . . . one of the world black revolution or world revolution of oppressed peoples rising up against their former slavemasters. Our movement is a movement of black people who are coordinating their efforts to create a 'new world' free from exploitation and oppression of man to man." The essence of the movement's social concern was the preservation, consolidation, and enrichment of black-held urban and rural territories. Specific demands were made for a separate black nation and economy financed by a substantial payment of reparations by the United States government. If these demands were not met, RAM threatened to embark on a campaign of guerrilla warfare against "the world's No. 1 imperialist nation." From clandestine headquarters in central-city black areas, RAM guerrillas would attack key business centers and communication installations. Agitators would harangue the crowds and whip them up to a riotous frenzy. Special attack squads recruited from street gangs and paramilitary organizations would initiate sporadic fire-bombing and sniper fire. During the night they would launch organized battles and unlimited terror. At first guerrilla weapons would be no more than a poor man's arsenal of rusting handguns and rifles, booby traps, and homemade acid and gasoline fire bombs. Later, they would be augmented by more sophisticated weaponry—flamethrowers, grenades, rocket launchers, machine guns, and light mortars—bought from servicemen or stolen from armories. Should there be a protracted conflict, aid was expected from a liberation front of political activists who would mobilize popular support and a workers' general strike to cripple the urban economy. Finally, if RAM's separatist demands were ignored, Stanford predicted an all-out war between the United States and "the reactionary white nationalism of Western capitalist nations" and a revolutionary liberation army and Afro-American government-in-exile supported by Africa, China, and the oppressed peoples of the world.

With RAM's collapse, Stanford fled New York, changed his name to Akbar Muhammad Ahmed, and started a new organization, the African People's Party, from a Cleveland address. His ten-point program, published in *Black Scholar*, May 1972, placed strong emphasis on territorial separation in the form of a black nation in five states of the Deep South operating a "cooperative communalist economy financed by $400 billion reparations from the U.S. government." Specific demands are made for an "immediate end to the racist war of genocide against black communities, freedom for all black people held in jails, and exemption of black men from military service." The program also advocated "a government of our own decided by a national Congress of Afrikan Peoples called together by a Black Liberation Front as a centralizing committee, and that our case for self-determination be put to the United Nations and the World Court." In Stanford's career his main skills seem to be taking ideas he developed in activist youth groups like SNCC, RAM, and later the New York Black Panther Party chapter, and setting them down as organizational principles for the formation of new groups. That he was able to do this was due in part to his background of collegiate politics at the black Central State University, Ohio, and his associations at different times with Malcolm X, Stokely Carmichael, Rap Brown, LeRoi Jones, James Forman, and Robert Williams in the founding of black-liberation projects. In 1968, then only twenty-five years of age, Stanford helped organize the Third National Black Power Conference and was co-chairman of its political workshop. In many ways, however, he proved to be a luckless amateur. He went underground after failing to return to face the New York conspiracy charges, but was arrested in an FBI raid in September 1972 while attending a conference of the Congress of Afrikan Peoples sponsored by Imamu Amiri Baraka (LeRoi Jones) in San Diego, California.

Territorial separation is also a central doctrine of a small black nationalist organization, the Republic of New Africa, founded in 1967 by Detroit attorney Milton Henry. Also known as Brother Gaidi, Milton Henry was an early acquaintance of Malcolm X and presided over the Malcolm X Society in Detroit. In recent years the republic's leadership passed into the hands of his brother Richard, who is known as Brother Imari Abubakari Obadele. A native of Philadelphia, Obadele is college-educated and a prolific writer of political tracts. As president of the republic's provisional government, he was instrumental in creating a tiny base of operations in Hinds and Leflore Counties, Mississippi, from which to launch a new black community and an independent black nation.

The principles of the Republic of New Africa are modeled after Ujamaa or the Tanzanian model of cooperative economics and community self-sufficiency. The goal is to establish a black nation in the Deep South states of Louisiana, Mississippi, Alabama, Georgia, and South Carolina. In its Declaration of Independence, entitled "Revolutionary Aims," nine major objectives are stated:

—To build a new society that is better than what we now know and as perfect as man can make it.
—To promote industriousness, responsibility, scholarship and service, initiative and devotion to the Revolution.
—To build a black independent nation where no sect or religious creed subverts or impedes the building of the new society, the

new state government, or the achievement of the aims of the
Revolution.
—To end exploitation of man by man or his environment.
—To assure equality of rights for the sexes.
—To end color and class discrimination, while not abolishing
solubrious [sic] diversity, and to promote self-respect and mu-
tual respect among all people.
—To protect and promote the personal dignity and integrity of the
individual and his natural rights.
—To assure justice for all.
—To place a major means of production and trade in the trust of
the state to assure the benefits of this earth and man's genius
and labor to society and all its members.

Obadele says the republic is prepared to wage military and
guerrilla warfare to achieve these objectives. A lengthy statement,
"The Struggle Is for Land," in *Black Scholar*, February 1972, by
Obadele suggests a fighting strategy to create a situation in which it
is cheaper and more advantageous for America to relinquish control of the five states than to continue a war against the republic to
take back or hold the area. According to Obadele's plan, the republic's troops will be recruited from young ex-Southerners, veterans of
ghetto uprisings, and trained black American soldiers. Recruitment
and training is the responsibility of the republic's Defense Minister,
Alajo Adegbola, who warns that the struggle will be long and ardu-
ous. The new recruits must come with their own equipment,
and it is suggested that this include radios, medical kits, field packs,
tents, and arms, such as M1 Garand rifles, 12-gauge shotguns, M1
carbines, and plenty of ammunition. In the meantime, financial
support for the republic's liberation army is being sought at the rate
of $70 per week per man.

To further the "land and power" goals of the republic, Obadele advocates a policy of dual attack. One is sporadic guerrilla actions in Northern cities supported by armed and sympathetic black
communities. The other is a major drive in the five Southern states
to win black control and the people's consent to a government
under the leadership of the republic. Obadele claims that the tradi-
tionally heavily populated black areas of the Deep South are black

by right—"our black homeland"—and he proposes a vigorous military campaign to free them. The liberation forces would also seek United Nations recognition and plebiscites in the disputed territory, and press for the right of black people to reparations, land, and development aid from the United States. Diplomatic missions would be established in friendly territories outside the South and seek support from the Afro-Asian nations and China to discourage attacks by United States federal power. Once independent, the republic would start Ujamaa-type cooperative communities in agricultural areas such as Hinds and Leflore Counties. Local officers would modify and improve the educational system and start new cooperative industries to end unemployment. Economic unions and a Common Market would be sought with black Caribbean nations, Africa, Asia, and Latin America.

In Obadele's opinion, the issues are quite clear—it is a matter of black survival. In Detroit, where he lived for seventeen years, thousands of workers are unemployed and many of these are young and black. By contrast, he feels that Mississippi, where he has lived for five years, is, despite its poverty, the economic salvation and potential homeland for America's blacks. But how much thought has Obadele given to solving specific problems associated with his grandiose scheme? How, for example, will the republic gain black support? Obadele acknowledges that winning the consent of Southern blacks will be a formidable task. The people are primarily low-income, unskilled land workers and semi-skilled town laborers, with little experience of direct democracy. He will rely, therefore, on creating an attractive program for the resettlement of Northern blacks, many of whom ran away from poverty in the South only to experience it again in the North. The new settlers would have the tasks of clearing the land, building new settlements, and defending them against attack. As for his proposal for guerrilla campaigns in Northern cities, Obadele expects widespread support from low-income blacks and unemployed youth. On the other hand, he expects opposition to his ideas from the black middle class, from old people, and from women. They tend to be conservative, he says, because after all these years in the North they either think they're free or, more likely, are too deeply dependent on established institutions and welfare programs. The black church will also be a conservative force, he says, because mass relocation of their congregations would threaten ministers with loss of their livelihood and political power.

How will the republic subsidize the Ujamaa production units and create strong economic centers? Obadele says he is seeking a $57 billion reparations payment from the United States government which will be used to fund development and provide cash assistance to settlers and existing communities.

Obadele believes that blacks should have the right to exercise an option for or against United States citizenship. He claims that the doubtful freedom granted to the black man under the Emancipation Proclamation and the Fourteenth Amendment to the Constitution is illegal. No referendum was held and the slaves were powerless in these matters. Furthermore, he says, under international law people released from slavery or colonialism should have the right to choose whether to return to their homeland, petition for citizenship rights, seek separate nationhood, or exercise the right to migrate to any other sovereign nation. American blacks had none of these choices, and for this reason Obadele demands reparations for the due process which was denied blacks and calls for a "freedom vote" or plebiscite to determine "the citizenship options for a kidnapped people under international law."

Because of his activities, Obadele has been charged with treason and waging war against the state of Mississippi. He has served time in the maximum-security unit of the Hinds County jail on a murder charge growing out of a shooting during an FBI and police raid on the republic's headquarters. Since then, further raids on the House of Uhuru (Freedom), the group's West Side Detroit office, have led to the arrest of several other members. In the decade since its founding in 1967, the Republic of New Africa's "Land and Power" slogan has not attracted support from black Americans, who see the Republic's settlement project as little more than a real-estate broker's ploy to profit from the purchase and resale of parcels of land to impoverished homesick urban-dwelling blacks, all on credit supplied by the United States government. The republic's tenuous associations with Malcolm X have long since ended. Its brief flirtation with the returned exile Robert Williams, who in 1969 was hailed as the President of the Republic of New Africa, terminated with his resignation. And lukewarm support by Black Panther Party leader Huey Newton, who once thought the republic "perfectly justified in demanding and declaring the right to secede from the union," has been withdrawn. Police and FBI actions have effectively silenced stalwarts of the republic and scared off would-be supporters, leaving Obadele as a somewhat pathetic figure groping for publicity and a means of covering up a series of disasters in his program.

Revolutionary black nationalism in the sixties triggered a resurgent interest in Pan-Africanism, and it too had a territorial separatist emphasis. Historically, men like Bishop Henry Turner, Edward Wilmot Blyden, and Marcus Garvey saw Africa as the fount of black nationhood and believed that a return to Africa was the solution to the black man's problems in the diaspora. Today, the Pan-African nationalism of Garvey is still a potent emotional force, albeit among a small following in East Coast cities. The esteemed figure of honor is Garvey's son, Marcus Jr. In recent speeches at Liberty Hall in Harlem, the spiritual headquarters of the movement, he reaffirmed the purity of his father's ideas. "A lot of people claim they know about Garveyism," said Marcus Jr., "but they don't know anything about the philosophy my father enunciated. They use the rhetoric of Garveyism to disguise their true intentions of confusing the Black masses about the Back-to-Africa Movement." His father, he claims, was one of the greatest men of this century. "He was the true Father of Orthodox African Nationalism and was railroaded to prison and exile because of his vehement words: 'Mr. White Man, are you mad? Are you insane? Do you think that you can rule the world on bluff? Do you think you can withstand the power of Africa and Asia combined? I say to you, Europe for the Europeans . . . Asia for the Asians . . . And above all, Africa for the Africans—those at home and those abroad.' "

Allied with Marcus Jr. are two key leaders of the Garveyite Universal Negro Improvement Association and African Communi-

ties League, Thomas Harvey, president-general of the national or-
ganization, which has its headquarters in Philadelphia, and Arthur
"Lumumba" Grant, president of the Harlem Vanguard Division.
Harlem is also honeycombed with many small quarreling groups
created by Garvey-inspired disciples: Carlos Cook, James Lawson,
Abdel Krim, Rabbi Judah, Conrad Peters, and Charles Kenyatta, a
burly construction worker and former confidant of Malcolm X.
The African National Pioneer Movement, founded by the late
Carlos Cook, is one of the most important of these splinter groups.
The ANPM calls for Afro-American unity, self-determination, and
racial separation. It sponsors annual Garvey Day celebrations in
black communities and works very closely with Ajass, a black-arts
group, and the Federation of Pan-African Nationalist Organizations
(FOPANO), a group of young militants devoted to "mobilizing Africans in this country to make practical contributions toward the al-
leviation of the conditions which exist in our Motherland today."
FOPANO leaders have been highly critical of the "genocidal lack
of American official concern" about famine relief in the drought-
stricken Sahel and West African areas. They are also linked by origin and kinship with a loose association of West Indian clubs concerned with Caribbean political affairs.

By far the most radical proposals to galvanize the flagging spirit
of Pan-Africanism in America have come from Stokely Carmichael, the former leader of the Student Nonviolent Coordinating
Committee. After many years in Ghana and Guinea, Carmichael
has returned to his old stamping grounds, traveling the back lanes
of the rural South organizing and preaching. But, in the small
clapboard churches and schoolhouses of Lowndes County, Alabama, where he first came to public notice, he is not talking about
the vote any more. The message now demands revolutionary Pan-
African socialism and a return to Africa—a view most sharecroppers in his audience have hardly heard before.

Stokely Carmichael left America disillusioned in 1969; he felt
that he no longer had anything to say. The euphoria of Black
Power had passed. America was still in one piece and a new strategy was needed. In the Republic of Guinea with his wife, the
South African black singer Miriam Makeba, Carmichael spent

many hours in discussion with President Sekou Touré and with one of his neighbors, the late Kwame Nkrumah, exiled in Guinea following his overthrow as President of Ghana in 1966. These two African socialists were instrumental in forming his beliefs about Pan-Africanism. It is, he says, an idea born as a movement of revolt against forces of exploitation, oppression, and alienation; and when infused with an Africanist scientific socialism offers a method of analysis and strategy for African development. Carmichael supports President Touré's vision of a revolutionary Africa stripped of all foreign masters, and where black dignity and power will flourish. He dreams of one united Africa—no individual countries—one leader, one army, and one representative at the United Nations.

Armed with his Pan-African socialist views, Carmichael is now concentrating his efforts on laying the foundations for another upsurge of black American consciousness. Carmichael contends that there is no future for blacks in a white-dominated society that bought their forefathers as slaves and later thrust citizenship on them without asking them what they thought of the idea. He believes that blacks should abandon America en masse. Black emigration would prove beneficial for Africa as well, he argues, for "Africa would not need to depend on foreign technicians to service and maintain sophisticated imported equipment. African technicians exist. They are in America . . . The land in Africa, not America, is ours. Our primary objective should be Africa."

Carmichael describes himself as a "devotee of Pan-Africanism which is scientific socialism down the line." But he does not lay claim to being a Marxist or Leninist. On the contrary, he once said in a speech at Algiers: "For me to always look to Marx is once again to give credit for everything to Europe. Once again I continue to stress my own inferiority as an African. Ready to unify my country, I continue to look to a European, Marx, to unify me . . . People with this approach do not believe that they themselves can originate something worthy, which becomes very damaging." He concludes that the only position for black men to take is Pan-Africanism. We need our own ideology, he says, and we need a land base, a power base, and this must be Africa.

Despite the efforts of the Garveyites and Carmichael, black

Americans have neither rushed to affirm their "Africanitude" nor shown much desire to return permanently to Africa, the black Zion. It is true, however, that small bands of settlers have taken root in Liberia, Ghana, and Tanzania, and jet-set safaris are an exotic lure for the affluent. Indeed, the mastery of the language and symbolism of Pan-Africanism is probably more widespread than ever before and there are an estimated two thousand black Americans living in Africa. Moreover, in America many more Africa-oriented organizations have been created since the demise in the late sixties of the American Society of African Culture, discredited by allegations of funding by the CIA. Scholars find expression through the African Heritage Studies Association established in 1968 by John Henrik Clarke of Hunter College and the African-American Scholars Council chaired by Professor Elliott P. Skinner of Columbia University since 1971. In addition, ad hoc groups have been organized to call attention to the pitiful conditions of nomads and peasants affected by the drought in Africa's Sahel region and to the dire problems of conflict and transition in Southern Africa.

What seems of paramount importance about modern Pan-Africanism is that it enables its adherents to place Afro-American problems in a wider context, geographically, politically, and ideologically. Many black moderates see Africa as an impoverished distant relative to be helped, not emigrated to, and urge black Americans to take a position to aid and to favor Africa on all issues that do not affect strategic national interests. Congressman Charles Diggs, Jr., and the U.S. Congressional Black Caucus stressed the importance of African independence to American blacks in discussions with Dr. Henry Kissinger and Presidents Ford and Carter, and as justification for their surveillance of United States policies in regard to Southern African affairs. Roy Innis, director of CORE, has adopted a Pan-African nationalist stance in his many discussions with President Julius Nyerere of Tanzania and President Idi Amin of Uganda, and claims recognition for CORE as "the authentic liberation movement of African people in the United States." In Greensboro, North Carolina, home of the civil-rights sit-ins, a small radical student group called YOBU—Youth Organization for

Black Unity, proudly proclaims from the masthead of its journal, *The African World*, a quote from Kwame Nkrumah: "The truly African revolutionary press must aid in the defeat of imperialism and neo-colonialism, hailing those who advance the revolution and exposing those who retard it. We do not believe there are necessarily two sides to every question: we see right and wrong, just and unjust, progressive and reactionary, positive and negative, friend and foe. We are partisan."

Admittedly, Pan-Africanism does not lend itself to a simple or precise definition; it is rather an umbrella for the assemblage of related ideas. But some historical reference is necessary to place what we shall see is a decidedly American emphasis on Pan-Africanism into perspective. Pan-Africanism was born at the turn of the century as a protest by black American, Caribbean, and colonial African peoples against the universal belief in the inferiority of their status. Essentially it insisted on the unity of black people, the right to self-determination, and treatment with dignity and respect. It linked the regeneration of blacks in the diaspora to the redemption of Africa as an independent and united continent. At the outset Pan-Africanism was undoubtedly race-conscious, and therefore susceptible to proclamations by many of its adherents that black is noble and beautiful instead of dirty and ugly. It characteristically involved a desperate search for a uniquely African personality typified all too frequently by a violent reaction to whiteness and an uncritical acceptance of all things black. With the appearance of Stalinist Marxism and the Marxist analysis of the close and exploitative relationship between capitalism and colonialism, and later with the increasing tempo of the march toward African independence, a new breed of Pan-Africanist emerged. It was clear to militant colonial intellectuals like Nnamdi Azikiwe in West Africa and to Marxisante expatriates like the West Indian theoretician George Padmore and Kwame Nkrumah in England that the goal of colonial freedom was a dynamic factor in its own right and that blackness alone was not sufficient to mobilize people to take their destiny into their own hands. Padmore and Nkrumah declared categorically that Pan-Africanism rejects both white racialism and black chauvinism; it looks beyond the narrow confines of class, race, tribe, and religion to a time when there will be equal opportunity for all. In the course of the development of these ideas, they also rejected the excesses of capitalism and Communism and strove instead to create a social democratic base for the decolonization and development of the economy and polity. Pan-Africanism today in Africa is Afro-centric; it emphasizes national and continental freedom, human dignity, and economic and social redemption. And this view holds a paramount place in the objectives of African states and the Organization of African Unity.

In the United States today, some form of Pan-Africanism has found verbal support across a broad range of opinion—from moderates to militants and from community organizers to college intellectuals. But there is a persistent tendency toward blackism which gives the concept a diasporic and peculiarly Americo-centric quality, and lessens its usefulness for the resolution of the problems of both the mass of black Americans and Africans. This tendency was identified by President Sekou Touré in a widely publicized message to the Sixth Pan-African Congress in Dar es Salaam in autumn 1974. President Touré spoke out against "the obscurantism of color identity and sterile emotions used by imperialists and false and opportunistic black leaders alike to anaesthetize the people . . . We must combat this tendency, whose most obnoxious and alienating characteristic is negritude." In his view, which found its most vulnerable target among the Black Power-imbued, 200-member United States black delegation, Touré said that "the reclamation of Pan-Africanist identity requires a fight against racist, segregationist and Zionist movements and any attempts to encapsulate the movement in a particularistic identity, for these are retrograde tendencies which place Pan-Africanism in a 'geological garden of stagnation.' " On the contrary, Touré declared, the destruction of imperialism in all its manifestations—cultural, political, and economic— cannot be racially based. It was now clear from his own experiences and those of other freedom fighters that "skin color, be it black, white, yellow or bronzed, does not indicate anything about social class, the ideology, the nature of behaviorism, or the qualities and skill of man or people." In conclusion, President Touré defined Pan-Africanism as the class struggle at the scale of Africa and all other black communities. In the pursuit of Pan-Africanism, he said, "one goal is the liberation of the continent and our peoples from imperialist oppression—another is a cultural revolution, quite different from the worship of African artifacts, whose purpose is to humanize and universalize us among the peoples of the world."

Against this background, Pan-Africanism in the United States seems more American than African. The fetishistic cult of black Zionists, with their exotic dreams of ebony kings and queens gamboling among the palm trees and mud huts, pursue a fantasy far removed from the realities of modern African life. Leaders of allegedly black-nationalist organizations, like Innis of CORE, posture at internationalizing the Afro-American struggle while meddling in the internal affairs of independent African nations and serving as a cover for spurious and provocative actions by United States government agencies and corporations. Black politicians use Africa to assume an air of foreign policy expertise and to curry favor with establishment policy elites. The fact is that too many blacks and so-called Pan-Africanists in America are filled with a romantic image of themselves as superior to indigenous African peoples, and in the mirror of their minds justify their schemes of technical, cultural, and business infiltration as a civilizing mission. Seen in historical context, Pan-Africanist programs are by and large a travesty of schemes proposed by American leaders from Thomas Jefferson to Abraham Lincoln to establish colonies of acculturated New World blacks in Africa as factors of American enterprise and pacifiers of African peoples. From this perspective, Pan-Africanism in America today seems less a revolutionary Afro-centric ideology than a vehicle for the creation of black agents of the American empire aiding the exploitation of whole regions and establishing United States hegemony over strategic African resources.

Dissent, protest, and resistance were all highlighted by militants in the post-Malcolm X period. But there was no decided shift toward mass revolutionary power based on collective black responsibility. The organizations which emerged were a mixture of three vital compounds. One was an abstract, almost metaphysical, phenomenon, the search for an identity. Another was the angry expression of deep discomfort at the daily grievances and problems of black people. A third was hatred for systems of exploitation and a desire for radical change. But in the process of combination the ideologists of revolutionary black nationalism and their organizations veered sharply toward disjointed rhetoric or racial chauvinism and away from a strategic conjuncture with historical forces capable of bringing about profound changes in the society and its institutions. Today the leading figures of this ill-fated venture are either dead, jailed, coopted, or compromised. Revolutionary black nationalism, for all its stress on separatism, reparations, territorialism, Pan-Africanism, or even the Panther version of black socialist unity, proved unable to achieve widespread involvement of the people. On the contrary, as we shall see, black thought and practice moved inexorably toward cultural, economic, and political forms of bourgeois nationalism. In culture and the popular arts, large segments of the population gave themselves over to joyful paroxysms of self-love, shouting "Black is beautiful." On the economic front the angry cries of "Black Power" and "Off the pigs" were muted and coopted into black capitalism and establishment programs for ghetto improvement. In politics, middle-class intellectuals, religious and business leaders encapsulated militant movements in a series of national conferences and there was a rise of moderate black elected officials. Meanwhile, between fits of darkest anger and apathy, the black urban masses wasted away in a gehenna of torment.

5 Images of Cultural Unity

The stunning events of the sixties stimulated a remarkable sense of black cultural consciousness. The legitimacy of black values and life styles—the common foods and cadences of everyday life—were emphasized by artists, writers, and poets. A black perspective was called for in all aspects of life—education, social science, the arts, and communication—and black culture was acclaimed as a major element within a pluralistic American society. Traditional aspects of black experience were elevated to a place of great esteem, and the black world of Africa, the Caribbean, and Brazil was scoured for exemplary cultural artifacts. New black fashions were modeled on imported African hair styles, names, multicolored cloth and garments, leatherwork, beads and bangles. Race pride became a major cultural factor, worn like an Afro halo around the head or a badge of honor by some; wielded by others like a Zulu warrior's assegai to ward off attacks against a fragile, budding sense of racial self-respect. There was widespread debate about the wisdom of assimilation into the white world, and moreover, there was a growing feeling that black values and strengths should have a distinctive and equal place in America after all legal and psychological barriers were removed.

The essence of black culture is undoubtedly religion. Black Americans are a deeply religious people. More than ten million adults and five million children are Christians and Protestants, of established black Baptist and Methodist persuasions, and pride themselves on going to church on Sunday. The church is for them the stable "Rock of Zion." Fellow church members are an intimate family of worship and support, and the ministers and deacons are esteemed community leaders who bury the dead, baptize the newly born, organize the Christmas parties and church outings, reward graduates of high school and college, and preach love, not hate, in the face of racism. Through its melodious hymns and spirituals, the black church, now almost two hundred years old, has made a unique contribution to Christendom. In their humble way, when black Christians raise their voices to the heavens, they affirm the glory of living by the Grace of God. "My Lord Is A-Writing All the Time" expresses their faith in God and his ultimate justice; "Nobody Knows the Trouble I've Seen" speaks of their patience and long suffering; "Go Down, Moses—Tell Ol' Pharaoh to Let My People Go" and "We Are Climbing Jacob's Ladder" are laments to freedom and a passionate cry for progress and salvation; and "Steal Away to Jesus" and "Were You There When They Crucified My Lord?" are reverential statements of belief in redemption. Nowhere are these folk-religious qualities more evident than in the rural Southern black church. A good example is the documentary "Let the Church Say Amen," in which the young filmmaker St. Clair Bourne illustrates the binding power and roots of religious worship in the rural traditional black church as he experienced it in Mound Bayou, Mississippi, the oldest black settlement in the United States. "Without a doubt," he stated in an interview, "the Black Church is the most stable, most representative community organization that Black people in the United States have."

In the course of rapid urbanization, however, as new problems of stress and strain engulf black communities in large towns and cities, new tendencies have appeared on the fringes of established religion. These are, most notably, evangelical and Muslim. There are thousands of storefront churches and pentecostal sects whose semiliterate preachers ply their religious trade in lower-class neighborhoods. Yoruba cults and temples offering worship to African gods are flourishing. And so are Moorish Science temples, black Jewish sects, and groups professing mystical Oriental-Eastern religions. The Black Muslims continue to win converts and influence untold numbers with their version of the "black man's religion," and Islamic proselytizing groups, like the Ahmadiyya Movement, flood black areas with the message of their spiritual founder, Hazrat Ghulam Ahmad, the "Promised Messiah."

A significant element within resurgent non-establishment religion is concerned with forging a path to black identity, unity, and development and owes its impetus to the civil-rights and Black Power crusades of the sixties. One well-known personage in this regard is Reverend Jesse Jackson of Chicago, an old associate of Martin Luther King, Jr., and former national director of Operation Breadbasket. He now preaches a brand of "civic economics" as leader of PUSH (People United to Save Humanity) and his slogan, "Soul Power," declares that meeting the social and religious needs of black people is the most important task of a liberatory religion. Other notable examples are the community-organizing projects of the Blue Hill Christian Center in Boston run by Reverend Virgil Wood and the Glide Memorial Church, led by the poet-theologian Reverend A. Cecil Williams. Broadly speaking, these groups aim to provide vigorous leadership in local communities and to compete for status and resources. They believe "there's power in coming together, man," as Reverend Williams has said, and desire "to move the Gospel from the pulpit to the picket-line." They also show an extraordinary catholicity of orientation, weaving together fundamentalism, Black Muslim dogma, and integrationist and black-power ideologies to win converts and influence communities and to negotiate support from established black and white churches, national political parties, and government welfare programs.

What is remarkable, however, is the gradual success of a new black nationalist theology movement, which offers "a black alternative to white Christianity" and owes much to the spirited intervention of Reverend Albert B. Cleage, Jr., pastor of the Shrine of the Black Madonna in Detroit and author of *Black Christian Nationalism* and *The Black Messiah*. Reverend Cleage argues that a black religious perspective is necessary to complement black nationalism and to counteract the integrationist tendencies of leading liberal churchmen. Integration, he says, is the name given to the black man's philosophy of self-hate, and the dream of integration is the mechanism by which black people permit themselves to be controlled. Since the white power structure created a segregated society, blacks can utilize their separateness as a basis for gaining political and economic power and maintaining their cultural values.

Cleage's brand of Christian black nationalism coincides with the emergence of a caucus of black theologians in the predominantly white Unitarian-Universalist Church. Combined, they form the elements of a black humanism or black nationalist theology, which retains a Christian form and structure but reinterprets it in the light of black experience. God's existence is assumed, but attention is focused not on abstract debates about the nature of the deity but on the quality of black life. Jesus Christ is accepted as the Supreme Liberator of man; however, he is conceived of as a Black Messiah whose life and work on behalf of the poor, the oppressed, and the rejects of society is unmistakaby paralleled by the black rebel prophets of the twentieth century.

Black nationalist theologians like Cleage and his colleagues teach that the message of the Black Messiah is likewise the message of Black Revolution and liberation. Jesus was a revolutionary black leader, they claim, and a founder member of the Zealots, an activist group that spurred the rebellions which toppled Rome. The resurrected Christ is alive and at work in the nation's ghettos, seeking to free men from racism. Thus, according to their belief, if the message of the Gospel is liberation of the oppressed, then it speaks directly to black people. Hence, Black Power is Christianity. By the same token, any doctrine of God, Man, and Christ which is inconsistent with the demand for black liberation must be repudiated. Black nationalist theology proclaims its concern with meeting the needs of blacks to create a collectivity of cooperation. A new value system must be created to guide black consciousness and reinterpret the meaning of truth and combat the reality of racism. Revolution and violence cannot be ruled out if the existing social system and its legal arrangements are in contradiction with God's purpose. Reconciliation with whites will come when they are capable of developing values which allow them to glorify and exalt in blackness.

It is still too early to judge whether the new black nationalist theology will advance beyond these formulations and win many converts. Certainly, at the moment unorthodoxy is an insignificant part of the religious outlook of black Americans. Established black Christianity remains as strong as ever and shows no sign of declining popularity in membership and attendance. There is still more than enough separateness, blackness, and beauty in it to meet the demands of cultural nationalism today.

The black Protestant church is not without flaws or challenges. Black Christianity is the spiritual watering place for Afro-Americans. It is the only institution from which black social movements have been launched consistently. But it is also a reservoir of "otherworldliness," of mysticism and folk superstition. The great contribution of black Christians to Christendom is not in theology or in implementing social change but in spirituals, religious fervor, and loyalty. The black church has produced scores of eminent leaders, among them Martin Luther King, Jr., and responded during the sixties with many cardinal examples of quiet strength and black righteousness, but it is also a haven of charlatans and hustlers and riddled with commercial opportunism. Furthermore, no matter how black and culturally distinct the church may be, its congregations share a common belief with whites in the Protestant ethic of capitalism and Christianity, with its inescapable emphasis on Euro-American values and attributes of a white god, a white Jesus, and a pantheon of white prophets. (This dualism is equally apparent in the case of non-establishment Protestant groups, such as the Black Nationalist Theology Movement, which in spite of its emphasis on blackness is officially affiliated to the predominantly white United Church of Christ.) Finally, it is all too apparent that rather than being in the vanguard for the radicalization of cultural consciousness, as some cultural nationalists would hope, the black church constantly drifts into conservative passivity and irrelevance, and serves as a mechanism for adapting black people to the status quo.

Professor Charles V. Hamilton has had much to say about the challenges facing the black church in his slim volume devoted to the one spokesman with the longest tenure of leadership, dating back to the moment black people landed as indentured servants and slaves, *The Black Preacher in America*. In it he explores the role of the preacher as a buffer and a bridge between blacks and the white world, with examples from Nat Turner to Malcolm X, Martin Luther King, Jr., and Jesse Jackson. He concludes with the observation that what black youth today want is not so much Princes of Peace but pioneers of protest. "Black Americans are a people developing, coming out from under a long period of subjugation and oppression." And he adds, "They need rigor and talent and discipline and a value system that contributes to unity of purpose and collective development—in this historical time and in this place. A leadership, secular or religious, that overlooks this and fails to respond, will be dysfunctional and will deserve to be discarded."

What Professor Hamilton fails to identify, however, are the steps the black church must take to make it relevant to the black community and what forces will bring about a radical reappraisal of the church in all its aspects. Within the church there are many schisms—between denominations, age groups, regions, and classes. There is the "low church" of the Baptists, which dispenses a soothing emotional balm of Gilead to black toilers, and there are the "high churches" of the Episcopal and Presbyterian denominations, which preach "doing good and doing well" to their neatly dressed, middle-class congregations. How is unity to come about? As Professor Hamilton points out, the black preacher is above all a community cultural leader who has learned to survive with his people. However, in a practical sense, the church is unable to render the services needed by people in slum-locked ghettos. It has a ministry inadequately trained to do the job. More than 90 percent of the entrants to the black ministry are professionally unprepared, in theology and social administration, and hence cannot develop the intensive service programs necessary for the uplift of a handicapped people. The black church is a vast, relatively wealthy, influential, and respected institution but has done little to rectify this situation. The suspicion arises therefore that existing multimillion-dollar church budgets could be better employed to finance an active urban ministry rather than larger buildings, salaries, personal displays of conspicuous consumption. But how, too, is this possible in the face of entrenched and selfish interests?

On the horizon is an external challenge to the black Protestant church. It is the startling fact that in the last three decades black membership in the Roman Catholic Church, now 800,000, has tripled and is at present one of the leading established religious groups among blacks—third after the 1.2-million-member AME church and surpassing at least two of the major black denominations. This trend may accelerate if recent attempts at cleansing racism in the Catholic Church are successful. Three historical events are crucial. First of all, in 1968 a newly organized Black Catholic Clergy Caucus of priests and religious brothers defined the Catholic Church as a white racist institution and called for a national office for black Catholics financed by a $500,000 grant from church authorities. Second, in the same year a National Black Sisters Conference challenged black nuns to be reborn into the black-liberation struggle. Then in 1970 the Black Catholic Lay Caucus was formed and called for black self-determination and lay leadership within the Church. These organizations are within, but "independent" of, the Church, and strive to make the Catholic Church more relevant to black people. They are committed to work for the survival of the Catholic Church in the black community, and if backed by the huge resources and personnel of the Church could present a formidable challenge in the next decades to the Protestantized religious culture historically associated with blacks.

Contemporary black cultural perspectives are associated with a widespread rejection of popular American values and the affirmation of black perceptions, images, and interpretations. This affirmation, while noting the excellent few who make remarkable forays into hitherto sacrosanct fields of Western culture, emphasizes the cultural expressions of the black masses with their themes of folk life and migration, rage and alienation, Negritude and religion, miscegenation, black-white love-hate, jazz and the blues, daring deeds and ribald tales, the ghetto, race and redemption, freedom and revolution. These thematic expressions are rooted in one fundamental principle: black culture is black people structuring reality, mentally and emotionally, in the dank stillness of tenements and shanty towns, in the long, slow-moving unemployment and welfare lines, in the military camps, the sweatshops, and the factories, and in the daily experiences of discrimination and deprivation.

Cultural nationalists, many of them the brightest figures in the arts today, challenge the assimilationist standards of the arts and media and the absurdity of blacks judging themselves by the skin color, hair texture, and features of Caucasians. "Our oppression is due to our color, and only our color unites us," they say, and they cite as the gurus of their belief well-known elder statesmen of black history and literature, such as John Henrik Clarke, editor of the journal *Freedomways*, and social critic, John O. Killens, the author and playwright, and the most widely read of the younger poets of the rebellious sixties, Don L. Lee (Haki R. Madhubuti). Cultural nationalists want no more white Santa Clauses, Tarzans, Davy Crocketts, and Daniel Boones; no more General Custer, Superman, and John Wayne–Marilyn Monroe cults of superwhite masculinity and pulchritude. Instead, they call for black heroes and heroines of all kinds, good, bad, and indifferent.

The hallmark of popular cultural unity and black pride today is an astonishing outpouring of creativity displaying the talents of a newly inspired generation of artists, actors, writers, and media personalities. Blacks have moved firmly into the mainstream of popular music, film, and television, and recaptured a place on Broadway, the show-business capital of America. In doing so they have come a long way since the mid-nineteenth century, when the actor Ira Aldridge and the playwright Victor Sejour fled to Europe to advance their careers.

The most widely acclaimed dance and theater groups include Arthur Mitchell and the Dance Theatre of Harlem, The D.C.

Repertory Company, Alvin Ailey and the City Dance Theater, and Douglas Turner Ward and the Negro Ensemble Company. Notable contributions have been made in black communities by Kasisi Jitu Weusi (Les Campbell) of The East cultural group in Bedford-Stuyvesant, Brooklyn, Elma Lewis and the Center for Afro-American Arts in Roxbury, Boston, and Bob Macbeth and Ed Bullins of the now defunct New Lafayette Theatre in Harlem, New York.

St. Clair Bourne, Gordon Parks, and Melvin Van Peebles have established names in filmmaking; the *Black Photographers Annual* and the works of photo-journalists Don Charles and Chester Higgins, Jr., of *The New York Times* have earned critical acclaim.

Artists like Nat Pinckney and Tom Feelings display their talent in major galleries. Ted Joans, Quincy Troop, Calvin C. Hernton, and young women like Nikki Giovanni, Elouise Loftin, and Wanda Robinson make their special contributions in poetry and literature.

Other major black writers have come to the fore, among them John A. Williams, Clarence Major, Ishmael Reed, Julius Lester, and a bevy of women writers, Alice Walker, Paule Marshall, Rosa Guy, Louise Meriwether, and Maya Angelou.

In music, black relevance takes on a disco beat in the performances of James Brown, Isaac Hayes, Stevie Wonder, Aretha Franklin, the Fatback Band, and the multimillion-dollar record sales of the Motown music corporation.

Black actors have starring roles in the visual media, and notable performances have been given by Jim Brown, Bill Cosby, Harry Belafonte, Sidney Poitier, Ossie Davis, James Earle Jones, Billy Dee Williams, and Earl Cameron. Ruby Dee in *Buck and the Preacher* and Cicely Tyson, acclaimed for her performances in Lonne Elder's film *Sounder* and Ernest Gaines's television presentation *The Autobiography of Miss Jane Pittman*, have done much to change the black image in films. Cynthia Belgrave, a well-known character actress, has been instrumental in training a new, more self-confident generation of actors, in her work as a professor of the performing arts at Staten Island Community College, New York. Black television artists are a common sight and family shows like *Good Times, All in the Family, Sanford and Son, Maude,* and *The Jeffersons,* have received rave reviews.

Black theater has flourished in Broadway and Off Broadway productions. Ron Milner's *What the Winesellers Buy* won critical applause. Joseph T. Walker's *The River Niger,* directed by Douglas Turner Ward was voted the best dramatic play of the 1973 season, and *The Wiz,* a rhythm-and-blues adaptation of *The Wizard of Oz* by Gilbert Moses and Geoffrey Holder won several Tony awards in 1975. In countless other productions around the country, black playwrights, actors, and directors weave their stories of funky street culture, ghetto life and love, dope addiction and criminality, and the struggles of black families to survive.

The most militant black creative artists generally reject all concern with whether their works are considered "good or bad theater" by white critics and reviewers. They are happy with making a living at producing "black art and theater," loosely defined as meeting the cultural levels of their black audiences. "Ours is a black-controlled organization, oriented toward utilizing black talent, and black people are our primary audience," says Douglas Turner Ward, artistic director of the Negro Ensemble Company. "Whites are welcome, but I'm not interested in integrated theater," says Ward in the program notes of his skillfully directed production of *The River Niger,* a play that was first produced Off Broadway and later attracted thousands of black theatergoers to Broadway's Brooks Atkinson Theatre. "I'm not interested in segregated theater either," he adds, "and that's no contradiction. I happen to be interested in a theater of Negro composition and of Negro orientation . . . our plays are picked for their relevance to the Black experience."

The logic of black relevance is simple but circuitous. Ward's associate, the playwright Joseph T. Walker, dedicated *The River Niger* as a "love poem to my folks," and said very candidly in a *New York Times* article, August 5, 1973: "Although I am a professor of speech and theater, I still have not forgotten how to get down with the nitty-gritty! And if the fantasy makes my spiritual fingers pop, then I'm going to dig it! But if it gets too embroiled in the mire of inconsequential logic, then I'm going to cut loose. Blacks will attend anything that moves them. And will not attend that which does not. How do I know? Because I'm black." Walker passionately believes that black theater is crucial to the survival of the American theater as a whole. He says; "The only vitality left in the theater is black vitality . . . In the same way that we are the juice which keeps this country spiritually nourished, we are helping to keep the theater alive in this country."

The new sense of blackness found acceptance and commercial success in the publishing field as well. New journals were launched with the word "black" prominently displayed on the front cover: *Black Dialogue, Black Theatre, Black Scholar, Black Creation, Black Poetry,* and *Black Enterprise. Encore* and *Essence,* both black journals, are geared to the successful middle-class market. The well-established monthly pictorial journal *Ebony* modified its conservative, integrationist leanings to reflect a new grass-roots emphasis on socio-political issues, women, the South today, and black history, and its companion journal, *Negro Digest,* changed its name and orientation to *Black World.*

New studies by black linguists have charted black speech, humor, gestures, and body language from their African origins to the New World. With great passion some authors declare that the essence of black culture is "soul." Soul revealed in the way Negroes get "sanctified" in church and in the way a mother cries out over a wayward child, "Oh, Lord, have mercy . . . Help me, Jesus." Soul in black hips swaying on the dance floor. Soul expressed in the satisfying knowledge that everything is going to be all right, "I've got my black self together." And when soul combines with black style—verbal display, colorful apparel, processed hair and "natural," or the way teenagers congregate on street corners with an air of insouciance that signifies "I'm cool, hip, and ready"—you get a supreme and unique demonstration of blackness. And this blackness pervades: it is defined and redefined everywhere across the country—in rural Southern homes, churches, and ramshackle juke joints, in urban street life, in campus and high-school student centers, and even in the "bourgy" life styles of middle-class professionals.

Soul, too, lies in a Muhammad Ali poem recited by him in a *Black Scholar* interview, June 1970:

You've had us in your lock, tight as a cage
and now you're acting shocked, we're in a rage.
Us on the bottom with you on top.
That's a game that we aim to stop.
That's all over now, Mighty Whitey.
That's all over now.

There are many conflicting aspects of emergent popular culture, however. In the sensitive fields of television, advertising, and fashion, where a few young black women have made a considerable impact, they have a greater chance for success "if they don't look too black." Beverly Johnson, a highly successful, brown-skinned young woman from Buffalo, New York, has made a million dollars for the magazines and fashion houses she serves because "she looks like a white woman dipped in brown paint." Miss Johnson has a universal appeal, it is said, because she fits the stereotyped requirements of the buying public, largely white suburban housewives. "She's just dark enough to be identifiably black but not Negroid enough to be offensive," a fashion agency director commented in a recent *New York Times Magazine* article. As for Beverly, she says she does not see herself as a black model but as a model who "happens" to be black.

Black television programs and family shows are spectacular imitations of white successes and come perilously close to farcical caricatures of black life. Four out of five of the most popular black family shows in recent season were comedies, and written by white scriptwriters. Black actors in them play their now stereotyped roles of corpulent, moral, and conservative mothers, weak ineffectual fathers, sexy teenage daughters, and clown-prince sons with an eye to the sponsor and the laugh meter rather than to the realities of black family problems in an urban setting. Critics of these shows, including many of the actors themselves, deplore the inability of scriptwriters to strike a balance between what is funny and relevant and what is outlandish, degrading, and embarrassing to black viewers. Similarly, the black characters in *Kojak* and countless other white-scripted-and-directed cops-and-robbers television productions have come under fire as mindless robots moving through the streets of death and despair impervious to the squalor, misery, and desperation.

With the production of *Cotton Comes to Harlem*, a screen adaptation of black author Chester Himes's novel of confidence tricksters, murder, and mayhem on the sleazy back streets of the ghetto, a new trend in "black films" was established. Later, the stark presentation of black masculinity in Melvin Van Peebles's picture *Sweet Sweetback's Baadasssss Song* grossed more than $10 million and the movie industry rushed in to capture the waiting black market. The outcome was a score of films—*Shaft*, *Superfly*, *The Mack*, and *Trick Baby*—trumpeting themes of what black critic Clayton Riley called "street-nigger royalty," of black violent, supercool, hypersexual detectives, pimps, dope peddlers, and hustlers. Black crime was featured in *Book of Numbers*, *Black Gunn*, *Across 110th Street*, and *Black Caesar*, a tired remake of the Edward G. Robinson hit *Little Caesar*. Hollywood also applied the tarbrush to hackneyed scripts to produce black Westerns like *Charley One-Eye* and *The Soul of Nigger Charley*.

These films proved extremely popular with blacks and bolstered a lagging industry, but broke no new ground in their portrayal of black characters. American cinema is replete with exaggerated images drawn from a very narrow sector of black life: little pickaninnies, tap dancing, shuffling, eye-bulging, grinning Rastuses, Sambos, and Aunt Jemimas, Hot Mamas and tight-skirted shameless Creole sluts, and shiftless, violent black rapists, murderous fiends, and criminals. One need only begin with the works of the founding fathers of American cinema, Edwin S. Porter's *Uncle Tom's Cabin* (1903) and D. W. Griffith's *Birth of a Nation* (1915), to find examples of the perversion of history to a point beyond the Big Lie. The common complaint today is still that serious black actors, themes, and directors find it difficult to get a foothold in a cinema industry which relegates blacks to a limited range of stereotyped roles. One can only conclude that "black films" is a misnomer. Most of them are conceived and financed by whites, and their entire distribution and showing is controlled by whites. While it is true that "black films" provide some temporary jobs in the industry and attract large black audiences to cinema houses and give

them a spurious sense of pride, nevertheless blacks remain culturally exploited and deprived as far as the film media is concerned.
The sixty-year transition from Sambo to Superspade marked little
change in the film industry's pattern of "blaxploitation."

The situation with black radio, the small minority of some
8,000 American radio stations, is not much different. Black radio,
that is the 330 United States stations devoting air time to black
programming, is hailed as a major achievement with a powerful
potential for educational and cultural development. But there is
much evidence that it has abdicated its responsibility for a fast
dollar. Black listeners receive a meager fare of packaged jazz, spirituals, and soul music, to the almost total exclusion of other forms
of musical and dramatic expression. They get superficial coverage
of news and information, and disc jockeys blatantly use "black
style" and "black involvement" to sell overpriced, inferior products.
Station owners are, of course, more concerned with selling radio
time and are convinced that this formula "sells." The crassness of
their single-minded view of what listeners want and will buy is also
expressed by black media advertising executives who believe listeners will be satisfied with any offering given a black label. The
philosophy is "Baby, all you need to sell these folk anything is a
picture of Reverend King or Malcolm X, or a black chick with a
fine Afro singing a groovy song." These views, coupled with the
fact that three hundred or more of these "black" stations are white-
owned, suggest that "black radio" is both a lucrative form of commercial exploitation and an electronic Trojan horse in the black
community, thinly veneered with false camaraderie and amplified
shouts of "Right on, brothers and sisters."

Cultural nationalists hold a particularly warm regard for black
music. Not so much for its place in the history of music and its
contributions to American society and the world, however. They
know little and care less about the impact of black music on Stephen Foster, the Dadaists, Irving Berlin, Igor Stravinsky, Darius
Milhaud, and John Philip Sousa. Most of them are not interested
in the early ragtime pianist-composer Scott Joplin, whose songs
gave the Robert Redford–Paul Newman film *The Sting* its authentic air of nostalgia. Nor would they be impressed by the way band

leader James Reese Europe, composer for Vernon and Irene Castle and inventor of the fox-trot, led his jazz-playing 369th U.S. Infantry Band down Paris boulevards in 1918. Today's cultural nationalists reject much of the musical past as irrelevant and somehow degrading—full of cake-walking buffoonery, banjo-strumming minstrelsy, and slave-like sentiment.

Rather, the contemporary musical expression of black cultural unity and autonomy is "soul music," considered a blend of all the other forms black music has taken. Soul music, say cultural nationalists, is a stream of messages of frustration, anger, pride, love, lust, and hope moving down from one generation to the next, charged with the moods and syncopations of black life, and electrifying everyone who really listens to it. And above all, the most rabid militants declare soul music is the inspirational theme of the struggle, the poetry of the black revolution. At its roots it is explicitly political in its message—a protest against white racism and a celebration of the beauty of blackness.

Yet there are severe constraints on the power of soul music to affect the black man's material condition—for it is whites, not blacks, who benefit from its popularity. Rolland Snellings (Askia Muhammad Touré) writing on the crises in black culture in the *Journal of Black Poetry*, spring 1968, takes the view that:

> We are cultural slaves! Dig it! Victims of what Bro. Harold Cruse calls "Cultural Imperialism." This means that since we didn't have any raw resources for whites to exploit, they were able to exploit our cheap labor and the products of our National Black Culture (mainly music). Broken down further, this means that the recording companies are white-owned (the booking agencies are white-owned; the radio stations, the theaters, and the night clubs where the music is heard, are white [usually immigrant]-owned). Broken down *even further*, this means, baby, that James Brown and the late Otis Redding, not to mention Aretha, are sending a lot of Jewish and Italian boys and girls to college and making their parents *rich* with the products of their Black souls. And further, *none*, or *very little of this bread is going into the Black communities that inspire the music*. Yes, Brothers and Sisters, "intellectuals," whether we dig it or not, we are supporting Zionist Israel and the Mafia (Italian Na-

tionalism) with our Soul Music—and further helping to impoverish the Black Nation.

What is needed, says Snellings, is a program for developing the "Black Cultural Philosophy and Ideology," and making the "Black Spirit/Awareness, or the Dynamic Black Psyche" pro-black and not anti-white. In the vanguard of these developments will be a new cultural intelligentsia—"The living mind of the Black Nation/Race"—drawn from radical campuses and the streets whose consciences have been awakened by Elijah Muhammad, Malcolm X, and Black Power ideologues. He claims that "the Black Musician became *and remains* the major philosopher, priest, myth-maker and cultural hero of the Black Nation," but is in serious trouble in a society and industry that exploits him. Rather than starve, black musicians should "return to the roots of 'Home,' the Black Community," and join with the intelligentsia to create a national congress of black culture, black musical and cultural institutes, and black repertory theaters.

Another critic of what he calls the "black cultural fantasy" is the writer Les Payne, who ridicules black moviemakers and playwrights that "put on grotesque shows as if the world had not been blessed with Aimé Césaire and Pushkin, or Fanon, or Dumas." Expressing his views in the journal *Encore*, July 1973, he says part of the problem is the incompetent imitativeness of talented blacks who have "made it" and accepted mediocre performances as the norm. Payne is more concerned with salvaging potentially gifted young people from the wreckage of black communities. "If Blacks are to build a Black culture," says Payne, "they must begin to save their warriors, their scholars, their artists, from the dungeons and the ash heaps of this nation."

Before black creative artists can save the race they will have to save themselves, however, and this requires a long, hard look at the contradictory nature of the black artistic psyche, its products and social role. The black American theater is in form Western theater, and its only distinction to being considered black is that it purports to deal with themes peculiar to the black American experience. The demands on it—a cry for return to Africa on the one hand and the urgent need for more social equity on the other—prevent it from achieving any kind of total commitment. Like black theater, black art is financially and artistically unstable and discontinuous, partly because it is deracinated and partly because it is entirely at the mercy of its white patrons and sympathizers. Contemporary black creative expression tends to adapt to, but does not excoriate, the triple evils of black urban life—drink, dope, and dissipation. On the contrary, it serves to emphasize the machismo and the male-chauvinist quality of "black players," the pimp culture of the ghetto, and glorify the combative instincts contributing to the high rate of black-against-black homicides, which currently outstrip those of whites. So much of black creativity in all the arts appeals to visceral emotions at the expense of the cerebral; it does not think, it only is; and in the search for ancestral identity it accepts all too easily mere Afro-exotica: semi-bare brown bodies, beating drums, shaking breasts and buttocks, stamping feet, and chanting in tight, deep-throated, hypnotic unison.

With each new show and each new "success" the black arts seem to retreat further from their oft-stated goals of relevance. To be relevant at this stage of black underdevelopment, the black arts would have to empty the vessel of outmoded traditions and subjective inhibiting attitudes and serve as a link between new ideological formulations and the practical daily tasks of advancement. The black arts must be related to raising the general standard of living and education, and must aid black people to rise from the cellar of the House of America. This means that artists and intellectuals of all kinds, to be worthy of their keep, have to be involved in the process of mass scientific, technical, and moral, as well as cultural, education. They have to be concerned with the resolution of social, economic, and political problems, or else they will be ignored as irrelevant. As one old man said to Bobby Seale in an anecdote reported in The New York Times: "Poetry ain't going to feed me always. . . . Poetry might be all right. You all talking about raising my consciousness, but you can't raise no hungry man's consciousness. His consciousness is on some food. Get him fed somewhat and relieve the agony somewhat and then he might be able to read the poetry and know what you're talking about."

Many black social commentators believe that black cultural expression is stifled and deformed by the power structure. Supreme among them is Harold Cruse, author of *The Crisis of the Negro Intellectual* and a faculty member of the Afro-American Studies Department, University of Michigan. Cruse emphasizes the important role of culture in the political and economic structure and calls for a black-led cultural revolution. American society, he says, is made up of divergent and contending ethnic groups. In it class divisions are transcended by ethnic divisions, and cultural pluralism is the dominant factor in all affairs. In fact, he argues, the Marxist concern with class is misplaced. The ethnic struggle is paramount over the class struggle. Control of the all-important mass cultural communications industry is in the hands of the dominant white Anglo-Saxon Protestants, and to a lesser extent the Jews, and they are in a powerful position to deform black culture and to thereby defuse any threat of black political development.

According to Cruse, Negroes have had a history of domination by other groups. First the Wasps provided models of attainment and then usurped and commercialized black culture. Later, Jews holding strategic positions in the left-wing and civil-rights movements distorted the expression of black unrest. Now it is necessary for blacks to create their own cultural role models in line with the objective requirements of the black-liberation movement. In Cruse's opinion, blacks are the "one group who have the motivation for democratizing American culture and forcing the return of the public arts to the people."

Intellectuals must play a special role, says Cruse, in the vanguard of the black cultural revolution against the communications-industry establishment. They must "assail the stultifying blight of the commercially depraved white middle class which has poisoned the structural roots of the American ethos and transformed the American people into a nation of intellectual dolts." Speaking forcefully and directly to black militants, Cruse says, "The only observable way in which the Negro rebellion can become revolutionary in terms of American conditions is for the Negro movement to project the concept of Cultural Revolution in America." The task, therefore, is "to locate the weakest sector of the American capitalist free enterprise front and strike there." And that sector, he claims, is mass cultural com- munications—its ownership, administration, and expression in films, plays, radio and television, music, performing arts, and pub- lishing, popular-entertainment booking, performing, and manage- ment.

Cruse's argument appears plausible enough until one exam- ines it a bit closer. It seems evident that the most vocal exponents and comforting allies of popular cultural nationalism are middle- class elements, including artists and entrepreneurs, who stand to gain economically from participation in the cultural arts business. As far as the question of power and control of the media is con- cerned, there is little evidence to support Cruse's assertion that the cultural sector is the weakest area of American capitalism. And how is his proposal for a cultural media revolution to come about? All that emerges is a plea for the democratization of relations between competing ethnic groups and for increased access by blacks to the mass media. What Cruse seems to be after is the creation of a new elite corps of black middle-class cultural administrators who would be more sensitive and responsible to their communities than has been the case up to now. Insofar as the system remains the same and blacks are last in line for media rewards (and Cruse gives no in- dication how the system and its allocation of rewards might be changed by black media men and women), then the black cultural revolution amounts to nothing more than token integration at best. And at worst it would increase widespread fears that the Establish- ment would use black media personnel to absorb black protest and disseminate a distorted set of images and values. Few would argue that the American economic and political system could not coopt more blacks and extend democracy into any field without altering its fundamental structure or existing power relationships. But unless these are changed, then how can "ethnic democratization" be any- thing more than a meaningless shibboleth, like "racial integration," which does little to help black people as a whole.

In regard to the cultural aspects of student youth activities, most black intellectuals would agree that students should play an important part in the resurgence of black culture, but what that role will be depends to a large extent on the result of major battles for Black Power and Black Studies on campuses around the nation. The student-led movement of black consciousness and separatism which in 1968–69 hit more than one hundred campuses has had widespread effects. Newly created Afro-American clubs and black student centers on white college campuses demanded greater representation in the student body, more blacks on the academic faculty, and the restructuring of curricula to emphasize Black Studies. Specific demands were made for the recruitment of inner-city blacks, the relaxation of educational standards of entry and performance, and increased scholarships, loans, and jobs. And in some schools demands included separate black dormitories, recreation centers, and even separate black colleges within the university.

Faced with recession and its inevitable effect on university finances, black students have intensified their protests against proposed cutbacks in the benefits from aid programs. In the spring of 1975, for example, a rash of black student strikes, sit-ins, and demonstrations struck many of New England's major campuses. Brown University's "Third World Coalition" of five hundred black and Latin American students seized the main administration building, and a group of fifty students occupied the building for two days. After negotiations with school authorities, the students won a partial victory in their demands for maintenance of minimum percentages of minority students and faculty members, and the continuance of present levels of funding for special minority programs.

The sociology building at Brandeis University, an institution largely dependent on the American Jewish community and heavily in debt, was occupied by minority students for six days. This action dramatized student fears of cutbacks in minority staff and the $82,000 remedial program for disadvantaged students. They also called for increased enrollment of Asian and minority students. Similar demands were made at predominantly Catholic Boston College, where students allege that the goal of 10 percent minority representation set in 1968 has not yet been met.

At Harvard University students demonstrated against increases in tuition fees and admissions policies, and burned President Derek Bok in effigy. Minority students also staged a sit-in at the main administration building. The chief concern of black students, however, was the role of Black Studies and research at the proposed W. E. B. Du Bois Institute of Afro-American Research, under discussion since 1971, which the students feared would not have enough independence from university authorities.

The Black Studies movement, which stems from cultural nationalism, has attracted much support. The views of one of its leading proponents, Dr. Nathan Hare, a sociologist and educator in California, are starkly simple. Existing educational systems train students to adjust to society, a racist society. So, to be relevant to the black predicament, education must be revolutionized, and Black Studies are one attempt to accomplish this. Dr. Hare makes it clear that he doesn't advocate racial separatism, but he does want to help create "a community with a sense of its cultural and historical identity, with a sense of its collective predicament, and the collective struggle to eradicate that predicament."

Dr. Hare, publisher of *Black Scholar* and author of the imaginative and controversial analysis of the black middle class *The Black Anglo-Saxons*, supports the recruitment of black teachers to teach Black Studies. In explaining his ideas, he says that they are needed to provide a positive role model for black students. Furthermore, black students should have priority in admission, and control should be in the hands of the black community. As far as academic standards are concerned, he says, Black Studies are not meant to turn out intellectually qualified students but rather to serve as a means of helping them shake off the shackles of inferiority.

Hare has special words of scorn for America's Negro colleges, which he feels have failed to respond to the needs of the black cultural revolution. Negro colleges were created by Northern abolitionists and missionaries and later reluctantly bolstered by state and federal assistance. Far from fighting to preserve a separate culture, he says, these colleges are militantly opposed to everything that made Negroes different from whites on the grounds that these tendencies are lower-class and disruptive of tradition. Today, Negro colleges are not serving as centers designed to salvage victims of injustice and mold young black revolutionaries, as Dr. Hare would like them to. Instead, they are becoming integrated schools at the behest of government authorities and are thereby coopted into the broader system of anti-black cultural forces. Dr. Hare notes with some regret that students on Negro college campuses have not fully raised their level of cultural consciousness and suffer under the worst forms of black bourgeois tyranny and management. But he points out that elsewhere more black students are attending white colleges and developing their consciousness as they militantly oppose campus and community racism and seek to implant models of revolutionary thought and practice. There are a number of reasons for this militancy, according to Dr. Hare. Black students on white campuses are isolated and are tired of being fed Western civilization and Western languages, and colonialist sociology and anthropology, which picture blacks as pathological and primitive. They feel that integration, and its companion tokenism, rewards a few individuals without altering the lot of the whole race, and weakens the collective racial thrust. Increasingly, therefore, black students are rejecting the white orientation of their education in favor of preparing themselves for a return to the black community to help build a new way of life. This new mood is born of a greater awareness of the glories of their own racial past, an image they now wish to convey to others. Hence the clamor for more "black courses" and subjects taught from a black perspective.

Not all black educators agree with these opinions. Greggory K. Spence, dean of Boston University's College of Liberal Arts, is sympathetic, but in an interview published in the college bulletin urges his students to get the knowledge necessary to be leaders of the future in all fields.

> "Dammit, suck this University for all that it is worth," he says to new black students. "Drag away from here all that the bags in your mind and heart can hold . . . No one is asking you to give up your life-style. Be cool, be Jive and Fly, or Superfly; dress like Shaft. Walk mean like Jim Brown. If you are high yellow, then smile! If you are ebony black, be happy! . . . But if you intend to slick, and hurt the Man, rip him off, and con the brother, this is not the place for you . . . What I am suggesting is that a new ideology of achievement and black excellence be born into the hearts and minds of you, who are the young black leaders of today and tomorrow."

One of the sharpest critics of Black Studies and black student solidarity is Martin Kilson, professor of government at Harvard University. He has publicly called on the university to depoliticize its recruitment of lower-class blacks, restore aptitude tests which discriminate in favor of more highly qualified middle-class blacks, and withdraw financial aid to separatist groups like the Afro-American Students Association. Black students should not recoil into solidarity groups, says Professor Kilson, but participate more in interracial situations. What is at stake, he says, is the future quality of Afro-American elites. The poor performance and maladjustment of Negro students hastily recruited in the late sixties to the achievement-and-success-oriented life styles of top-rank white colleges must be corrected. In his opinion, "The situation has never been better for the full-fledged development of the black professional classes in American society, and it will be tragic if the nation's leading colleges fail to seize this opportunity because of misplaced sentimentalism."

These charges, further elaborated on in a lengthy correspondence in *The New York Times*, reveal the vast chasm that exists between young black students and the older generation of black scholars like Kilson, many of whom might never have obtained permanent high-ranking posts in white schools without the impact of the turbulence of the sixties on the liberal academic establishment. Black Harvard students were quick to point this out in the pages of the *Harvard Bulletin* and *The New York Times*. They reject Kilson's views of the "pathology of intra-black association" and his desire for "individualistic acculturation" to Harvard life. "We submit," they concluded, "that such an absurd and total mimicry by blacks of the dominant American culture would not only be antithetical to the purported American ideal of cultural pluralism, but also (and more so) antithetical to every natural and human inclination toward love of self."

Meanwhile, out in the ghetto streets, advocates of black cultural nationalism and unity like Maulana Ron Karenga and his followers have made strident claims for black militance and separation from the dominant culture. Karenga, the son of a Baptist minister, claims he went through the "integrationist thing" while getting his college education. He was the first black elected student president at his junior college in Los Angeles, and he obtained a master's degree in political science and African Studies at UCLA. After the Watts riots in 1965, he turned to the cause of the black cultural revolution.

Karenga organized a small group of followers to promote African culture and to aid blacks in their struggle. He called his group US (as opposed to Them) and members were sworn to learn Swahili, to adopt Afro-Swahili surnames, to shave their heads and wear African-style clothing. Karenga, whose title "Maulana" means master-teacher, espoused a "black value system" called Kawaida—the seven principles of blackness—which, he says, is "traditional to black people and is our Ten Commandments." Specifically, the movement's goal is nation building or national liberation, and its basic principles are Umoja (unity), Kujichagulia (self-determination), Ujima (collective work and responsibility), Ujamaa (cooperative economics), Nia (purpose), Kuumba (creativity), and Imani (faith).

Listening to a Karenga speech is like undergoing a sustained bombardment, his words explode with a passion akin to frenzy:

> We're fighting a revolution to win the minds of black people
> . . . Let me tell you, brothers and sisters, black people suffer because they have a lack of culture . . . US don't trust black professionals, Marxist-Leninists or any other kind of white men . . . US is against bush-smoking, wine-drinking black hippies and don't give a damn for any kind of white liberals . . . US is for race pride and the pursuit of blackness . . . The issue is racism, not economics; not a class struggle but a global struggle against racism.

Karenga's particular brand of race politics, broadcast from the secular pulpits of nationalist meeting halls and through a collection of excerpts from his speeches during 1965 to 1967, *The Quotable Karenga*, has found response in the ghettos of many cities. On the West Coast in San Diego, Mahidi Ken Msemaji runs the NIA Cultural Organization. On the East Coast in Newark is Karenga's most notable convert, LeRoi Jones, better known as Imamu Amiri Baraka. Baraka, a graduate of Howard University in Washington, D.C., gained fame and notoriety as the prodigious author of many literary works on themes of black culture: *Home: Social Essays, Tales, The System of Dante's Hell, Dutchman, Black Magic Poems, Four Revolutionary Plays,* and *Raise.* Like his acknowledged mentor, Baraka has argued for separation from "assimilationist brainwashing or subjugation by the mind of the white nation." He founded the Congress of Afrikan Peoples, to advocate nationalism, Pan-Africanism, and black political power, and converted an old building in Newark's black quarter into the Temple of Kawaida, a community center and school of spiritual values. Baraka's followers affected African styles of dress and conversed in Swahili, the required second language. They also dutifully attended classes in African music and dance, homemaking and training in the observance of the organization's holidays, for example, Kwanja, a substitute for Christmas. In addition, the Congress journal, *Black New Ark,* served as a vehicle for the ideas of Baraka and Karenga, which in the late sixties were ferociously nationalist, anti-Communist, and anti-black bourgeoisie. In every issue Baraka stressed the goals of black nationalism: nationhood, Black Power, and black identity, and supported the work of an equally militant cultural nationalist influenced by Karenga, Kasisi Jitu Weusi, editor of *Black News* and director of The East organization in Brooklyn.

Despite his moderate prominence, Ron Karenga's influence was curtailed by his imprisonment in 1971 for one to ten years for a murderous assault on a female US member. There were also schisms among followers who resented their leader's fanatical personality. Others were astonished at Karenga's involvement with the Los Angeles police in quelling the Watts riots in 1968 following the assassination of Martin Luther King, Jr., and the way he curried favor with arch-conservative politicians like California Governor Ronald Reagan and Los Angeles Mayor Sam Yorty. Furthermore, Karenga has never overcome the stigma of involvement with US gunmen in the grudge killings of two Black Panther Party members John Huggins and Alprentice "Bunchy" Carter, in 1969 at the University of California, Los Angeles, campus. He has always been at the center of controversy and violence and this has limited his credibility among many sectors of the black community.

In retrospect, one sees that Karenga and Baraka had during this period a starkly simple and limited view of the scope of the black cultural revolution, much different in language and meaning from the academics, Clarke, Cruse, and Hare, and the radical street warriors, the Black Panthers. In the name of a return to the roots, they created a mystique of black culture and reactionary African social forms. This mystique hid the chauvinism and impotence upon which their militancy and black awareness rested and was especially evident on matters of great social importance, such as male-female relationships, fertility, and family planning. The role of the black woman is considered to be horizontal: she is supposed to inspire her man, educate the children, and take care of the home, and is expected to be an available and willing sex partner and avoid the use of contraceptives. The argument being that "we need to produce black warriors for the revolution." This despite the fact that the black family is in dire straits, that black women have far too many unwanted children, that as breadwinners they must compete for jobs with often better-educated white women and must fight against economic and sexual exploitation by both black and white males in society.

In 1975 Baraka and Karenga, arch high priests of cultural nationalism, executed a *volte face* which threw their followers completely off balance and triggered a new round of ideological quarrels among nationalists. Baraka and Karenga publicly jettisoned cultural black nationalism and embraced the class war dogma of the twenties, proclaiming that Marxist-Leninist scientific socialism is the solution to the black man's problems.

In Baraka's case he was clearly responding to some new initiatives. Trends among revolutionary black nationalists indicated a shift away from debates about integration and separation toward discussion of the importance of class factors, as opposed to color and culture, in the resolution of the problems of black people. These new trends, at once intellectual and international, reflected a wide range of contacts made while militants were traveling abroad during the sixties and seventies. Peripatetic militants were impressed by socialist experiments in Cuba, Vietnam, Tanzania, and Guinea. In Cuba, particularly, it was apparent that working-class blacks could play a leading part in the revolutionary struggle against imperialism and for socialism in concert with other Cubans of differing complexions and social status. Stokely Carmichael had returned and was preaching about Pan-African socialism. There were also new ideological formations emanating from the Sixth Pan-African Congress, convened in Tanzania, June 1974. Baraka, for example, claims to have been deeply influenced by the socialist ideas of national liberation movements and the writings of Amilcar Cabral, the slain leader of the Guinean movement for independence from Portuguese colonialism. It was obvious also that Baraka's involvement in local and national political activity required a vigorous injection of new ideas. For all these reasons Baraka now tells his followers in the Congress of Afrikan Peoples that blacks should join with poor whites, disadvantaged minorities, and labor unions to bring about revolutionary socialist change. Speaking disarmingly of his own culpability, he says his new ideological perspective has helped him to see the imperfections of black nationalism and the narrow view that the white man is the enemy. It is, he says, a "sickness or criminality akin to fascism which uses the same pseudo-science and charlatanism to justify a black super-race as is used to justify a white super-race."

Ron Karenga reportedly underwent similar ideological changes during four years at San Luis Obispo Prison in California. When released in May 1975, he claimed allegiance to the principles of Marx and Lenin which he had read in prison and denounced his errant support of "backward cultural nationalism." He assured his audiences and newspapermen that he is a confirmed supporter of "scientific socialism and multi-ethnic alliances." In Karenga's new view, black nationalism is reactionary because in the pursuit of an elusive ideal of unity it masks class contradictions among blacks. He has come to realize that despite the seeming universality of "soul" in the form of chit'lings, black-eyed peas, fried chicken, music and rhythm, there are basic conflicting class differences. Now living in San Diego with his wife Tiamoyo, Karenga is writing a book on his new ideas and completing work on a doctoral degree.

The abandonment of black cultural nationalism by Baraka and Karenga marks the loss of its most radical exponents and the political demise of the militant cultural revolution of the sixties. But having said this, the new ideas coming from Baraka and Karenga should not be lightly dismissed. On one level they confirm the general trend among many militants in the post-Malcolm X period away from a black-centered philosophy to one of shades of gray, if not white. Baraka and Karenga's complete change in attitude is, in this context, as remarkable as, say, the shift by the Black Panthers to socialist internationalism and later middle-class reformism, and no less striking than Malcolm X returning from Mecca and telling his followers that all white men are not evil. On another level, the ideological *volte face* of Baraka and Karenga opens up an old rift in the race versus class debate. It adds grist to the continuing debate among nationalists, sparked by the Black Panthers, on the correct relationships of political and cultural ideologies inherent in modern black nationalism, e.g., Black Power, Pan-Africanism, African socialism, capitalism, and Marxism. For this reason it is worthwhile tracing briefly the recent development of Baraka's neo-Marxist leanings.

Writing in *Black New Ark* in August 1973, Baraka was still a rabid cultural nationalist when he declared: "Black vs white is the principal contradiction in America! (Not the rich vs poor, the bourgeois vs the proletariat, white men vs white women, Democrats vs Republicans) . . . Marx and Engels don't apply." This is, of course, the classic race over class, black-nationalist position. He then went on to elaborate his views on a trio of revolutionary objectives of the world African liberation struggle: Nationalism, Pan-Afrikanism, and Ujamaa (Afrikan Scientific Socialism). Baraka said:

> Yes, we are Nationalists because we will not submerge our identity to the whites or be absorbed by them. We are also Pan Afrikanist, because we understand that unless the continent of Afrika is Unified and Independent under an Afrikan Socialist Union Government, we can never maximize our political and economic power wherever else outside Afrika we are. Yes, we are Afrikan Socialists, advocates of Ujamaa, because we understand that the Familyhood of Humanity

is our ultimate goal, but we also know that we must apply an Afrikan approach to scientific socialism, i.e. one that takes into consideration our culture and context, giving a national form to our internationalism.

Following the crucial Sixth Pan-African Congress, Baraka began to downgrade "skin nationalism" and to advance the theory of economic class struggle and the overthrow of capitalism, imperialism, and racism based on the ideology of scientific socialism associated with Marx and Lenin and Mao Tse-tung. By January 1975, the slogan "Black liberation is a struggle for socialism" assumed a prominent place in Baraka's new organ, the newspaper *Unity and Struggle*. He described it as "a revolutionary socialist paper published by the Congress of Afrikan Peoples—carrying news and information on the concrete struggles of oppressed people against imperialism—and discussions of various ideological positions being taken in the revolutionary movement today." Several pages were devoted to an article presenting Baraka's new beliefs, in which he stated categorically: "We are saying that in order to liberate black people or any other oppressed people, capitalism must be smashed and replaced with a system of public control of the means of producing wealth—the land, factories, machines and mineral wealth—and furthermore, that such a change can only be brought about by socialist revolution." "Our principal enemies are the Ruling Class, the big capitalists, and not all whites," he said, and called for the mobilization of "all the energies of the diverse peoples in the United States—the entire multi-national working class." His guide, and that of his followers, should be the theories and practice of scientific socialism; and he assured his readers that armed with "the revolutionary science called Marxist-Leninist-Mao Tse-tung thought integrated into the day-to-day concrete struggle of the Black Liberation Movement, ultimately we will be part of the triumphant force that annihilates capitalism forever."

By July 1975 Baraka had moved confidently toward a political view that would not have sounded out of place in the postwar Communist movement. He said: "Being socialists gives us the correct methodology for struggle. It means we understand that Black Liberation is a struggle for socialism. That it is only socialist revolution that will bring about the Liberation of the Black Nation in the United States. That the social force to wage that socialist revolution will be the multi-national working class in alliance with the great majority of oppressed nationalities." As evidence of his new orientation, Baraka introduced changes in the Temple of Kawaida. The custom of wearing African-style gowns was ended. Photos of Marx, Lenin, and Mao joined that of Malcolm X. Baraka granted media interviews in which he recounted the errors flowing from his infatuation with Black Power ideologies and Black Muslim demonology. He spoke of his seduction by bourgeois nationalist values, and the difficulties stemming from his involvement in internecine quarrels within the national liberation movement. He assured his readers, nevertheless, that he had not abandoned the black struggle *per se*. In fact, his newspaper supported Black Women's Solidarity Day, a Stop Killer Cops Campaign, and advocated the release from jail of Ron Karenga and Rap Brown and a pardon for fugitive-exile Eldridge Cleaver. In a veiled reference to the Black Muslims, whom he now considered political enemies, Baraka heaped scorn on their small business activities, saying: "Philosophies that tell us that 'the white boy is the devil,' so that their proponents can have an exclusive market for their fish sandwiches, are simply part of the system that ultimately oppresses all of us."

In sum, Baraka's new approach is marked by two important modifications. First of all, he overhauled his Pan-African philosophy, seeking to unite blacks everywhere, and added elements of the "scientific socialism of Marx-Lenin-Mao Tse-tung." Second, he revamped his goal of temporal and spiritual leadership of Newark blacks, whom he intended to organize into the most politically conscious black community in the nation, and added an emphasis on "multi-national coalitions and ethnic alliances." These modifications have had powerful repercussions within the movement, however. Baraka's followers in Newark have not accepted his new approach with as much enthusiasm as he expected. His original appeal to them was based on a call to throw off the cultural yoke of the white oppressors and to smash the relationship between bourgeois blacks, politicians, and the power structure that subverts the black struggle. Small groups of dissidents are now openly critical of his abandonment of cultural nationalism for the socialism of Marx, and are particularly upset at his increasing support of Newark's Puerto Rican and white workers.

The socialist stance of the new black Marxists has, like a lightning rod, attracted thunderbolts of anger from major figures on the cultural nationalist scene and sparked a tremendous debate. The issue is race or class as the correct ideological basis of the black revolution, one of the most significant developments in black thought in the post-Malcolm X era. In the front ranks of the new black Marxists are Baraka and Karenga. Their allies are lesser-known figures, such as Owusu Sadaukai (Howard Fuller), formerly head of the now defunct Malcolm X Liberation University in Durham, North Carolina; Mark Smith, former vice-president of YOBU—Youth Organization for Black Unity; and S. E. Anderson, a poet, essayist, and mathematician at Old Westbury College of the State University of New York. Activists like Smith and Sadaukai, fresh from their experiences organizing textile workers, now believe that "all white people are not devils—you must form coalitions to gain power." In their view what is needed is a strategy of building unity between black and white workers. They contend, however, that they are not Communists. They reject all association with the white socialist parties and the United States Communist Party and their black theoreticians; they claim instead a special place for blacks at the forefront of a multinational vanguard of revolutionary change.

The cultural nationalist counterattack is led by John Henrik Clarke, John O. Killens, and Haki Madhubuti, who have been joined by Ronald Walters, a political scientist, Kasisi Jitu Weusi of The East cultural organization, and Kalamu ya Salaam, a Louisiana-based playwright and author. They argue for "race to work for race" and criticize Baraka and Karenga as instant Marxists, faddists, and opportunists seeking to maintain white friendships and resources at the expense of the race. Furthermore, they allege that the black nationalist movement is being infiltrated by the white left, which claims to place black people at the vanguard of the world socialist revolution only to manipulate them. Some extreme nationalists say the socialist theories of Marx, Lenin, and Mao do not hold the solution to black problems, and they oppose any coalitions with white groups. But moderates suggest that there is no contradiction between nationalism and socialism. The thrust should be for the development of black working-class leadership.

The color-class debate is not without its casualties; one of these is the outstanding journal *Black Scholar*, in whose pages an intense ideological confrontation took place in 1974–75 between new black Marxist and cultural nationalist factions. This debate is seen by some observers, notably black journalists Charlayne Hunter and Mel Watkins of *The New York Times*, as the chief development in black thought since the civil-rights movement culminated in Black Power in the late sixties. *Black Scholar* was founded and first published by the non-profit Black World Foundation in 1969. It aimed to fill an intellectual hiatus after the sit-ins, freedom rides, campus protests, and urban riots had fragmented black opinion. The guiding figures at the helm of the journal were the publisher Dr. Nathan Hare and the editor Robert Chrisman, a poet and professor of English at San Francisco State College. The dominant focus was "race," and Hare and Chrisman assembled an advisory board and contributors who could replace the "dictatorship of the white definition" with fresh ideas about the black struggle. The goal was to provide a forum in which a revolutionary ideology of black liberation might evolve. The audience was students, intellectuals, and professionals who were prepared to take a new and hard look at all aspects of black life.

Disunity at the journal results from the growing tension in the class versus color debate, and in its style the debate is reminiscent of an earlier period of schism and factionalism, the thirties. Then, too, the dilemma of black intellectuals of all persuasions was "how to argue constructively about a means to an agreed set of goals while maintaining a united front." As of the moment, the cultural nationalists have lost out to editor Chrisman and his supporters, who lean to a modified Marxist and nationalist approach. Dr. Hare resigned in March 1975 and now devotes his energies to completing a clinical-psychology degree. In an "Open Letter,"

Dr. Hare denounced what he calls the Marxist takeover of the journal's board, a charge denied by Chrisman, and "their narrow devotion to conventional Marxist interpretations and an iron-clad intolerance for and resistance to opposing views." He holds no brief for either extreme cultural nationalists or Marxist-Leninists and says that both groups have substituted ritual for rigor. Other resignations have come from a moderate, Professor Charles V. Hamilton, and two cultural nationalists, Haki Madhubuti and Kasisi Jitu Weusi, who contend that the shift from race to a concern with class alone obscures many facets of the black problem.

It is generally felt among intellectuals that the demise of *Black Scholar* would be a tragedy. In its brief lifetime a broad cross section of black opinion was represented on its board. There were notable political figures like Representative Shirley Chisholm of Brooklyn, Imamu Amiri Baraka, Angela Davis, the musician Max Roach, the actor Ossie Davis, the social historians Shirley Graham Du Bois and Lerone Bennett, Andrew Billingsley, assistant chancellor for academic affairs at the University of California at Berkeley, the psychiatrists Alvin Poussaint of Harvard and Price Cobbs of the University of California Medical Center, Floyd McKissick, John O. Killens, Ron Karenga, and Milton Henry.

The journal offered a forum to a wide variety of thought and experience. The first issue, for example, focused on the politics of black culture and included articles by President Sekou Touré, "A Dialectical Approach to Culture"; Stokely Carmichael, "Pan-Africanism, Land and Power"; Eldridge Cleaver, "Education and Revolution"; Imamu Amiri Baraka, "A Black Value System"; and John O. Killens, "The Arts in the Black University." Later issues introduced the work of young writers and social analysts, among them the sociologists Joyce Ladner and Walter Stafford, "Black Repression in Cities"; James Turner, "The Sociology of Black Nationalism"; and Linda La Rue, "The Black Movement and Women's Liberation." There were also well-researched special issues on black cities, black labor, black psychology, Pan-Africanism, and black politics, as well as informative interviews with black militants.

Over the years, however, *Black Scholar* failed to live up to its promise. Mel Watkins, in his review of the journal in a *New York*

Times article, May 30, 1971, points out that much of its material was lightweight intellectual froth and a repetitive classification of past events. The journal failed to come to grips with serious issues of maximum importance to black people, e.g., the black economy and its relationship to the national monetary system, the crises in black religion, and the ideologies of revolution. There was no comprehensive analysis of research findings to provide an overview of black life and new directions for the amelioration of conditions. Watkins, an astute observer, notes especially the failure of "blacks to look at blacks." Writers enamored of the ethos of integration extolled the black community's progress in adopting white manners. White "objectivity," and even its myths, were used as the standard of judgment and debate, and periodic alliances with Communist and socialist groups further inhibited the development of nationalist concepts and independent analyses of black culture.

The color and culture versus class debate has clearly revealed deep divisions among black intellectuals over ideological directions and there is no clear-cut victory in sight for either side. The scope and mode of debate is wide-ranging. As Charlayne Hunter of *The New York Times* indicated in an article, April 28, 1975, "The conflict is at once national and international, scholarly and emotional, courteous and acrimonious, confused and lucid, serious and humorous." What seems absolutely central to the debate is the question: Are race and culture the most important factors in the oppression of black people or is it being poor? This question has been crucial and dominant among black thinkers since Emancipation; it takes on a particularly bitter reality today as the severe recession forces black breadwinners and youth out of jobs and into the streets.

Now that the tumult of the sixties has died down, two things are clearly evident. Cultural consciousness was a predominant element at the beginning of the post-Malcolm X period but was soon encapsulated by bourgeois nationalism, which commercialized and exploited it. The young radicals primarily responsible for the upsurge of Black Power and rebellion were not able to bang the drum of black consciousness as loudly as artists and entrepreneurs. It is also obvious that the Age of Cultural Demagoguery is dead. Power does not grow out of the sleeve of a dashiki, and an Afro haircut can hide a very timid heart indeed. Any remnants of blackism, of "skin nationalism" and the mad pursuit of blackness that exist are like funeral wreaths on a dead past. Yet what strikes one forcefully is that cultural consciousness is a persistent fact among black people. Blacks, at once dispersed and compressed, challenge those aspects of the dominant values in society that weaken their search for a healthy, unifying, collective consciousness and equality of access to opportunities for development. "Pride of race" is therefore a natural response and both dominant modes of thought among black people—integration and separation—emphasize the need for a greater awareness of black history and culture. Both are reformist on a continuum from moderation to radical change. Within the integrationist camp, which broadly advocates greater assimilation into American society, there are many leaders who wish to maintain separate but cooperating strands of black and white culture. The doctrine of racial self-help through individual and collective action to reshape black consciousness is applauded by both integrationists and separationists. And even separatism itself is seen by some of its advocates as a means of mobilizing race pride, self-help, and black enterprise toward ultimate integration of blacks in America. Similarly, in the culture versus class debate there are no clear-cut distinctions between one side and the other. There are Marxist-Leninist-Maoists among Pan-Africanists; and there are black nationalists who hold socialist views.

These endless permutations can be seen as evidence of the sharpening of the instruments of debate or as a sign of deep confusion. What seems apparent is that a decade of racial dialectics—of the cut and thrust of white racism and Black Power—has touched the emotional roots of ethnic ambivalence. Blacks exhibit a high degree of fluidity and moodiness in their ideas about themselves and their future in white society. They are plagued by the question: Are we merely mirrors of white culture or do we exist in our own right? Registered on their minds is the memory of how Europeans exterminated African peoples, seized their wealth, and forced them into slavery. This memory of victimization and group oppression, reinforced daily by poverty and racism, accounts for so much of the anger, confusion, and suspicion that exists. At the same time, the rhetoric of democracy holds out the promise that all men are equal under the law. Many blacks believe this, and for them whites are models of attainment whose values and behavior should be imitated, regardless of the loss of the parent black culture. But others, perhaps a minority, hate whites as symbols of menacing oppression.

Continually denied full acceptance in society, and without the material and status resources for collective advancement, much of contemporary black cultural thought and expression tends to move in a sphere of unreality and futility. At the top of the black cultural world few escape involvement in a sad pantomime of black and white minstrelsy. At the grass-roots level, black opinion seems in a state of perpetual readiness to express contradictory and conflicting views. Blacks can meekly weep with the devout, nonviolent Martin Luther King, Jr., yet pray for the coming of the Lord's terrible swift sword to avenge them. They can feel "black and proud" at the machismo of the Panthers and Baraka, but share the dream of interracial brotherhood and harmony, and, in so doing, still fear the pitfalls of psychological and cultural exploitation by whites. They wish to preserve group culture and identity without destroying the opportunity for freedom of association and collaboration with other groups. Given certain pressures, they can support a chauvinistic pro-black, anti-white separatist movement, or see themselves allied with whites in the vanguard of loyal democratic forces fighting to preserve American and Western civilization, or, again, with a passive cynicism born of centuries of denied aspirations, they can occasionally try to relegate the whole matter to the farthest corners of their minds.

6 The Quest for Equity

Black militancy and civil-rights agitation in the sixties instilled a new sense of urgency into urban economic affairs and stimulated concerted efforts by blacks to get a "fair share of the American economic pie." The goal was to create more earners, producers, consumers, owners, and businessmen, and to translate Black Power into dollars and cents. Thousands of black enterprises sprang up. Retail stores opened on the charred sites and vacant premises of white shops on the main streets of black communities, and black-managed manufacturing and service industries began operation under franchise and subsidiary agreements with large corporations.

Black economic nationalism, or the drive for black-owned equity within and outside the ghetto, is a dominant goal today based on an almost universally shared desire for economic equality, self-determination, and advancement. Basic is "shopkeeper capitalism," which advocates small-scale local business, "buy black" campaigns, and boycotts of white businesses in black communities which practice discriminatory hiring and upgrading practices. Ownership of "Mom and Pop" candy stores, groceries, and newspaper kiosks is hailed as typical of local family enterprise. Black ownership of barber shops and beauty salons, liquor stores, and Laundromats is also heartily approved, along with clothing stores, food and drink shops, real-estate and employment agencies, funeral parlors, store-front churches, and radio and television rental and maintenance stores.

Perhaps the Black Muslims have been the most successful organizers of shopkeeper capitalism. Under the leadership of Elijah Muhammad they achieved what the young Black Power militants were unable to achieve—a measure of economic independence. The Black Muslims have property and holdings valued at more than $80 million, an estimated 250,000 dues-paying members, and 120 temples throughout the nation, and the group is probably the richest black organization of all time in total assets. The Muslims own farmland in Georgia, Alabama, and Michigan; in Chicago and several major cities the sect operates supermarkets, clothing stores, bakeries, restaurants, dry-cleaning shops, and other small businesses. The Muslims' official weekly newspaper, *Muhammad Speaks* (now called *Bilalian News*), is published in a large mul-timillion-dollar printing plant; in one recent headline it boasted MUSLIM BUSINESSES PROSPER WHILE ECONOMY FAILS.

A second aspect of black economic nationalism is "black capital-ism," which calls for alliances with major government and cor-porate institutions to encourage black participation in the economy of the ghetto and the nation. Every city has its nucleus of well-dressed, fast-talking black entrepreneurs vying for the attention of white executives. Black publicists in Washington, D.C., have com-piled an *Impact Directory* aimed at "white industries and corpora-tions who are interested in patronizing black business but who don't know who or where they are." In New York, the Council of Con-cerned Black Executives, an organization of black managers in major corporations formed after the assassination of Martin Luther King, Jr., is dedicated to increasing black participation in industry and improving conditions in the black community.

Black capitalism was first proposed not by blacks but by men like Henry Ford II and President Richard Nixon and business, labor, religious, civil-rights, and government leaders seeking to curb black militancy and tame the ghetto. Two prominent organizations were the National Urban Coalition and the National Alliance of Businessmen, chaired by Henry Ford II. President Nixon thrust the concept into the spotlight in 1968, when he declared that America must give black people a share of economic and political power or risk permanent social turbulence. He called for "imaginative enlistment of private funds" and pledged government support in the form of investment assurances and tax incentives to corporations that locate in ghettos, train local people, and expand opportunities for home and business ownership. "People who own their own homes don't burn their neighborhoods," he said. Then in a remarkable statement Nixon coopted the demands of black nationalists into the establishment vocabulary: "From this can flow the rest—black pride, black jobs, black opportunity, and yes, black power in the best, the constructive sense of that often misapplied term." Furthermore, he continued, "it's no longer enough that white-owned enterprises employ greater numbers of Negroes, whether as laborers or as middle-management personnel. This is needed, yes—but it has to be accompanied by an expansion of black ownership, of black capitalism." Inherent in this view was the belief that government, in active partnership with business, could create economic opportunity and that the energetic elements in the nation's black population could thereby share more equitably in the rewards of the economic system.

Shortly thereafter, the Nixon Administration assembled the enabling legislation and governmental structures deemed adequate to cope with the needs of America's estimated 322,000 minority or non-white businessmen, some 4 percent of the nation's businessmen. The Office of Minority Business Enterprise coordinated new and existing programs and served as a "wholesaler" of ideas. The General Services Administration, the government's procurement agency, opened business advice centers in eleven cities. The Small Business Administration, which provides the bulk of government loans to entrepreneurs, encouraged industrial and financial corporations to contribute capital through minority enterprise small-business investment companies. Large corporations responded by setting up service and manufacturing subsidiaries with written commitments for future black ownership, and extended franchises and dealerships to black entrepreneurs. Expertise and skills were offered by the Interracial Council for Business Opportunity, and its associates, the National Urban League and the American Jewish Congress, to provide credit, management, and technical assistance. In addition, multimillion-dollar commitments for aid came from the life-insurance companies, the American Bankers Association, and the American Institute of Certified Public Accountants.

Nixon's idea that Black Power and black capitalism, supported by the government and American business, would lead to black economic progress, found many willing supporters. Indeed, thousands of middle-class blacks thronged to Black Power conferences financed by corporations and foundations, and endorsed resolutions calling for more capital and assistance to black entrepreneurs, and for the organization of the ghetto as a separate economic base.

Black Power enthusiast Roy Innis of the Congress of Racial Equality is perhaps the best-known proponent of black capitalism. Writing in a Columbia University publication of black economic development, Innis argued for "separatist economics—a black nationalist philosophy for survival" which would involve "the manipulation of the economy of black areas in a preferential way to obtain an edge and protect the interests of the black community." It is as if one were "to place a membrane around the community that allows full commercial intercourse with outside business interests while setting preconditions and guidelines advantageous to the community." In Innis's view, "Black Power is Black Business." Black economic bases in the ghetto would be created and supported by major companies, foundations, and government, and community self-development corporations would be established with a measure of local control. Ultimately, said Innis, this would lead to the takeover of local economic and political institutions, and the creation of separate and parallel institutional systems to those existing in the dominant economy.

Floyd McKissick, one-time leader of CORE, also took up the cause of black capitalism. McKissick argued that "the very existence of Black and White in this society is threatened. It is my belief that the development of Black Economic Power offers White America its last chance to save the Republic. If we are to exist together, it will be as equals. Equality depends on Black control of its own institutions." To further his aims, McKissick formed a company to propagate black economic development through the formation of a strong black business class with the assistance of wealthy whites. McKissick Enterprises will, he said in a publicity statement, seek to initiate technical assistance and funding services, new housing and building programs, and to redistribute profits among local black communities. Capital attracted from whites will be used to open restaurants, shopping centers, publishing companies, and social clubs in existing black urban areas and to build "Soul City," a new town in rural North Carolina. The goal is to provide "a means for Black People to become a part of the American capitalist system and thereby achieve social and economic parity with the white community."

The most adventurous proposal for black capitalist development, however, came from Robert S. Browne, a black economist and long-time supporter of many separatist causes. In the early seventies Browne received a million dollars from a "perceptive benefactor" and launched three associated institutions: the Black Economic Research Center, the Emergency Land Fund, and the Twenty-first Century Foundation. "What unifies the outlook of these organizations," says Browne in his *Report of Activities 1972–73*, "is their insistence that, while they must rely on funding external to the black community, their activities will give priority to encouraging and supporting those efforts which will extend the area of black economic independence in the hope that at some far off day there will have developed an array of financially independent black institutions which can fund the needs of the black community without reliance on sympathetic whites or on special government programs."

The Research Center, first of the three organizations to be formed, publishes *The Review of the Black Political Economy* and offers technical assistance to rural and urban communities seeking development aid. Current staff activities include contract economic research on land ownership and income changes. The Land Fund seeks to stem the decline of black land ownership in the South and improve rural living. Legal, educational, and financial assistance is provided to help farmers retain and develop their properties, and in the future the fund plans to acquire land for distribution to poor and landless families. Finally, Browne says, the Twenty-first Century Foundation aims to create a $10 million, and later a $100 million, funding program for economic-development efforts. Current investment grants on the order of a modest $30,000 to $50,000 per project are earmarked for support of the Mound Bayou, Louisiana, Cycle Products Company, feasibility studies for a black-controlled petroleum company, SECRUOSER, and community projects in areas of heavy black concentration. Browne has high hopes that the foundation will become an important adjunct of aid-granting foundations and the corporate world, and provide guidelines for the allocation of their funds to black-oriented programs. By its very existence and the creative use of capital assets, he says, the foundation will directly raise the aggregate economic status of the black community in America. His goal is to overcome the disheartening fact that black business enterprise is less than one tenth of one percent of the nation's Gross National Product and that there is not a single black foundation with capital assets in excess of $1 million.

What emerges from this brief review of black economic nationalism is that there is no lack of ability among some groups, for example, the Black Muslims, to organize profitable small enterprises, or in the case of McKissick and Browne to create schemes to attract and utilize on a limited scale resources offered by white benefactors and government agencies. But clearly, black rural and urban communities do not themselves have the resources and skills to deal with the mammoth problems they face. They lack full ownership and sovereignty over their land and resources, and hence cannot be self-taxing, and even if they could, the money gained thereby would not match the need.

There remains, however, one alternative source of funds proposed by black economic nationalists, and that is reparations, a one-time single transfer of capital to black people as payment for unremunerated slave labor and discrimination. The argument for reparations gained vociferous support in the speeches of James Forman, former executive director of the Student Nonviolent Coordinating Committee during its halcyon days in the mid-sixties. Moreover, Forman chose to buttress his argument by an attack against black capitalism and a defense of a revolutionary and socialist perspective. The broad outline of Forman's case for reparations was presented in his "Black Manifesto to the White Christian Churches and the Jewish Synagogues of America, and All Other Racist Institutions," adopted by the National Black Economic Development Conference in Detroit early in 1969. The conference, it should be noted, was sponsored by the Interreligious Foundation for Community Organizations (IFCO), an interfaith coalition created by major white Christian and Jewish organizations to fund militant local and mainly black community-action groups.

Forman's "Black Manifesto" opens with a biting attack on black capitalism. He says: "We must separate ourselves from those Negroes who go around the country promoting all types of schemes for Black Capitalism . . . They are pimps; Black Power Pimps and fraudulent leaders and the people must be educated to understand that any black man or Negro who is advocating a perpetuation of capitalism inside the United States is in fact seeking not only his ultimate destruction and death, but is contributing to the continuous exploitation of black people all around the world." Blacks, he says, are a vanguard force in America and must assume total leadership. "We must commit ourselves to a society where the total means of production are taken from the rich and placed in the hands of the state for the welfare of all the people." And he further states that the black man "must be committed to building the new society, to taking the wealth away from the rich people such as General Motors, Ford, Chrysler, the Du Ponts, the Rockefellers, the Mellons, and all the rich white exploiters and racists who run this world."

Then Forman makes a direct plea in support of a "socialist ideology" and says: "There is no need to fall into the trap that we have no ideology. We HAVE an ideology. Our fight is against racism, capitalism and imperialism and we are dedicated to building a socialist society inside the United States where the total means of production and distribution are in the hands of the State and that must be led by black people, by revolutionary blacks who are concerned about the total humanity of the world."

Forman had now arrived at the point of no return; throwing caution to the winds, he plunged wildly on, saying:

> Racism in the U.S. is so pervasive in the mentality of whites that only an armed, well-disciplined, black-controlled government can ensure the stamping out of racism in this country. And that is why we plead with black people not to be talking about a few crumbs, a few thousand dollars for this cooperative, or a few thousand dollars which splits black people into fighting over the dollar. That is the intention of the government. We say . . . think in terms of total control of the U.S. . . . . We work the chief industries of the country and we could cripple the economy while the brothers fought guerrilla warfare in the streets. This will take some long range planning, but whether it happens in a thousand years is of no consequence. It cannot happen unless we start.

Forman's "Black Manifesto" demanded $500 million from churches and synagogues as partial reparations for past racial discrimination, to be used for economic development of black communities free of any control by the donors. The manifesto's demands were part of a revolutionary strategy which if ignored threatened to cripple the United States economy by sabotage, armed rebellion, and guerrilla warfare "to help bring this government down" if necessary.

Despite the revolutionary rhetoric, the specific demands called for were merely another version of territorial nationalism and black capitalism. The reparations would be used primarily to create a Southern land bank, small business enterprises, and a mass-communications industry and training center to counter racist propaganda. In addition, reparations would be used to support the activities of the National Welfare Rights Organization among the poor and welfare people, to create a national black labor strike and defense fund for the protection of militant black workers and their families, and to launch an international black appeal for development funding. Assistance would be given to establish a black university in the South and a black anti-defamation league, with additional sums allocated to create cooperatives in Africa and support African liberation movements.

Needless to say, reparations on the scale suggested by Forman never materialized, though token contributions were made by some churches and synagogues to community-action groups. Forman's case for reparations gained no support from government or the white community, and blacks themselves view it with the utmost skepticism as an improbable scheme with no chance of funding or success. From time to time, the demand for reparations appears in the programs of black nationalist groups, but on the whole, the pursuit of capital for black economic development still requires holding out the begging bowl to white institutions for piecemeal contributions.

Of all the ideological positions today, black economic nationalism in the form of shopkeeper capitalism and black capitalism is, nevertheless, the most potent idea in the minds of aspiring blacks in the upper-working-class and lower-middle-class strata. The feeling is that "we have two choices before us"—either to enter the mainstream of the American economy or to set up a separate black economy. Since the first option does not seem fully possible, the argument continues, or only offers an inferior stake in the economy, then let us try and bring about black people's control over their own destiny. Armed with this idea, enterprising blacks like Cora T. Walker, a Harlem attorney who launched a cooperative supermarket in 1968, have introduced small locally based business initiative with a fervor unparalleled since the time of Marcus Garvey and Booker T. Washington.

Why does black economic nationalism persist? The answer given by nationalists is that black business instills race pride and is the only genuine equal-opportunity employer in a racist society. It offers, they say, a chance to capture some of the non-wage portion of national income and, by comparison with white-owned ghetto business, leaves a higher proportion of profits in the local community. In the long run, it is said, black business has an important multiplier effect—it generates employment opportunities for local people, introduces new decision-makers into the productive sector of the economy, and gives blacks the crucial lever of economic power.

There seems little doubt that as long as identifiable and vulnerable black communities exist, the drive for black capitalism, "economic self-determination," "fair shares," and "economic autonomy" will remain a powerful motivation for many blacks, whether for reasons of personal ambition, lucrative profits, crass greed, or idealism. The goal of its most militant supporters is not the radicalization of moderate blacks toward the overthrow of the system but rather to control the black segment of the marketplace within the prevailing system. Despite occasional references to cooperatives and African-style socialism and communalism, the concepts of both shopkeeper capitalism and black capitalism accept the premises of capitalist society and differ from integrationism only in the emphasis given to the creation of a separate black market of opportunities parallel to the dominant economy. Thus, black economic nationalism occasionally finds favor among white corporate interests and among certain white ethnic elements which serve as middlemen between the ghetto and the urban economy. For a relatively small investment, given at little risk and monitored by dependent black intermediaries, sales and profits can be made in the ghetto and the world informed that America does not practice apartheid but rather is supporting the expressed desires of her black citizens for separate development.

Separate black economic development has not proven successful, however. The ghettos do not have within them either the resources or the skills with which to repay a mortgaged future. Furthermore, the urban private and public sectors controlling basic community services—food supply, schools, transportation, housing, sanitation, and jobs—do not place a high priority on the expenditure of scarce economic resources for black and poor citizens. The situation remains one in which black workers, entrepreneurs, and professionals are totally dependent on the national and urban economy over which they have no control. Confronted with the inescapable dependence on external forces for capital, resources, and technical skills to foster their programs of black economic development, none of the leading black spokesmen has formulated set conditions concerning economic assistance. If the plea that blacks are the needy darker brothers of America, a domestic version of a poor Third World nation, will get money, then that ploy is used. The same is true of the reparations argument. And, if all else fails, the tendency is to fall back on government grants, philanthropy, and the largesse of guilt-ridden white benefactors. There exists a vague belief that once the money is in hand future economic independence will somehow be achieved. It seems apparent, however, that even the most vehement cries of "black economic power" often mask a desire for personal gain and a willingness to accept the relatively slow growth of a black middle class occupying a special and dependent place within the national economy.

Beneath the ritual and cant of economic nationalism there rests, however, a solid bedrock of established black business enterprises which should not be ignored. The oldest and richest sector is life insurance. The giant North Carolina Mutual of Durham founded in 1899 has assets of $129 million, and not far behind are Atlanta Life Insurance with $80 million, Golden State Mutual of Los Angeles with $44 million, and a string of competitors with from $20 to $40 million in assets. Furthermore, the shift of corporate finances to black insurance companies in recent years has added to their financial stature. North Carolina Mutual and Golden State Mutual have been designated to receive about $25 million of group life coverage from the International Business Machines Corporation which were previously assigned to Prudential Insurance Company. A similar switch was made in the early seventies when the Ford Motor Company assigned to Golden State Mutual about $90 million group life coverage formerly held by John Hancock Life Insurance Company.

In the last four decades, a handful of manufacturing, sales, and service companies have gained secure markets and their founders have risen to the forefront of black business. George E. Johnson is the king of the cosmetics and hair-conditioner market and his company has annual sales of $17.5 million. John H. Johnson of Chicago built *Ebony* magazine and a stable of other black publications into a large, well-equipped publishing company with $23 million sales per annum. H. G. Parks sausage products company in Baltimore has a reported $13 million volume of sales each year. Paschal's Motor Hotel, a popular rendezvous of Atlanta's middle-class blacks, provides sales and services worth $1.5 million, and Greenwood's Transfer and Storage of Washington, D.C., was built up from a horse-and-cart haulage business into a modern company with a $1 million per annum sales record and the United States government as its prime customer.

Today these older companies have been joined by a flood of new enterprises. There are some one hundred top black businesses and most of them were founded since 1968. Yet, despite this dramatic rise, black America has only a slender foothold in the national economy. The central and dominant forces in the American economy are the large industrial corporations, banks, life insurance, diversified financial, retailing, transportation, and utility companies. For example, the top American corporations have industrial aggregate sales of more than $500 billion, according to *Fortune Directory*, and account for two thirds or more of the total sales, profits, and employees of the nation's industry. In this context, the contribution of black business to America's trillion-dollar Gross National Product is negligible. It is capital- and credit-poor and subsists on the extreme periphery of the economy.

Black companies are in the minor leagues of American business. The Top 100, described in the May/June 1973 issue of *Black Enterprise*, showed gross revenues of $473 million. Most of them hover around the $1 to $3 million mark, while three had reached $20 million, and one, the highly successful recording and artists' company Motown Industries, had sales of $40 million. The Top 100 black companies are predominantly in the consumer-oriented retail and fast-food business, though a dozen or more are in the new and used automobile sales market, and at least one is a defense equipment supplier to European markets. They have small work forces and serve mainly black communities in six major urban centers with large black populations—New York, Los Angeles, Chicago, Washington, D.C., Baltimore, and Detroit.

The premier black enterprise in the country is Motown Industries, headed by Berry Gordy, a skillful promoter of recording artists like the Jackson 5 and Diana Ross, whose portrayal of the late Billie Holiday in the Motown production *Lady Sings the Blues* won five Academy Award nominations. Other notable successes in the last decade were TAW International of New York, an exporter of $10 million worth of capital equipment; Garland Foods in Dallas, which sells $12 million worth of meat products per year; and FEDCO Foods Corporation of New York, a supermarket chain with sales of more than $23 million.

In banking there are thirty-seven black-controlled institutions. Again, most of them are fledgling concerns and they shoulder an incredibly large share of the loans granted to black and minority entrepreneurs. They supply more than one third of minority business loans while possessing less than 1 percent of the nation's bank assets. It is very doubtful whether they can stand this pressure on their resources much longer. Many black banks are threatened with bankruptcy due in large part to errors of judgment, overextended credit, and bad debts. Some, like the Skyline National Bank in Denver, Colorado, face transference to white ownership to write off these losses. To redress these difficulties, black banks have had to tighten up on loan procedures and cut back on their hopes of expanding loans to minority entrepreneurs.

Similar problems face other major black financial and insurance institutions—among them forty-four black savings-and-loans associations and forty-two black-managed insurance companies. They are in a double bind. Their successes attract competition from white companies for the black market, and their failures bring a hardening of attitudes among white financial institutions against further guarantees of support. One notable success is the North Carolina Mutual Life Insurance Company of Durham, the most stable and wealthiest black business in the country. Mutual's history epitomizes both the promise and potential failure of black business development. Founded to serve a segregated market, it has now shifted to providing group coverage for industrial corporations. In the process its rating with the National Underwriter Company jumped from 897 to 207 on the list of accredited insurance companies. At the same time, white insurance companies are seeking new black customers and are hiring black salesmen away from Mutual to chase them. Conversely, to maintain its competitive position, Mutual is going after the general white market and has been forced to take on white salesmen to make the initial penetration.

In advertising, despite an initial spirit of elation over the estimated $51 billion annual consumer market among blacks, America's fifteen top black advertising agencies with billings of more than $200,000 are now facing a difficult period. No doubt there has been a phenomenal rise in black agencies, and there are six with annual accounts doing $1 million in billing each, and four having accounts of $300,000 or more. But these are low figures in comparison to the large multimillion-dollar white agencies. The black-owned John Small Company in New York, which focuses on selling to the white market, has done well, and the smaller, black-oriented Vince Cullers Agency of Chicago, which introduced the Afro and dashiki into black consciousness, has also been successful. Nevertheless, white agencies are capturing the black market advertising black-oriented products and creating sales-promotion campaigns to reach the black markets; as a result, the future for black advertising agencies seems bleak.

By all indications, it will be a long time before blacks gain parity in the American business community. To achieve parity on the basis of population they would have to attain a seven- to tenfold increase in their present holdings and a twentyfold increase in their portion of the nation's gross business receipts. Achieving parity on the basis of color is even unlikelier for blacks than for other minority groups. Blacks comprise two thirds of the nation's minority population, yet they operate little more than half the minority-owned businesses, and take in less than half the receipts. By way of contrast, Hispanics, who are about a fourth of the minority population, operate about one third of the minority-owned businesses, with commensurate gross receipts, and have easier access to loans and credits.

The growth of black business in the sixties was followed by a heavy failure rate. Inexperience and lack of management skills, chronic shortage of capital needed to catapult enterprises beyond the break-even point, and a downturn in the economy all contributed to the large number of bankruptcies. Black entrepreneurs constantly complain that they are unable to make long-range development plans or free themselves from dependence on single-line products and so enlarge their markets. In this respect they are victims of a situation confronting all small companies. One half of all small businesses (and most black and minority firms fall into this category) fail within the first three years, and three quarters of them fold within five years.

For all these reasons, it is extremely difficult to maintain black-owned and black-oriented businesses of any size, a situation made more difficult by cutbacks and discontinuance of government subsidies. Given this fairly gloomy prospect, some black economic experts like Andrew Brimmer, a former member of the Federal Reserve Board, are advising black entrepreneurs not to place so much reliance on minority enterprises that seem destined to remain Lilliputian in a land ruled by gargantuan corporations. It might be wiser, they suggest, to enter executive jobs in major industries or take up partnerships with whites in building large-scale businesses. The implication is that blacks ought to prepare themselves for careers as managers, directors, and salaried professionals, and not as self-employed entrepreneurs.

A new phenomenon unheard of in the past has come into existence: black elites are moving into positions on the boards of directors of major corporations. In a nation where there are some fourteen thousand directors serving the one thousand largest firms, there are now seventy-five to one hundred black directors. These Black Titans of the Board Room are a new breed spawned in the aftermath of civil-rights agitation and urban rebellion and are heavily represented on the boards of banks and life-insurance and public-utility companies, according to recent surveys conducted by the journal *Black Enterprise*. Six of the ten leading life-insurance companies and five of the ten leading banks of America have at least one black director, while Chase Manhattan, one of the largest banks, and Metropolitan Life, the largest insurer, have two black directors each. Chase Manhattan's board includes Washington law-

yer Patricia R. Harris and Thomas A. Wood of TAW International
Leasing in New York. Among Metropolitan Life's thirty directors
are George E. Johnson, president of Johnson Products, the Chi-
cago-based cosmetics company, and Robert C. Weaver, former
Secretary of Housing and Urban Development and now a professor
at Hunter College in New York.

The new recruits represent a cross section of the moderate
middle- and upper-class black elite—Ivy League graduates and professionals, community and religious leaders, educators and college
presidents, businessmen, civil-rights and political leaders, former
federal appointees and diplomats. Dr. Jerome H. Holland, former
Ambassador to Sweden and former president of Hampton Institute,
a black college in Virginia, is said to hold more directorships than
any other black American, including the New York Stock Exchange and four companies which control billions of dollars and
employ thousands of workers: American Telephone and Telegraph,
the nation's largest private corporation; Chrysler Motors, the third
largest auto maker; Manufacturers Hanover Trust, the fourth largest
bank; and the New York Stock Exchange. Franklin A. Thomas,
president of the Bedford-Stuyvesant Restoration Corporation, a
community improvement organization in a large black neighborhood of Brooklyn, has memberships on the boards of Columbia
Broadcasting System, the First National City Corporation, and the
New York Life Insurance Company. Clifton R. Wharton, Jr., president of Michigan State University, is on the boards of Burroughs
Corporation, Equitable Life Assurance Society, and the Ford
Motor Company. Vernon E. Jordan, Jr., executive director of the
National Urban League, holds memberships on the boards of
Bankers Trust Company and the Celanese Corporation. Mrs. Pa-
tricia R. Harris, in addition to being a director of Chase Manhat-
tan, also holds directorships in Scott Paper Company and IBM.

The black recruits serve, for the most part, as non-staff or "outside" directors on newly created board committees concerned with
company affairs and public responsibility. From this arises one of
the fundamental conflicts in the way black directors understand and
perform their roles. Many are not sure which side of the fence they
are on, that is, whether they represent the stockholders or are

spokesmen for black people. Some believe that they are "directors first and blacks second," and that they should not recognize any constituency other than the stockholders and board members who elected them. Dr. Holland, for example, says that "all of us first have to conceive of ourselves as being directors who have an interest in the overall spirit of the American free enterprise system," and Vernon Jordan feels that those who expect a black director to represent the black community misunderstand the nature and functions of a board of directors. Furthermore, Jordan has declared that he would not entertain complaints directed to him specifically by minority employees because "I don't think board members should function as personnel directors." Hobart Taylor, Jr., a Washington, D.C., lawyer and former director of the U.S. Export-Import Bank, has said almost proudly that the chief executive of Standard Oil of Ohio, one of the companies in which he holds board membership, never consults him on matters of race.

An opposing view is held by a minority of black directors who believe that their role is to "help black people." Reverend Leon Sullivan, pastor of Zion Baptist Church in Philadelphia, is one of those who say their commitment is to act as spokesmen for the black community. Reverend Sullivan, who is on the board of General Motors and two Philadelphia institutions, feels that black directors should be first and foremost auditors of company policies affecting black people. He is joined in this attitude by H. G. Parks, a prominent businessman who sits on the boards of a radio-electronics firm, a Philadelphia bank, and an aerospace-instruments company. Parks recognizes that he has certain special skills in the marketing field but that he has an important role to play as a "burr in the britches" in regard to minority employment problems.

Broadly speaking, black directors recognize the importance of community relations and the implementation of equal-opportunity programs. Moderates all, they nevertheless hold contrasting views, and the differing emphases on their roles reveal a fundamental conflict between directors of both nationalist and integrationist persuasion. The views of Reverend Sullivan, for example, are essentially a moderate form of black nationalism which has as its primary goal prising open the door of opportunity for blacks at all levels and manipulating company policies to favor black communities. By contrast, Holland and Jordan are essentially integrationist in their attitudes and see their role as applying expert knowledge and influence to maximize the public responsibility and profitability of company policies, and if this helps black people, then the system works.

Regardless of these differing and often opposing views, there are severe limitations on the action and effectiveness of the new black directors. It is clear that they found their place on company boards because of the pressures of the late sixties, though few of them admit it. The new appointees are seen by the boards as convincing proof of their commitment to black economic progress and equal-opportunity employment, and no further decisions of a precipitous nature are deemed necessary. In some cases, the boards encourage black directors to express a special point of view and interpretation of issues of minority affairs which might otherwise be overlooked or inadequately understood. Too often, however, the boards see the new black directors as a welcome, least-cost effort to keep black communities happy and tame.

Nonetheless, racial discrimination at all levels of American industry continues. Many of the companies with black directors lag far behind in minority employment, and even when they wish to, the black directors are in no position to deal effectively with minority problems. Most often the board agendas are filled with corporate problems, such as capital expenditures, declarations of dividends, and acquisitions and mergers, requiring expert knowledge or silence. And what is more crucial, blacks arrive on the board of directors scene at a time when, according to some recent studies of corporate structures, there is a diminishing power of company boards over management policies and practices. They are more like social clubs, and when the boards meet, members tend to enjoy themselves rather than ask embarrassing questions. This element of impotence, when coupled with the tokenism inherent in their appointment, suggests that the new black directors are captives of a gilded ghetto within the nation's board rooms. They are a select group of token appointees, paid comfortable retainers of $5,000 to $15,000 per year, and generally beholden to the company chief executive. It seems likely that even if their numbers increase over the next decade they will have little impact on institutionalized racism in American corporate economic and social structures.

At the bottom of the corporate structure is organized black labor pausing uneasily after the first major breakthroughs for blacks in the mid- and late sixties, and now regrouping for a new onslaught against the citadels of power. Black workers have progressed a long way since the efforts by political and labor militants and civil-rights leaders in the 1940's to gain acceptance at national trade-union conventions of the right of blacks to full trades-union membership. Three million blacks have since entered the ranks of the nation's 20 million union members. Furthermore, unionized black workers account for about one third of the total black labor force, a figure which represents a higher ratio of union membership among blacks than prevails among whites in the country, according to a survey article in *Black Enterprise*, July 1972. Their strength lies in the industrial unions, especially the three largest national unions. Two hundred thousand blacks are in the 1.8-million-member Teamsters Union, 200,000 are in the 1.2-million-member United Steel Workers union, and 500,000 are in the 1.5-million-member United Auto Workers union.

Black workers in the UAW, comprising one third of its membership, constitute the largest concentration of Black Power in organized labor. Long-standing members speak with some pride of the history of black participation in union affairs and of the achievements of men who have attained high-ranking posts. Nelson Jack Edwards, for example, has been a dedicated union man since the terrible thirties, when Henry Ford tried to stifle working-class organizations in Detroit; he has held posts on the executive board and as vice-president and is considered the most powerful black man in organized labor. Marcellius Ivory was the first and only black to hold the position of UAW regional director; and Robert Battle gained the presidency of the big Local 600. The union has a progressive record on issues such as full employment, rebuilding slums, and providing better housing, education, and medical care. Wages are high; in fact, blacks in the UAW have higher wages than any other group of unionized black workers in the country.

Yet the automotive industry has within it the most powerful centers of black discontent. The main causes of unrest are low wages and bad working conditions in comparison with whites. Black wages are almost 20 percent lower than those of fellow white workers. Customary discriminatory practices relegate blacks to the hot, heavy, and tedious jobs which white workers refuse to take, and they are effectively excluded from supervisory and skilled positions and from well-paid posts on the union's international directorate. Among the steel workers the situation is the same. As one worker commented, the black man is "never a highly paid crane operator, always a lowly 'hooker' assisting the operation from the ground."

These grievances were clearly evident to young blacks in the sixties. As *Black Enterprise* points out, the young black worker, particularly the Vietnam veteran, felt a kind of "gut frustration and anger" at the slowness of change. "He has paid his dues and he wants his just due today," commented a union member about youth. "To tell him things are getting better or will be better some time in the near future is to play with dynamite." The union had to be questioned. Management, too. And also the black union leaders trapped between the wishes of the white rank and file who flocked to hear Governor George Wallace at the UAW hall and the blacks who responded with equal fervor to the cry of "Black Power." Black leaders like Marcellius Ivory admit they have a two-way communication problem: "The top white leadership won't listen to our reasonable demands and neither will that young, angry militant black out there in the plant. He assumes because I'm past fifty and a member of the executive board and I'm on the board of the NAACP, he assumes I'm a conservative, handkerchief-head nigger," says Ivory, but "he never talked to me, doesn't know what I think about, what I represent or what I feel."

It soon became clear that the goals of Ivory and other black union leaders for moderation and peaceful petitions were not shared by young workers on the assembly lines. Sporadic protests and walkouts led to the formation of small activist cells in company plants. In 1969 the League of Revolutionary Black Workers was formed "to challenge racism in industry and the trade union movement." Essentially the league is a confederation of "revolutionary union movements" among black workers in Detroit, and the most significant of these is the Dodge Revolutionary Union Movement (DRUM) started in 1968. Its constitution urges members to "break the bonds of white racist control over the lives and destinies of black workers, particularly the United Auto Workers, and the management of Chrysler Corporation." DRUM's motto is "Dare to Fight, Dare to Win," and its specific objectives are better working conditions, the end of white harassment, black control over union locals, and community control over the expenditure of union funds. The DRUM constitution also expresses solidarity with oppressed Third World peoples and calls for the equalization of the hourly wage rate at Chrysler plants throughout the world, including South Africa.

DRUM and the league have initiated highly effective work stoppages and wildcat strikes in the auto industry and on several occasions crippled production at Chrysler plants. In August 1973 their members held a thirty-hour sit-in protesting the dismissal of a leader of a local group, the Workers Action Movement, an affiliate of the Maoist-oriented Progressive Labor Party. The sit-in dramatized demands for proportionate representation of blacks in the union and the motor companies and an end to discriminatory practices which relegate blacks to the most onerous and lower-paid jobs. Limited gains have been won in token upgradings and appointments. But each small victory has brought deeper divisions rather than unity between members who want to accept incremental gains and those who wish to wage a broad struggle based on a well-constructed political orientation. Nevertheless, though tokenism and internal schisms have blocked the drive for black workers' rights, in the current climate of economic stringency and unemployment black activism against the auto companies and within the unions may emerge again as a means of drawing attention to the underlying grievances of black workers. As one militant said, "The message is clear—black workers will be heard or organized labor will face its most serious threat since Henry Ford set out to break UAW."

Militancy at Chrysler has inspired other workers to form a Black Workers Congress and triggered organized wildcat strikes at Dodge plants in Michigan and at the Ford assembly plant in Mahwah, New Jersey. The result at Ford was the formation of the United Black Workers organization and a journal, *The Black Voice*, to "educate, expose, inform and agitate fellow workers to deal with the many problems facing workers on the job, in the community, country and around the world." The militancy of auto workers also stimulated the growth of unions and caucuses among black hospital personnel and construction workers, and sparked the efforts of activists among striking transit workers in Chicago, sanitation men in Memphis, and shipbuilding workers in Newport News, Virginia. The basic tactic of the small but widely spread revolutionary workers' movement is to form separate black and minority workers' organizations and encourage alliances in a struggle against the leadership and management of both trade unions and companies.

In other sectors of organized labor where blacks face discriminatory practices, the situation is far different. The AFL–CIO affiliated unions in the building trades and the rail unions remain notoriously closed to black membership. Blacks among the Locomotive Firemen and Rail Trainmen can literally be counted on the fingers of one hand, and blacks are only 1.7 percent of all iron workers and less than a half of 1 percent of all unionized plumbers, sheet-metal workers, and elevator constructors. In the public services, recent surveys indicate significant increases in black workers and a growing protest against discriminatory job assignments, pay, and upgradings. The nation's 400,000 black federal employees are clustered in the lowest five grades. Most of the forty thousand postal workers in the National Alliance of Postal and Federal Employees union are in the lower grades and are threatened by the introduction of automation and reorganization schemes. Blacks in the American Federation of State, County, and Municipal Employees, about one third of the union's 525,000 membership, are concentrated in the low-paid menial categories in public works, sanitation,

transit, hospitals, parks, and recreation departments, and are subject to periodic layoffs during crises in municipal finances.

The sixties will be remembered as a time when many blacks
saw their struggle for civil rights more as a battle for economic
equality than for the right to eat a hamburger or an ice-cream soda
anywhere they wished. Since then uneven progress has been made
in comparison to whites, a middle class has developed, and important changes have taken place in the relations between black socio-
economic classes. Indeed, the black gains of the period encouraged
claims of enormous black economic progress leading to a thin majority of blacks in the middle class, a view put forward by political
analysts Ben Wattenberg and Richard Scammon in an article,
"Black Progress and Liberal Rhetoric," in *Commentary*, April 1973.
Subsequently, more sober research has questioned this "illusion of
black progress," most notably the work of Dr. Robert B. Hill,
Director of the National Urban League Research Department, and
Dr. Herrington J. Bryce of the Joint Center for Political Studies.
Although blacks made steady progress during the sixties, their economic status has deteriorated since 1969, as characterized by high
rates of unemployment and declining median incomes for blacks
relative to whites. Furthermore, the black middle class remains significantly underrepresented in high-wage occupations, and only
one in four black families is "economically middle-class," with
an income over the Labor Department's "modest, but adequate" in-
termediate living standard of $11,446 in 1972. In general, incomes
in America remain grossly and unequally distributed along racial
lines.

America's 23 million or more blacks still lag behind whites in
most social and economic factors, and there is a widening gap in
family income between the two races. Median family incomes for
blacks are less than 60 percent of those earned by whites.

Uneven gains over the last decade deepened the pressure on
the majority of black families and left them insecure and frustrated.
More blacks are in employment, mainly low-skill, low-paid jobs,
but there are continuing high rates of unemployment and un-

deremployment, especially among youth, and disproportionately few blacks are in high-status, high-paid jobs.

Black enrollment at school and college levels has increased, but there is still a high proportion of high-school drop-outs. Black college graduates are catching up with white in incomes, especially in the case of women. In most cities, however, the average black college graduate earns less than a white high-school graduate. The overall picture indicates that black men at each educational level earn less than whites and the gap is greatest at the college level and least among the uneducated.

Black poverty, defined by national standards at less than $4,000 per annum, dropped dramatically from 12 million to 7.1 million persons midway in the sixties; and this was hailed as an important gain. But since 1971 the black poor have increased by 600,000, while at the same time the white poor continued to drop by 500,000 from 16.7 million to 16.2 million. Contrary to popular belief, most poor black families are not on the welfare rolls; their breadwinners are more likely than whites to be low-paid earners with children to support.

Many blacks live in low-income poverty areas with the terrible problems of family earnings well below $3,000: large numbers of children in broken homes, low education levels, high proportions of unskilled males, and families living in substandard housing. According to studies published in the mid-seventies, there are 1.6 million black families in fifty-one urban low-income areas, accounting for a massive 40 percent of all black urban families. These urban ghettos contain about 4.3 million persons sixteen years and older, and more than a third of the families are single-person households headed by a woman.

But frightful poverty is no longer the common lot of all blacks. What was generally conceived of in the early sixties as simply a race problem in which all blacks faced all whites in a struggle for equal rights and opportunities has now been blurred by the growth of economic class distinctions among blacks.

It is clear that the decade produced extensive gains for the most favored segments of black America—the middle class and the organized and better-off sections of the working class. Those who entered the decade with the best marketable skills were more easily able to exploit the newly created opportunities. Many of the men and women who were involved in the boycotts, sit-ins, and freedom marches are now in well-paid executive, professional, teaching, and political positions. Government-financed anti-poverty programs, race-research centers, and urban-aid task forces, begun as the result of agitation in the ghettos, placed a generation of talented blacks in managerial, technical, and paraprofessional posts that hitherto were the province only of whites.

Blacks also gained access, in the gradual time-honored way, to jobs vacated by white ethnic groups in manufacturing, personnel, sales, and clerical work. There were heavy gains for white-collar workers in government and municipal employment—in social work, teaching, health and medical services, post offices, City Hall, and the federal civil service. Gains were also made in entertainment and sports, and in the security forces and armed services. On the national level, new prestigious posts were filled, and on the local and state level more than three thousand blacks took up elective office. Significantly, the national black college student population climbed dramatically toward one million, more than three quarters of them in white schools. At elite colleges like Harvard, Yale, and the University of California at Berkeley, blacks constitute between 5 and 7 percent of the student population.

At the top end of black society today are a tiny minority of highly paid black elites earning over $25,000 per annum, about 2 percent of all black families. They include big-city mayors and politicians, top-flight lawyers, business and educational executives, representatives of white churches, community-development corporations, and civil-rights organizations, diplomats and senior civil servants, heads of crime syndicates, sports figures, and media celebrities. Stylish and well-fed, they are the peacocks of black chic. Sometimes when talking to them in their lavishly furnished homes, their well-appointed offices, at late-night soirees, or in brilliantly lit theater lobbies, one feels they have lulled themselves into a state of fairy-tale-like complacency from which only a brutal shock will awaken them.

Below them is a growing solid core of professionals, white-collar and blue-collar workers who give the black middle class a depth and breadth it never had before. They constitute 30 percent of black families and earn salaries from $10,000 to $24,999. About one in four of the adults has a college education and holds a white-collar job in industry, government, commerce, and education. Many families have two wage earners, working full time all year round. Most have cars. About half own homes. About a third have two or more electric home appliances—air conditioners, food freezers, automatic washers, and dishwashers.

Next in rank are the better-off sections of the black working class, about 24 percent of all black families. They include self-employed artisans, small shopkeepers, foremen, clerks and sales personnel, many government employees, and automotive and factory workers. Their wages range from $6,000 to $9,999 per annum but cannot effectively support middle-class aspirations or buy security for their families. The crucial fact is that they are comfortably above the poverty line and are marginally better able to cope than the 44 percent of lower-class black families whose wage earners are in low-paid blue-collar service, operative and casual jobs, like porters, cleaners, or deliverymen, and sweatshop laborers.

There is no doubt that more blacks have rapidly achieved a perch on the middle rungs of the American ladder of economic opportunity. Though there is no agreed definition of "middle class," about 30 percent of all black families are in the income range $10,000 to $25,000, as compared with 56 percent of all white families in the same category. But "making it" hasn't solved all the problems of middle-income blacks. Black incomes are not keeping pace with those of whites, and black job holders and job seekers live in fear that the ravages of inflation and recession will claim them as first victims. They are a troubled class with deep feelings of insecurity bred by centuries of second-class citizenship.

True, today's black middle class is blacker in complexion and style of life, less clannish and more open to change than their precursors, the light-skinned, tightly knit, WASPish *ancienne bourgeoisie noire* of the post-Civil War period. True, they have more income, education, and talent. But they are also rootless hostages to fortune as defined by white society, culture, and economy.

Many of those who make their living in black communities can exist only because these communities offer a captive, closed, segregated market for black monopoly enterprise. And thousands of others are totally dependent on wages and salaries provided by external economic forces, particularly government-protected employment opportunities. The most socially conscious of them are guilt-ridden at the widening chasm that separates them from their "brothers," and the least are puzzled by the emotional and moral obligations they sometimes feel they owe to the impoverished mass of blacks. In many of the racially mixed suburbs, "integrated" blacks feel grossly ashamed when their white neighbors flee as other blacks arrive, and are compromised when they join demonstrations against incoming blacks to hold the line against "upsetting the racial balance of the area."

On the whole, the black middle class favors integration as a solution to the race problem. It is a means of advancement for them and offers the prospect of shedding the hated aspects of the black-poor image. However, when racism affects them, or when they face barriers to their progress, or when society shuts the door on integration, the black middle class responds by adopting a nationalist stance. It appears to reject the white world and instead flaunts its blackness. National conferences are called, manifestos are promulgated, and delegations meet with white political and business leaders. Even militant black nationalists are accorded a modicum of respect.

These actions have several important functions for middle-class blacks. They give them legitimacy in the eyes of the black masses who believe that at last the "brothers who have made it" have come home to their people. They allow sections of the black middle class to launch grandiose schemes for black business and professional growth upon the community and to assert general leadership over the black masses. In effect, the black middle class steps between the community and white society and, acting as mediator between the two groups, seeks advancement for itself. In this perspective, the recent growth of black caucuses among the better-off sections of the black community—teachers, municipal workers, organized labor, professionals, and the like—are less examples of a quest for racial unity than they are of combative syndicalism with racial overtones. Through these mechanisms the "black problem" comes to the attention of influential whites and the public, and moderate adaptations are made to relieve pressure points that reflect tensions in the delicate balance of race-class relations.

The notable rise of an affluent black bourgeoisie has been accompanied by the growth of serious class divisions between blacks and constitutes an important barrier to the attainment of the oft-stated quest for black unity. It is a question of unity around the interests of which group, which class, and which slogans. The black-middle-class response to these problems and contradictions has been to emphasize the interests of "the race" and to call on each class to make sacrifices at its own level of race consciousness. There are, it is said, "different strokes for different folks." But this plea has found no responsive chord among the mass of black people who are still battling with basic questions of survival. For most of them the sixties was not a revolutionary experience in any sense of the word. Patterns of abject dependence on the good will of whites and governmental administration, developed during slavery and its aftermath, continued. Urban problems of unemployment and low standards of living remained, and worsened for lower-class blacks. And there was even less change in rural areas. Special difficulties face the black poor, the 28 percent of all black families below the $4,000 per annum "poverty level," particularly low-paid workers, the jobless, and the deprived. The black poor are frustrated and hostile to white society for not fulfilling its pledges; they criticize the expanding black middle class for being more concerned with their own well-being than with completing the unfinished Black Revolution. It is patently clear to them that the black community is sustained not by the "free-market economy" but by the welfare system—food stamps, dependency payments, and unemployment checks—and occasional doses of congressional or corporate guilt. They know that in the ghetto the most successful entrepreneurial activities are preaching, betting, and gambling, drug-pushing, pimping, and usury. In New York City alone, racketeers siphon off $300 million a year from the black areas of central Harlem, the South Bronx, and Bedford-Stuyvesant. The tenements are like crowded reservations, filled with sullen and anguished people. In them one sees countless inconsistent cultural adaptations and hears a thousand curses hurled against the barren darkness of their lives. On the whole, throughout the nation, the black poor remain numerous, unskilled, and disaffected. They are a brooding, shadowy partner in a *ménage à trois* whose other principals are white society and the black middle class.

7 The New Black Politics

The drive for cultural and economic self-determination has its counterpart in politics. In every county, state, and city where a generation ago whites were dominant and deeply resented a lusty challenge arose—Black Power. Crudely formed and highly critical of the status quo, the emergent Malcolmist-inspired ideology denounced the white power structure as an illegitimate sovereign ruling black communities through unrepresentative leaders. Blacks were urged to mobilize their votes behind a nationalist program and to elect militant independent people's leaders to positions of power. These leaders, moving forward with the people in an unceasing ferment of activity, would redress grievances, raise income and social-status levels, and strengthen community institutions. Once armed with a newfound sense of unity and purpose, they would negotiate with the power structure for the resources of development. Eventually, black core areas would be liberated, claimed as autonomous states, and organized as planned economies based on self-reliant African communalist and socialist models.

In retrospect, it now seems quite apparent that the separatist *cri-de-coeur*, for all its fervor, underwent substantial modifications in the crucible of American race-class politics, and in all respects now bears the imprimatur of non-violent integrationist philosophies. The legal and legislative strategy of the sixties has shifted to the task of capturing party political office and transforming influence at the ballot box into effective group power within the existing political system. In these years, a veritable golden age of black political activity took place and a new generation of moderate and reformist black elected officials emerged from the grueling, agonizing battlefield of popular and party politics.

Black politics today is unmistakably linked with the remarkable emergence of black elected officials. Taking their cue from the protests and organizing drives of civil-rights groups and Black Power activists, black political aspirants bargained with the white leadership of major parties for positions in the political machinery controlling the black vote. In due course, blacks rose to elected positions at all levels of government, from county officials and mayors to congressmen. Their numbers leaped from 100 in 1965 to 1,185 in 1969, and had nearly tripled by 1975, when there were 3,503 black elected officials in forty-five states and the District of Columbia. The major gains were in the seventeen states of the South which account for 55 percent of all black elected officials.

In the Southern states of the Old Confederacy, where in 1960 civil-rights protesters were dragged from lunch counters and bus stations to hastily erected county stockades, there are now black sheriffs, probate judges, and elected officials. Charlottesville, Virginia, home of Thomas Jefferson, gained a black mayor, Charles Lee Barbour, a hospital cardiac technician. Three northern Louisiana towns—Tallulah, Lake Providence, and Waterproof—installed black governments. Charles Evers became mayor of Fayette, Mississippi, and Robert Clark entered the state legislature. More than fifty black candidates campaigned for legislative positions in South Carolina, Alabama, and Georgia in the 1974 state elections. And three Southern blacks were elected to Congress—the Democrats Barbara Jordan of Texas, Andrew Young of Georgia, and Harold Ford of Tennessee.

In the urban North, the voting power of large black districts, harnessed to citywide coalitions and party machines, elected more than a dozen congressmen and swept blacks into office in scores of cities. Anna R. Langford became Chicago's first black woman alderman and Albert Wheeler, professor of microbiology at the University of Michigan, became the first black mayor of Ann Arbor. Walter Washington and a majority-black council took over the city affairs of the nation's capital. State executive positions were captured by Michigan Secretary of State Richard H. Austin, California Superintendent of Public Instruction Wilson Riles, and Henry E. Parker, State Treasurer of Connecticut. Notable victories were won by Mervyn M. Dymally of California and George L. Brown of Colorado, the first black lieutenant-governors in the nation since P. B. S. Pinchback served in Louisiana during the Reconstruction period.

Most of the new elected officials tallied in June 1975 are persons of stable means and above average social backgrounds. Among them are 530 women, including 9 mayors and 35 state government officers. The largest number, some 1,438, are in small municipal and local constituencies and serve in a wide range of posts—health supervisors, sheriffs and tax assessors, education officers, and city councilmen, mayors and county officials. Most are Democrats; few of them are professional politicians, and as is often the case, they serve only on a part-time basis while earning their livelihoods as real-estate and automobile dealers, lawyers, morticians, insurance salesmen, and ordinary working people.

The crucial factor in the rise of black elected officials was the Voting Rights Act passed by Congress in the summer of 1965. The act followed a spring of mounting racial violence which claimed among its victims Malcolm X and the white civil-rights activists Mrs. Viola Liuzzo and Reverend James J. Reeb, Jr. It was, as well, a federal response to an eloquent plea for voting rights by Dr. Martin Luther King, Jr., at the close of the Selma-Montgomery voter-registration campaign and protest march. "We are on the move now, and no wave of racism can stop us," Dr. King told his 25,000 foot-weary followers gathered on the steps of the state capitol, and a petition handed to Governor George C. Wallace declared: "We have come not only five days and fifty miles, but have come from three centuries of suffering and hardship. We have come to declare that we must have our freedom NOW. We must have the right to vote; we must have equal protection of the law and an end to police brutality." As a result of these events, Congress hastened to stop the exclusion of blacks from the voting process in seven Deep South states—the worst offenders. Federal protection was offered to registrants and voters, and the states were barred from erecting further barriers to the exercise of black voting rights.

In the following ten years, black registration in the Deep South states doubled from one to two million and made its impact at the ballot box. The Voting Rights Act stimulated a wave of confidence among blacks in the South and had repercussive effects in elections in every state in the nation. As of 1975, Illinois, Louisiana, and Michigan topped the list of states having the most black officeholders, with more than 220 each, and North Carolina and Mississippi followed with more than 190 each. At the forefront of these emergent blacks is a small band of elites holding key offices in the American political structure—135 mayors, 276 state senators, 2 lieutenant governors, 17 congressional representatives, and 1 U.S. Senator, Edward Brooke, a Massachusetts Republican. They are the leaders of a fledgling, black-oriented political force, and the enthusiasm with which these neophytes are organizing caucuses and conventions to rally voters indicates that black politics is the new civil-rights movement of the seventies and eighties.

Once begun, black participation in the American political establishment was organized into loosely structured conclaves, or caucuses, meeting frequently to examine common needs and problems. The caucus strategy owes its inception to two veteran politicians, Mervyn Dymally, a Trinidad-born, former California state senator, and Percy Sutton, Borough President of Manhattan, New York. Both men were influential in convening the first conference of black elected officials in Chicago in 1967 and subsequent meetings in Washington, D.C., in 1969 and 1975 to assess political needs and resources and promote non-partisan strategies aimed at improving the quality of life. Now, after a decade of organizational efforts, black officeholders have formed seven major caucuses representing the interests of local elected officials, the judiciary, school-board members, county officials, mayors, state legislators, and congressmen, and are increasingly active in national life at the polls and in policy-making posts. Within the caucuses there is a broad spectrum of age groups and opinions, largely dominated by political affiliation, as the sociologist Hugh H. Smythe and the former mayor of Cleveland, Ohio, Carl B. Stokes, point out in their summary article on politics in *The Black American Reference Book*. Their most important influence is the Democratic Party-oriented U.S. Black Congressional Caucus formed in 1969, and its collaborators in local and state constituencies. The caucus clearly aspires to be the high command of black political power in public office. Its members maintain friendly and cooperative relationships with national and regional civil-rights leaders, the NAACP and the Urban League; and because of their commonly shared view that black political power should be integrated with "green power," they are allied with wealthy white supporters.

Black caucuses in the political sphere are special-interest groups within, or related to, a larger white organization. In this regard they are not far removed generically from earlier forms of associations. Their precursors are the ad hoc grievance committees of "free colored gentlemen" and the "Jim Crow" organizations formed when blacks were denied entrance to white groups. More recent forebears are conclaves of elites, like the civil-rights organizers of the March on Washington, 1963, who petition government for succor from actions and policies threatening to blacks. Today's black caucuses are nominally concerned with expressing and implementing black opinion. They differ from their predecessors in one crucial respect—there is a broader base of elected members who have attained their offices and titular positions as black spokesmen through the electoral system. In practice, however, the caucuses serve as consultative bodies offering "representative" black opinion. More often than not they are black parallel organizations, that is, ethnic carbon copies of white organizations, and have a dual orientation of purpose and perspective, one toward the black community and other black leadership groups, and another toward more power-

ful white groups controlling access to higher-level posts and sine-
cures, as well as needed resources.

One example of this dual orientation is the National Black
Caucus of Local Elected Officials (NBCLEO), formed in 1970
with Mayor Robert Blackwell of Highland Park, Michigan, as
chairman. It is a formidable ally of the seventeen-member U.S.
Congressional Black Caucus and the embryonic Black Caucus of
State Legislators. At the same time, the immediate arena of power
politics for the NBCLEO is the predominantly white association,
the 15,000-member National League of Cities, and its sister organization, the prestigious U.S. Conference of Mayors. Soon after its
formation, two NBCLEO members, first Mayor Carl Stokes of
Cleveland and later Mayor Kenneth Gibson of Newark, gained
seats on the league's executive board, and blacks are now prominent on policy committees dealing with community development,
employment and income security, and human resources. More
recently, in 1975, Gibson was elected vice-president of the Conference of Mayors and subsequently became president of this influential body. Another black mayor, Richard G. Hatcher of Gary, Indiana, is a member of the conference's board of trustees, while five
black mayors sit on the advisory board: Robert Blackwell of Highland Park; Doris A. Davis of Compton, California; William S.
Hart, Sr., of East Orange, New Jersey; Maynard Jackson of Atlanta;
and Clarence Lightner of Raleigh, North Carolina.

Blacks in these high positions contributed to a shift in league
policies from vague statements of constitutional idealism to a call
for affirmative action by government on behalf of blacks and disadvantaged minorities, with special insistence on aid to local entrepreneurs and industry in depressed areas. This "strategy of infiltration," the NBCLEO leaders claim, will siphon off for blacks some
of the flow of government services, 95 percent of which is directed
toward whites. It will also aid their bid to replace the leadership
position left vacant by moribund civil-rights groups who until recently were the only channel through which blacks got access to
government resources. In the NBCLEO view, the traditional
methods by which whites dealt with blacks through self-

appointed leaders like King and the NAACP have lost their effectiveness, and the government must respond by utilizing the burgeoning leadership of black elected officials.

The U.S. Congressional Black Caucus is another example of organized black political activity with a duality of purpose and perspective. Most of the year its seventeen members are engaged in the long, tedious job of legislating and lobbying, but once a year during the last weekend in September, the caucus devotes its energies to a fund-raising dinner and a round of activities directed at black leaders and influentials. The 1974 schedule, for example, included meetings with fifty minority aides to governors and U.S. senators and congressmen to make sure that minority views are heard in federal legislation. There was also a workshop on black legislative priorities for 1975, with panels led by Senator Hubert Humphrey (D.–Minn.), former Cleveland mayor Carl Stokes, Vernon E. Jordan, Jr., of the National Urban League, Assistant U.S. Attorney J. Stanley Pottinger, and John Lewis of the Voter Education Project of the Southern Regional Council. The annual fund-raising dinner was a sellout at $100 a plate and gave tribute to black women, especially "widows of leaders of the black liberation struggle": Mrs. Myrlie Evers, Mrs. Coretta Scott King, and Mrs. Betty Shabazz. Meetings were held with the NBCLEO, and caucus member Congressman Parren Mitchell (D.–Md.) was host of a conference of leading black economists and businessmen to grapple with the implications of the deteriorating black economic condition. Other meetings included combined sessions with representatives of national associations of minority architects, mortgage bankers, contractors, and housing specialists.

The highlight of the U.S. Congressional Black Caucus's efforts to influence national policy came in August 1974, when the members, fifteen of whom had voted against his confirmation as vice-president, met with Gerald Ford shortly after he took over the presidency from the discredited Richard Nixon. The caucus spokesman, Charles B. Rangel (D.–N.Y.), expressed concern about the budget and inflation and went on to outline the views of the caucus on matters of prime importance to black people. Unemployment relief topped the list, followed by housing, economic development, health care, education, and extension of the Voting Rights Act. Of broader significance was reform of the criminal justice system, expansion of urban mass transportation, and a review of American foreign policy toward Africa and the Caribbean. Congressman Rangel expressed pleasure at President Ford's stated intention to appoint blacks to decision-making positions in the White House, in the federal bureaucracy, and at every level of his Administration. But, he went on, "We know, however, that our optimism cannot be sustained unless it is fed by concrete accomplishment, and although we stand ready to work with the President if he proves his good will, we stand equally ready to oppose him if he does not."

In the following year the caucus announced a legislative agenda, "Priorities for the Future," outlining the issues they intended to pursue during the 94th Session of Congress. Two economic programs were stressed: reducing the 8 percent nationwide unemployment rate by expansion of public-service jobs and unemployment benefits, and closing tax loopholes which benefit rich oil companies and multinational corporations and deprive the government of $50 billion in revenue. Wider public participation in the political process was encouraged. Emphasis was placed on extension of the Voting Rights Act for another ten years, with assurances that the Attorney General would prevent shifts of legislative boundaries to dilute black voting strength. The caucus also supported the introduction of a system of universal voter registration by mail. Expanded domestic assistance programs and the repeal of punitive amendments in welfare legislation were seen as being of utmost importance. The caucus agenda called for renewal of the Higher Education Act, more funds for needy students, and enforcement of the affirmative action clauses requiring institutions to hire and promote minorities. It also sought renewal of the Vocational Education Act, ensuring benefits to handicapped and disadvantaged students. Proposals were made for a permanent and comprehensive health-insurance scheme and programs involving community residents. Finally, echoing the views of their allies in the NBCLEO, the caucus agenda proclaimed the aim of tightening the revenue-sharing statutes to ensure effective enforcement of civil-rights provisions and provide greater benefits to low-income communities.

The growth of black political influence from the sixties to the present has not been confined to politicians and elected office-holders. Black appointees dramatically increased in the top ranks of government, the federal judiciary, and the diplomatic and civil-service corps. Some of them achieved instant national and international notice. Under President Lyndon B. Johnson, Hobart Taylor, Jr., was appointed director of the U.S. Export-Import Bank and Robert Weaver to the post of Secretary of Housing and Urban Development. Andrew Brimmer was appointed to the Federal Reserve Board and Thurgood Marshall was named to the Supreme Court. Key posts in Congress were attained by Adam Clayton Powell as chairman of the House Committee on Labor and Education, and William L. Dawson became chairman of the powerful Government Operations Committee. Others worked further from the glare of publicity. Hazle R. Crawford, assistant secretary in the U.S. Department of Housing and Urban Development, took charge of a vast public-housing division and multibillion-dollar mortgage insurance and property disposition program. Robert L. Carter, a distinguished civil-rights attorney who helped pioneer the 1954 NAACP desegregation case, is U.S. District Court judge for the Southern District of New York. Black Americans served as U.S. ambassadors in Europe, the Middle East, and Africa. Lieutenant-General Daniel James, Jr., was appointed Principal Deputy Assistant to the Secretary of Defense. Jewel S. R. Lafontant, a Chicago lawyer, became Deputy Solicitor General of the U.S. Justice Department, and Barbara M. Watson served as an administrator in the U.S. Department of State.

By virtue of their appointments, these men and women were raised to positions of "black leadership." Despite their undoubted individual merits, their elevation highlighted the uncertainty of white politicians about the black vote. Caught between the surging militancy of urban blacks and the ugly manifestations of white resistance to change, the national political machinery responded with token appointments. There is a story, apocryphal perhaps, which went the rounds of Washington's political circles when President Lyndon B. Johnson appointed Andrew Brimmer to the Federal Reserve Board. President Johnson had decided on Brimmer, but it was necessary to elicit the approval of Senator Russell B.

Long, chairman of the Senate Finance Committee. LBJ had promised that if possible the candidate would be from Long's home state of Louisiana. On being told that Brimmer was the man, Senator Long said, "But I've never heard of him; how come he's from my state?" The President was silent but passed him a photograph, upon which Senator Long let out a howl. "Oh, my God, he's a nigger." To which LBJ replied: "But look at his qualifications." "But what can I say in Louisiana?" said Senator Long. "Tell them you didn't have a qualified white man in Louisiana," snapped Johnson, "so it had to be a nigger."

Of less strategic importance than black appointees, but with a more widespread following and roots in the organized middle and working classes, are America's black civic elites—the leaders of traditional institutions—who have reasserted their claim to prestige and influence in national halls of power. They are the Grand Polemarches, Supreme Commanders, and Grand Basileuses of fraternities and sororities, and the presidents and chairmen of professional associations, colleges, and large businesses. They also include the executive directors of civil-rights organizations and trade unions, the heads of church councils and large religious congregations, and a sprinkling of national celebrities like the award-winning baseball player Hank Aaron, and show-business personalities like Pearl Bailey and Sammy Davis, Jr.

Together, these three groups, the black elected officials and politicians, the appointees, and the civic elites, make up America's black influentials—an educated middle-class stratum holding positions of power and national influence whose policies and actions significantly affect the black population. Their advice and consent is sought, as required, by city hall, the governor's mansion, and the White House. They are available for consultation at hastily convened "Calls to Action" and "Black Summit" conferences seeking information on attitudes and conditions prevailing in black quarters.

The heyday of black political development was marked by a triumphant pageant of national conferences attracting a cross section of black opinion—civil-rights moderates, young radicals from

SNCC and CORE, militant black nationalists, bearded members of the Revolutionary Action Movement, and clean-shaven, dark-suited Black Muslims. Dressed in variegated costumes—flowing African robes, Ivy League seersucker suits, miniskirts, faded blue jeans, hippie love beads, and brightly colored head ties—black people came together to affirm their newly found belief in Black Power and the necessity to alter racial inequities.

The first steps in this direction were the National Conferences on Black Power held in Washington, D.C., in 1966 with the sponsorship of Congressman Adam Clayton Powell, and again in Newark in 1967 under the chairmanship of Reverend Dr. Nathan Wright, Jr., urban-affairs director for the Newark Episcopal Diocese. The Newark Conference attracted a thousand delegates to the city one week after racial disorders and bloody street fighting had left twenty-six dead and many hundreds injured. In an ugly atmosphere of rumor and racial tension, the delegates discussed an agenda of political issues influenced by the widely differing ideologies of the cultural nationalist Ron Karenga, the separatist economist Robert Browne, the former national director of CORE James Farmer, and the actor Ossie Davis, who had eulogized Malcolm X. The now familiar themes of black nationalism and Black Power were reiterated. In prominent display were placards urging delegates to "buy black" and support neighborhood credit unions, cultural autonomy, community control of school boards, guaranteed incomes, and more congressional representation. The needs for black economic development, an educational fund, and an international congress were strongly stressed and many delegates favored a separatist-inspired resolution seeking "a national dialogue on the desirability of partitioning the United States into separate and independent nations, one to be a homeland for white Americans and the other to be a homeland for black Americans." Carried forward on a wave of racial confraternity, the delegates demanded in a babel of voices "empowerment," "fair shares," and "race solidarity." Though no consensus was achieved about the definition and scope of Black Power, the spirit of debate reflected the new sense of self-determination blossoming in black communities.

But these communities, lacking the power to influence future events, were in fact communities in peril buffeted about in the stormy turmoil of the American political system. What was needed, said many black leaders, was the awakening of a sleeping giant, the black vote, and a call went forth for a national black political convention sponsored by Mayor Richard G. Hatcher of Gary, Indiana, Congressman Charles C. Diggs of Detroit, and Imamu Amiri Baraka, the poet-playwright-strategist. The convention, held in Gary in March 1972, was proclaimed as the most significant mass gathering of the era. It was aimed at America's 14.2 million voting-age blacks and brought together an assembly of eight thousand people, half of whom were delegates, observers, and representatives of community organizations from all over the nation.

Three dramatic issues were at the heart of the debates: the crisis of black people, the inadequacies of the political system, and the need for a "new black politics." Delegate after delegate mounted the rostrum to describe in vivid terms the cities where blacks live as dope-ridden, crime-haunted, and stricken with unemployment, especially among youth. A mother fought back tears of anger as she condemned ghetto schools unable or unwilling to educate her children for the real world of their struggles. A young college student said the plight of black people is the same everywhere. At home, the American institutions in which blacks have placed their trust are unable to cope with the crises created by a single-minded dedication to profits and the maintenance of white supremacy. And abroad, he added, blacks and the peoples of the Third World have fallen prey to the same forces of domination, exploitation, and deceit.

Ringing manifestos brought an avalanche of sustained applause with allegations that the American system does not work for the black masses and cannot be made to work without radical surgery. Dependence on white men has continued for too long without success, it was suggested. Wasn't it obvious, came the arching question, if white liberalism could have solved our problems, then Lincoln, Roosevelt, and Kennedy would have done so? If the nation's difficulties could have been solved by aggressive, crafty politicians, then wouldn't Ol' LBJ have retained the presidency? And, furthermore, if American monopoly capitalism and military imperialism could have saved the nation, why did Nixon run in panic around the world seeking to stabilize relations with Moscow and the so-called Communist Chinese enemy?

In the closing sessions at Gary there was mounting support for a new political approach, perhaps a black political party, designed to serve black needs. Prevailing political structures were dismissed as "white politics" dedicated to the preservation of white power and hence incapable of serving black people. Instead of blindly supporting morally corrupt Democratic and Republican Parties which treat blacks with savage disregard, black people should organize to advance their own interests. What was needed, it was stated, was a new black politics which places community above individualism, love before exploitation, a living environment before profits, peace before war, justice before unjust order, and morality above expediency.

Twelve crucial demands were highlighted in the reports of city-based coalitions, state caucuses, and national organizations. These were compiled by the convention steering committee and disseminated as a National Black Political Agenda calling for:

—Proportionate black congressional representation or a minimum of sixty-six representatives and fifteen senators.
—Community control over the police, schools, and other institutions affecting the lives of black people.
—A Bill of Rights for black victims of America's "criminal justice system" and the release of political prisoners.
—An end to political surveillance of blacks by the FBI, the CIA, and the Justice Department, and a shift of their attention to ending organized crime and drug traffic.
—The right of cities with black majorities whose population exceeds that of the nation's smallest state to vote on whether they want to assume the status of states.
—A national black commission to calculate the amount of reparations due blacks because of their legacy of slavery and racial discrimination.
—A black United Fund to solicit money from blacks to be used for black charitable and development purposes.
—Black labor unions parallel to those unions excluding blacks.

—A government-guaranteed minimum annual income of $6,500
for a family of four.
—Free academic and technical education for all blacks up to their
highest attainable level.
—Black control of the mass media.
—National Health Insurance for all citizens and free medical care
for all families earning less than $10,000.

In the aftermath of the Gary convention two aspects of political debate behind the scenes were destined to haunt the conveners. One had to do with political in-fighting, the other with the convention's black nationalist emphasis. The initiation, planning, and leadership of the Gary convention was almost entirely in the hands of middle-age, middle-class black Democrats whose objective was to increase pressure on the Democratic Party to support black candidates and appointees and deal with black needs. Within the party, however, young black intellectuals were critical of the established party leaders and were hoping to get on the bandwagon of welfare liberalism associated with Senator George McGovern (D.–South Dakota), a candidate for the Democratic presidential nomination. Meanwhile, a sprinkling of older Republicans was trying to win votes for their candidate, Nixon. In effect, the convention was a scene of intense political party debate, not non-partisan racial unity, and this fact continued to plague the efforts of the convention committee many years later.

The difficulties over the black nationalist and separatist emphasis at Gary were manifest in 1974. Hatcher and Baraka, acting on behalf of the steering committee, mobilized a Second National Black Political Convention on the theme "Black Unity without Uniformity," and two thousand delegates swarmed into Little Rock, Arkansas, in answer to their call. But despite pretensions of racial solidarity, there were notable absences of prominent politicians and civil-rights leaders, some of whom had been at Gary but who had grown increasingly uneasy at the fervor of black nationalist debate. As it transpired, the Little Rock resolutions were in the main relatively mild exhortations to group unity. What did stand out, however, was the nationalist demand that the new black politics find fruition in an independent black political party incorporating all tendencies—moderate integrationist, nationalist, and revolutionary. This demand proved unacceptable to delegates with clearly Democratic or Republican affiliations or sympathies and was the straw that broke the back of black unity at the convention. Following Little Rock, there was dissension within the steering committee amid accusations that Baraka and his nationalist band of followers had manipulated the convention to advance their own purposes and muzzle opposition from moderate elements. Indeed, Congressman Charles Diggs subsequently vacated the presidency of the interim policy-making arm of the convention, the National Black Political Assembly, and Ron Daniels, an avowed black nationalist, was elected in his place.

Imamu Amiri Baraka is perhaps America's best known and angriest black poet and playwright. Writing from the decaying slums of Newark, Baraka first came to public attention during the 1967 riots in which twenty-six persons were killed and hundreds injured and jailed. Something of his own awakening consciousness during that period was on every page of his play *The Slave*, and the cry of Black Power seemed perpetually in formation on the quivering lips of Clay, the doomed hero of *Dutchman*. But more important for our understanding of trends in black politics, Baraka was an outstanding advocate of black political autonomy and community control and was the first of the militants to effectively capitalize on the power and potential of the black vote in Northern cities. He also sensed that when the militant offshoots of the civil-rights and embryonic Black Power movements came North, they would find fertile ground among disenchanted youth, the unemployed, and community-action groups. Through his writings and speeches he wedded civil-rights protests to Northern issues of curriculum reform, busing, police brutality, and urban renewal. He espoused the cause of black nationalism, Pan-Africanism, and liberation, and preached reverence for a pantheon of black heroes like Marcus Garvey, Malcolm X, Elijah Muhammad, and W. E. B. Du Bois.

Following the Newark Black Power Conference in 1967, Baraka set about organizing a campaign to influence the municipal elections. The key element in this campaign was a coalition of groups called the United Brothers of Newark, which in June 1968 nominated two candidates for city council. Its work was enhanced by a Baraka-inspired demand for a commuter payroll tax on non-residents, and for local control of federally sponsored Model Cities housing programs. This emphasis on local control by central-city blacks, which effectively highlighted their grievances against uncaring suburban-dwelling commuters, became an important component in Baraka's vision of a black-run urban government. For him, community control meant the "mobilization of black people with black consciousness to take control over the space which they already inhabit and to achieve programs so that they can defend and govern that space and survive the onslaughts of white society." Community control could implement three strategic sets of actions, according to Baraka's plan. One was a strategy of urban renewal and community development based on the expropriation of a local renewal site, NJR–32, funded by the federal government through the Newark Housing Authority. A second strategy involved a series of limited incursions into surrounding white areas to open up housing and jobs for blacks. An example is Baraka's proposal to build Kawaida Towers, a black housing project, in the Italian north ward of the city. The third strategy was to assist in the election of a black mayor. Taking on the corrupt political machine of the incumbent mayor Hugh Addonizio—who later was indicted for bribery and extortion—Baraka successfully helped place Kenneth Gibson in office.

Throughout the early seventies, Baraka managed to keep pressure on Mayor Gibson and political hopefuls by organizing the Committee for a Unified Newark and a program of public propaganda on the meaning and role of black politicians. The essence of black political power, said Baraka, is the nomination of candidates for office by the community, not the Democratic and Republican Parties or the blacks under their control. Furthermore, candidates should represent a black electorate organized into a permanent body to assist the leadership in reconstructing the community. Black politicians should expose the system as corrupt and unworkable. Black elected officials should have a portfolio of skills to analyze the problems of moribund city governments and their deteriorating relationships with federal agencies. They should be prepared to battle with labor and management in the public and private sectors, said Baraka, because blacks will never gain employment for their unused labor within the existing framework of white racism. Black mayors must understand how to use the time-honored device of patronage to the advantage of blacks. They must hire the directors and control their own police, fire, health, education, and social-welfare services. Above all, they should understand the difference between what can be done legally through city hall and what must be done through the political activity of black people armed with the ideology of Black Power and black nationalism.

Success in Newark was linked in Baraka's mind with the extension of Black Power and community control to all major cities throughout the country. The National Black Political Conventions he co-sponsored were important steps in this direction. He advocated the broad goal of a National Black Political Assembly whose august chambers would resound with manifestos of black nationalism and self-determination. An allied goal was a Pan-African Nationalist Party representing all America's black people and acting in concert with organizations in Africa and the Caribbean. These ideas would be spread through the medium of Baraka's creations: an African Free School, a journal, *Black New Ark*, and the Congress of Afrikan Peoples, a broad membership organization emanating from his Newark headquarters, the Temple of Kawaida. In addition, Kawaida youth cadres would be specially trained to spearhead community action against retrograde black officeholders, to initiate desirable alliances and coalitions, and, when necessary, to cause disruption and controversy.

Baraka was undoubtedly fascinated by the game of politics, the confrontations and even the inevitable compromises which he would cavalierly dismiss as the result of the evil machinations of white and black "lackeys of the system." There was, however, a perceptible move in Baraka's Black Power ideology toward electoral politics. This was noted with polite approbation and much private skepticism by black politicians, mayors, and civil-rights groups, but was not without cries of "traitor" from small militant ghetto groups committed to attacking the system and extending armed violence and confrontation into a black revolution. Baraka's reply to his moderate and militant critics was short and sharp: Black political power is a potent force, and must be used to gain what we want for our people in Newark and in the rest of the country. In his most recent pronouncements, Baraka has taken a sharp turn to the political left and says that it is no longer enough to have a black-middle-class face at the helm, important as it is psychologically; the question is how to get a black face that will push through the socialist policies necessary to help the really poor. When black nationalism is combined with scientific socialism, he says, we have a powerful ideological weapon in our struggle. Still critical of the rise of the black political establishment, Baraka dismisses Mayor Gibson with a scornful comment: "Another grin. But nothing for the masses. Nothing to change the horror of this giant slum. Nothing to make real change. Just another bourgeois nigger with a gig he thinks is hip."

There are some signs that Baraka's star is on the wane. His vitriolic attacks on Mayor Gibson and the black middle class are seen by many black people as cruel and divisive. Furthermore, all the political candidates supported by the Congress of Afrikan Peoples for election to Congress, state, county, and local offices have been defeated. These setbacks, when coupled with the continued delay of Baraka's urban-renewal proposals and pet housing project, Kawaida Towers, indicate a sharp decline in his Newark political base. This is unexpected considering that the Congress of Afrikan Peoples has offices in at least eleven cities, including St. Louis, Cleveland, and Houston. In addition, Baraka faces heavy opposition in his power bid within the National Black Convention and National Black Assembly of which he is secretary-general. One seasoned observer of Baraka's political career, C. Gerald Fraser, writing in *The New York Times*, February 3, 1975, has pointed out that "at the center of the assembly's difficulties are several factors. Most of the nation's more than 2,000 black elected officials do not participate in the assembly. The assembly has done little political organizing. It has no concrete program. And it has been divided over the issue of Imamu Baraka's 'dominance.' " Whichever way Baraka turns, he faces a dilemma. On the one hand, black elected officials and moderate integrationists have boycotted the assembly because they believe it to be too nationalistic. And on the other hand, when Baraka espouses his belief in "a broad coalition of black, brown, white, yellow and red people," criticisms arise from militant nationalists who fear that black nationalism will be diminished in importance and the assembly will be coopted by the new allies.

If Baraka's cry for political and economic autonomy for black communities was a minor irritant to establishment politicians, then the new political consciousness of the welfare masses during the decade was destined to be a persistent thorn in their sides. It was a period of intense micro-politics at the street and neighborhood level. Low-income groups in many black communities heightened their struggle for tenants' rights, fair rents, and community control of schools and social services. Concern was expressed for the rights of women with dependent children, the unemployed, and families on welfare. Grass-roots leaders emerged—many of them illiterate, some of them house-bound mothers, others working women. They condemned government programs as "welfare colonialism" and "genocidal bureaucratic attacks" calculated to dehumanize black people. Asserting themselves as the natural and legitimate heirs of the struggle of the black masses, the new welfare-rights and community-action leaders denounced the collusion of black and white politicians to "sell out" the poor. They claimed that "race help" and "race pride" are too simple ways to approach black political and economic goals. For the most deprived and poor the key issues are welfare rights and public assistance, income maintenance, and access to jobs, dignity, and justice. It followed from this, they claimed, that the real proving ground of black political development centered on achieving victories on specific issues. Foremost in their minds was the necessity to defend the rights of welfare recipients from arbitrary government power. Broad support was given to budgetary increases in allowances for children and for money for clothing and improved summer camp facilities. Consumer boycotts were launched to lower prices and establish more lines of credit in department stores; delegations were organized to protest unfair cuts in local and state social welfare budgets.

In the course of their activities, grass-roots leaders developed ideas about the political organization of the ghetto poor and their relationship to the wider black-liberation struggle. Black Power, yes; but it should not deprive the welfare masses of immediate relief. Something was better than nothing; a steady diet of poverty could not nourish revolutionary action. Later these points were reemphasized as protest groups came under the influence of white and black intellectuals and community organizers like Saul Alinsky and Dr. George Wiley. In Wiley's view, the protests of welfare and tenants'-rights groups would be inconsequential if they were not part of a broader effort involving the poor of every creed and color, and misguided if they did not seek aid from any source—government, industry, or trade union—which offered a real opportunity for respite from the travail of daily impoverishment. Attention should be given to creating forms of community organization and action which encouraged fellowship and prepared the participants for a struggle to bring about the redistribution of the benefits of the economy to aid those most in need. In due course, many black protest groups were attracted to the successes of Alinsky's community-action experiment with the Woodlawn Organization in Chicago and became involved in Wiley's National Welfare Rights Organization—a non-violent movement advocating redistributive justice as a solution to the economic and political inequities of American society.

However, neither welfare rights nor community action grass-roots movements are dominant forces in black communities. They are weak and vulnerable to manipulation, and there is too great a gap between the local community and centrally located decision-makers. Some organizations, like Baraka's, suffer from an excess of cultish symbolism. Others are afflicted by a paralysis of leadership. The groups influenced by Alinsky tend to be led by the crusty black gentry whose ideas of advancement are at odds with those of the welfare masses; and Wiley's organization of some thirty thousand members, mainly black women, went into decline after his death in 1973. What is important, however, is that the surge of welfare and community protest in the sixties did herald the emergence of leadership cadres primarily concerned with the creation of community-based institutional structures which could support them as adequately as the broader society supports the new black elected officials. Nevertheless, the future of black politics seems destined to remain firmly in the hands of elected blacks responsible to multiethnic constituencies and devoted to electoral and reformist strategies.

The dominant trend today is the "new black politics," a skillfully devised strategy of ethnic politics played by a new breed of elected officials, public appointees, and civic elites. The new black politics has all the earmarks of a fledgling movement seeking social and economic reform through participation in the political structure of society. It is predicated on the belief that most blacks are wage earners and want to "get in" rather than overthrow society and that full equality can be best achieved through the electoral system. Its adherents are committed to the slow task of gaining parity of representation with whites and revitalizing existing political institutions. Bloc voting and mass political action have their place within this scheme, but greater emphasis is given to negotiations and coalitions across racial lines to win elections and participation in the political decision-making process. In essence, the new black politics represents the Americanization of Black Power; it has interpreted Black Power as a symbol of the desire "to be somebody" in the society and oriented its thrust toward the ballot, the union card, interracial coalition politics, and the attainment of civil rights, equality, and integration.

The darling of the embryonic movement is young Julian Bond, a former member of SNCC who gained a reputation for respectable radicalism after his controversial support for United States withdrawal from Vietnam and his long and stormy fight for admittance to the Georgia state senate. Now a much-sought-after speaker at colleges and Radical Chic dinner parties, Bond argues persuasively for a politics based on the initiative of the black community. "Racial self-interest must always be paramount," he says, and adds that this is a basic rule of the movement and a primary requirement for survival in a racist society where "appeals to justice and fair play are outmoded and useless when power, financial gain and prestige are at stake." In a speech at the Institute of Black Elected Officials in Washington, D.C., in 1969, published in the pamphlet *The Black Man in American Politics*, Bond described the essential characteristics of a democratic black-oriented movement:

> It must extend to every member of the black community the opportunity to have a say in who gets what from whom. It must cast its votes in a unit, it must deal with problems on a local, regional, national, and international basis, and it must decide that freedoms not enjoyed in Watts or Sunflower County cannot be enjoyed in Westchester or Los Angeles County. It must declare itself in the interests of laboring people, but not become the mistress of organized labor. It must pay as much attention to a street light in a fifty-foot alley as it does to national legislation involving millions of people, and international complications involving the future of the world. It must maintain a militance and aggressiveness that will earn it the respect of those it challenges.

Adherents of the new black politics justify its black orientation by reference to the pluralistic nature of American society. Mayor Richard G. Hatcher, a prominent spokesman for the movement, argues that the black man's emphasis on integration after the Second World War was misplaced. In his speech to black elected officials at the Washington meeting, Hatcher said there is no single monolithic white culture, America is a nation of many cultures, each providing its members with a sense of identity, self-respect, solidarity, and protection. Furthermore, political action based on identifiable constituencies of culture and color has been a crucial factor in the rise of other groups—the Protestant Anglo-Saxons, the Irish, and the Jews—why can't blacks do the same? Blacks are entitled to, nay, *must* develop their own sense of nationalism, says Mayor Hatcher, and play their own brand of ethnic politics within the pluralistic society.

But the meaning of Hatcher's "nationalism" and Bond's "racial self-respect" is quite different from that of militant nationalists. "I am not talking about a black nationalism that is racist or reactionary," said Hatcher to his audience, and this he described as a nationalism which glorifies in separation, clamors for a return to

Africa, or seeks to set up its own black capitalist enclave. It should be, he said, a form of nationalism which instills pride in black culture and its past, and banishes self-hatred and self-doubt through strong organizations, unions, and caucuses. To which Bond adds a peremptory challenge to race-conscious nationalists by saying that the new black politics should have a threefold task: it "must address itself to solving America's white problem, to developing a new sophistication and consciousness in the black and white communities, and to making democracy safe for the world."

Bond and Hatcher are not alone in these opinions. Most black political figures believe that black people have a dual responsibility—they must fight for the right to be themselves and the right to share in the determination of a common American destiny. There is also much agreement with the beliefs held by Congresswoman Shirley Chisholm that blacks should help organize the unorganized—the low-paid farm, sanitation, and hospital workers—and champion the rights of all underprivileged groups. In her contribution to Nathan Wright's book *What Black Politicians Are Saying*, Mrs. Chisholm says, "As a black politician, I feel that my most important task is to work to create a climate within the American society where blacks, native Americans [Indians], Chicanos, Puerto Ricans, women and the poor can have stronger voices within the decision-making process." Moreover, there are many political figures who see the new black politics as having the utmost importance for the whole society. Reverend Nathan Wright, sponsor of a number of national Black Power conferences, clearly believes that the post-sixties generation of black politicians are the liberal heirs of the great popular and cultural revolutions of modern times. Black politicians, he says, can bring to the nation unique gifts born of these struggles which public life needs for its revitalization and redirection along a more salutary path. He deplores violence and extremism and believes that change will come about through political action aimed at social and economic rehabilitation and national fulfillment.

In all these respects, the new black politics appears to be an integrationist version of Black Power, not too dissimilar to that described by Dr. King in his book *Where Do We Go from Here: Chaos or Community?* Dr. King accepted the positive aspects of Black Power as proof of the life-giving qualities of the civil-rights struggle. It represents an emergent "rugged sense of somebodyness," he said, a desire to work for group identity through existing black institutions, and a need to constructively use existing freedoms to eradicate the vestiges of racial injustice. Black Power in its positive meaning is a call to black people to amass political and economic strength to achieve their legitimate goals, and a call for pooling of black financial resources to achieve economic security. But he emphatically rejected what he called its doom-laden, nihilistic, destructive, and separatist values on moral grounds and because "we cannot go it alone, we need allies."

Essentially Black Power, according to Dr. King, means "joining the system." In his book he says quite clearly:

> The American racial revolution has been a revolution to "get in" rather than to overthrow. We want a share in the American economy, the housing market, the educational system and social opportunities. This goal itself indicates that a social change in America must be non-violent. If one is in search of a better job, it does not help to burn down the factory. If one needs more adequate education, shooting the principal will not help. If housing is the goal, only building and construction will produce that end. To destroy anything, person or property, cannot bring us closer to the goal that we seek.

In the process of change from the rebellious sixties, black elected officials have emerged as the champions of black freedom in *locus standi*. They are acclaimed by a broad cross section of opinion as the new leaders of the civil-rights movement, elected by the people, and therefore the legitimate spokesmen of their hopes and desires. The intellectual doyen of the movement, Dr. Kenneth B. Clark, sees them as the realistic expression of integration, their posts are won with the support of blacks and whites; hence they are a concrete denial of separatism. And this is right and proper, he concludes. The days of the charismatic loner are gone, as are the days of the black nationalist demagogue and the petty ward politician. In their place are black elected officials at all levels of national life who are increasingly informed professionals capable of intelligent strategy and a genuine communication and identification with their constituencies.

The growing political sophistication of black leaders was clearly evident in the 1976 presidential elections, particularly in the campaign of Governor Jimmy Carter of Georgia, in which the initial and sustained support of black Congressman Andrew Young of Atlanta was crucial. Black leaders were convinced that any Democratic candidate, Carter especially, was better than the Republicans Ronald Reagan and President Gerald Ford. Black voters decided that Carter, a peanut farmer and small-town businessman, was their man and steadfastly stood by him; many of them felt that he had lived among them, understood them, and had fought for their civil rights. Of key importance were massive pre-election voter-mobilization campaigns by black organizations, national labor unions, and the Democratic National Committee. The National Coalition on Black Voter Participation, an ad hoc group of black organizations, including the Southern-based Voter Education Project, launched "Operation Big Vote," a series of voter-education, registration, and turnout campaigns in thirty-six target cities chosen on the basis of size of potential black vote, past political behavior, and significance of the state's electoral vote.

These efforts became the hallmark of the new black politics. On election day, November 2, 1976, an estimated 6.6 million black Americans gave Governor Carter 94 percent of their vote and provided him with the margin of victory in several states without which he could not have been elected. Election analyses showed that Carter won because blacks, the poor, various ethnic groups, and sufficiently large numbers of workers and middle-class whites voted for him. Quite clearly the majority of voters wanted a Democrat in the White House after eight years of Republican Administration. Blacks, however, were the crucial factor in the election, according to a national survey conducted by the Joint Center for Political Studies, a non-profit organization providing information and technical assistance to black and other minority officials. The JCPS survey, which covered five hundred heavily black sample wards and precincts in twenty-three states, indicated that 70 percent of all registered blacks went to the polls, and their votes proved to be the margin of Carter's narrow victory in such key states as Missouri, Pennsylvania, Ohio, Louisiana, Texas, Mississippi, and Maryland. In releasing the survey results, the JCPS president, Eddie N. Williams, said: "This is the first time in history that the black vote has played such a major role in the nomination of a presidential candidate and in the election of a president. The size and strategic impact of the black vote gives clear evidence of the black community's determination to use the political process to achieve its goals and to participate fully in shaping the nation's policies and programs."

It is still too early for hymns of praise, however. Blacks are a long way from implementing the mandate of the sixties, namely, independent political power through the ballot box. Severe restrictions remain on black involvement in the political process as voters and elected officials, and as custodians of their communities and influencers of public policy. On closer examination the gains of the golden age of black politics, from 1965 to the present, seem more apparent than real.

Political power in America is in all its essential characteristics white power. Blacks exist at the margin of national politics as an 11 to 12 percent minority population. They are by tradition, since Roosevelt's New Deal of the 1930's, overwhelmingly committed to one political party, the Democrats, and this at times can be a fatal loyalty. On many occasions their loyalty has been taken for granted by the Democrats without more than token recompense. At times blacks have been used as scapegoats; in 1968, for example, the Republican candidate, Richard Nixon, conjured up a racialist image of the ogre of the black vote to scare middle-class whites, split the South, and lure the white ethnic vote into his "new majority."

Voter registration and voter turnout among blacks is sluggish. Of the 14 million potentially eligible black voters estimated in 1974, only 7 million reported having registered, and a large proportion of the other half reported "no interest" or a dislike of politics to opinion researchers. Indeed, a mere 34 percent of all voting age blacks cast a ballot in the congressional elections of 1974, and perhaps of more importance, only one in six black youths, eighteen to twenty-four years of age, bothered to go to the polls. In the 1976 presidential elections only 43 percent of all blacks of voting age went to the polls (compared to a national turnout of eligible voters of 55 percent), according to estimates by the Joint Center for Political Studies. This turnout was some seven to nine percentage points lower than in 1972, but nearly as many persons voted in 1976 as did in 1972 due to massive voter-mobilization campaigns. Generally, blacks lag behind whites in registration and voting by some 12 to 18 percent, and these gaps, while decreasing to some extent in the South, have increased considerably in the North and West.

It is estimated that 2 million of the nation's unregistered black voters are in the South. Yet, with the exception of the limited activity of the Voter Education Project run by the former SNCC leader John Lewis, there has been no concerted voter-registration effort, regionally and in every state. On the national level 7 million unregistered black voters is a severe loss of political power at the polls, and despite "Operation Big Vote," the silent 7 million did not respond to a call to participate in the 1976 presidential elections.

When one looks at the seven states of the Deep South, the prime targets of the Voting Rights Act of 1965, a rather dismal picture emerges. The act released a trickle of black representation, but a large proportion of black electoral power remains isolated in stagnant pools of racism and apathy. Blacks are underrepresented in all elected posts and have a grossly lower ratio of representation by their own race than do whites. Blacks in the seven states range from 18.5 to 36 percent of the state populations, but hold only 2 to 4 percent of all elected posts. For every ten thousand blacks there is only one black elected representative, while for every ten thousand whites there are sixteen white elected representatives. Even more striking is the fact that there are forty-five majority-black counties which have no black elected officials at all.

There is ample evidence in many places of continued illegal barriers and, as a result, massive disenfranchisement. Seasoned observers of the South Carolina political scene report that black electoral power is severely reduced by the manipulation of voting dis-

tricts and registration procedures, to such an extent that blacks
would have to have a 60 percent majority in a voting district before
their victory at the polls could be assured. In Mississippi, where
there is a 36 percent black population, there were 192 black officeholders, as of 1974–75, principally in heavily black counties and
districts. But there is a bleaker prospect on a statewide basis. Only
one black served in the 122-member state legislature and there were
no blacks in the fifty-two member state senate. On the county
level, Mississippi whites defuse political change by combining
heavily black counties with larger white counties in order to dilute
black voting strength. In municipalities, the conduct of elections
on an "at-large" basis rather than by constituent districts means that
the election of a black alderman is a virtual impossibility if blacks
do not constitute a clear majority of the total qualified electorate.
These techniques of disenfranchisement, in direct violation of Section 5 of the Voting Rights Act, have been subject to judicial inqui-
ries and action by the office of the Assistant U.S. Attorney General.

Political emasculation appears in many subtle forms in the
Deep South, even where blacks are the majority in population and
registered voters. In Claiborne County, Mississippi, for example,
blacks are three quarters of the population, two thirds of the registered voters, and have one half of all elected county officials—a
seemingly acceptable balance of population and political power.
But research by the Joint Center for Political Studies and the results
of a report by the Black Economic Research Center in Jackson, entitled *The Mississippi Property Tax: Special Burden for the Poor*, indicate that all is not well. The stronghold of political power is the
all-white County Board of Supervisors, which controls county officials and influences the state legislature on county-related matters.
The board uses its power arbitrarily to reverse decisions of black
county officials and to safeguard white interests, especially that of
landowners, banks, and national companies, against the interests of
blacks and poor whites. Unequal property tax laws that favor the
rich and discriminate against the poor are vigorously protected by
the board, while proposals to solve key rural problems of road transportation, water and sewage facilities, housing and social programs
are continually rejected.

But why, one might ask, don't Southern rural blacks rise up and vote out their oppressors? The answer, simply put, is three-fold—entrenched monied and political interest, racism, and apathy. Powerful white groups control the land, business, and all sources of income. The mass of unskilled day laborers, sharecroppers, and domestic servants are most vulnerable to threats and economic pressure. Annexation and redistricting schemes, and "at-large" voting requirements, sap black political strength. There are conspiracies of white officials and citizens to interfere with voter-registration drives, provoke violence, and prevent black political expression. Frequent change in the location of registration offices and the failure to publish widely the opening and closing times of registration places all serve to frustrate the will of black majorities. Ignorance, fear, bribes, and sterile promises add their inevitable toll. And finally, there are the incontrovertible demographic and social disabilities of black political life—high percentages of persons under the required voting age, low rates of registration and voting among qualified persons, and manifest difficulties in organizing bloc voting for black candidates.

Several observations can be made at this point about mass political behavior among blacks. Blacks are a "nation" of non-voters, with respect particularly to the low rates of voter registration among persons of voting age, and their patterns of political behavior are not unlike those of other largely low-income, low-skilled social and ethnic groups. Blacks do not vote *en bloc* for "race" candidates; most are represented by unresponsive whites and do not take the trouble to radically change this state of affairs. (In the 1976 elections, blacks failed to make any dramatic inroads in the House of Representatives or the Senate; though all seventeen members of the House won re-election quite easily, twenty-eight of the forty-five blacks who stood for election were defeated. Furthermore, the total number of blacks in state legislatures increased only modestly by ten, from 277 to 287.) Advocates of the new black politics believe that if mobilized the black vote could be a decisive electoral factor, tipping the balance in dozens of cities and electing to office black and white candidates committed to advancing black interests. Indeed, it is said that black votes can be directly credited with sweeping the Democrats, Truman, Kennedy, and Carter, into the White House. However, until voter mobilization takes place to a far greater extent, at all electoral levels and in off-years of congressional and local contests as well as in presidential election years, and until the widespread manifestations of powerlessness, apathy, and cynicism are banished from the political culture of black people, all talk of black electoral power shaping public policies is debate without heat. The unrestricted right to vote secured by the Voting Rights Act, to have its fullest meaning, requires the removal of all voting and registration barriers, more and sustained voter education and registration drives, and a universal method of voter registration free from manipulation and intimidation. As for the militants behind the banner of Black Power, raising the level of political consciousness and activity of the actual and potential black electorate, clarifying the political interests of the mass of deprived blacks, and mobilizing bloc voting for black candidates most responsive to black needs remain the biggest challenges to the achievement of independent black political power through the ballot box.

Black-led agencies like JCPS and many black politicians will undoubtedly continue to stress in the 1980's, as they have done in the 1970's, the achievement of ever higher election turnout rates among voting age and registered blacks. But it is essential to recognize the danger in all debates about the political power of the black vote, especially since the election of President Jimmy Carter, of placing more emphasis than is due on voting as a mode of resolving black problems. One is reminded here of the remarks of Professor James Q. Wilson, a long-term observer of black politics, that modern black political activity must be judged as a strategy of limited objectives. He says in a contribution to *The American Negro Reference Book*:

> Where Negroes can and do vote, they have it in their power to end the indifference or hostility of their elected representatives, but the representatives do not have it in their power to alter fundamentally the lot of the Negro. The vote is a legally important, morally essential weapon for the protection and advancement of individual and group interests. It can force the passage of laws, the ending of obvi-

ous forms of state-sanctioned discrimination, and the removal from office of race-baiters and avowed segregationists. It can only marginally affect the income, housing, occupation or life chances of Negro electorates.

The powerlessness of blacks will not be resolved by the vote, essential though it is. There must be fundamental changes in the exclusionist policies barring blacks from positions at all levels of activity and authority in white-controlled institutions, the eradication of constraints upon the growth and strength of black-controlled institutions, and an end to the racialist norms maintaining the mass of black people in a state of impoverishment and second-class citizenship.

Black elected officials are a mere token force within the white establishment—one half of 1 percent of the 520,000 elected officials in the nation, and only 17 out of some 435 members of the U.S. Congress. In many localities, especially in larger or more urban constituencies, a significant number of black officeholders are elected by majority-white voters, as was the case, for example, with Georgia state senator Julian Bond, Fayette's mayor Charles Evers, California congressman Ronald Dellums and Tennessee congressman Harold Ford. To stay in office and wield power they must always delicately balance the interests of the white voting public against those of the black community. In this context the highly valued goals of "black orientation" and "meeting black needs" are made extremely difficult because the black populace, disproportionately the most needy, is not the majority voting population and normally has a lower turnout rate at the polls than do whites. Given these facts, a crucial political dilemma results. Moderation gains white approbation and votes and some hope for small incremental legislative gains on behalf of blacks; militancy, if carried too far, loses all. The result is that "shared power" is the key slogan in renascent black political circles and "serving the general welfare," not blacks alone, is considered the desirable norm.

In financing, as well as in tactics, the oft-stated goal of "independence" is compromised. Black political and voter-registration campaigns are not financed by the nickels and dimes of impecunious, freedom-loving black supporters; rather, they are almost totally dependent on money from white sources: political parties, voluntary associations, and individual contributions. The standard techniques are direct-mail solicitations, speaking tours, and cocktail parties geared to a small market of wealthy white donors. Personal pleas are made to chambers of commerce, business associations, religious and fraternal groups, and the country-club set. Though solicitation of white contributions for black causes is a time-honored practice, defended by many militants as well as moderates as a laudable Robin Hood-like operation, there is every reason to believe that when whites are literally the sole source of finance black confidence in their leaders is eroded and the proclaimed desire for independent political action is corrupted and compromised.

Political independence may also be endangered by slavish adherence to the pluralist-coalitionist emphasis of the new black politics. The pluralist arguments of Hatcher and Bond, for example, predicate a political structure made up of a "balance of groups" in which no one group has complete power or can wield its power save through coalitions with other groups. Even if this proposition offered a true picture of the political structure, and there is evidence to suggest that it is a grossly inaccurate appraisal, for such a politics of group interaction to work successfully there would have to be a broad consensus about basic aims so that no group could or would attempt to force its views and policies upon the rest to the point of civil strife. The events of the past decade indicate that the political structures determining "what America is or ought to be" are viewed in vastly different ways by blacks and whites. Cleavages induced by war and economic crises are expressed in racial and class strife; few blacks can accept without challenge as whites can a system based on what one political leader defined as corporate control and racism at home and a warlike policy and contempt for colored peoples abroad. There is a current of opinion, even among moderate blacks, that the political and economic structures of society must be revised if the status of black people is to be improved. Coalition is called into question by the authors of *Black Power*, Charles V. Hamilton and Stokely Carmichael, when they write:

We do not see how those same institutions can be utilized—through the mechanism of coalescing with some of them—to bring about that revision. We do not see how black people can form effective coalitions with groups which are not willing to question and condemn the racist institutions which exploit black people; which do not perceive the need for, and will not work for, basic change. Black people cannot afford to assume that what is good for white America is automatically good for black people.

Questions about the independence of black political action also arise when one considers the structure of the urban political machinery serving blacks, who are now a significant metropolitan population. Black politics, notwithstanding the organization of "non-party" caucuses and conventions, is essentially urban politics. That is, black politics is inextricably bound to political systems designed in earlier periods of urbanization and industrial growth in America to govern the urban masses, their activities and deployment, and their participation in the electoral process. These political systems involve formally constituted political parties, their candidates and followers, and a hierarchy of party-dominated elected and appointed officials from local wards to executive offices. There is a centralized leadership of the party machinery as well as informal systems of a religious, ethnic, and class nature through which the parties relate to local constituencies. The cement which binds the party machine and its supporters together is voter loyalty sustained by money and patronage, and the whole is subject to the iron law of oligarchy—the preservation of entrenched power. These interlocking systems also regulate the entry and flow into political power of successive ethnic contenders for "a piece of the action"— Germans, Irish, Jews, Italians, and belatedly, blacks, Puerto Ricans, and other minorities.

The relatively feeble black onslaught has not destroyed, influenced, or captured the party machinery, far from it. The internal political structure of urban black communities is an appendage and handmaiden of the political organization of the city—dominated by the white party machine. Hence, it is the form and rules, and patterns of incentives and rewards inherent in the party ma-

chinery, which determine how and when black politicians emerge
and the way issues, candidates, platforms, and election appeals are
treated. The rise of black politicians normally occurs when the
machine, to ensure its strength in black wards, coopts black leadership into its ranks. Only secondarily is it the result of pious hopes
or a bitter struggle by blacks to realize "race purposes" and elect
"race men." Where variations occur, or more rapid entry into the
political arena takes place, it may often be solely the result of
demographic and geo-spatial factors, such as the size of the basic
political unit, the rate of in-migration or build-up of black populations, and the density of the black area.

Furthermore, the major urban political parties in alliance with
unions, white elites, and ethnic associations still control access to
most of the better jobs and political offices that blacks want. The
party apparatus is instrumental in all important urban matters about
which blacks are concerned—the quantity and quality of welfare assistance, the adequacy of municipal services and schools, access to
public housing, the granting of business licenses, the award of construction contracts, and the establishment of priorities for the rehabilitation of rundown areas.

Black politicians are, perforce, agents of the party machinery,
and voter loyalty in the black community is obtained and sustained
by money and patronage, rather than by appeals to lofty racial principles. In this respect, the city is a vast political plantation in which
blacks are as surely bound to the white machine as they were to the
white master during slavery. And this latter-day plantation has its
black overseers as well. According to Anna R. Langford, who
fought the Cook County Democratic Organization to gain her alderman's seat, "black lackeys" are ever-present in the ghetto. In her
contribution "How I 'Whupped' the Tar Out of the Daley Machine," published in Nathan Wright's book, Mrs. Langford says:

> No matter how terrible conditions became in Chicago—the con-
> struction of concrete concentration camps known as public housing,
> the murder of a Black alderman, the notoriously open buying of
> votes and the unashamed stealing of votes at elections—there was
> always a Daley-controlled Black lackey to pass out political goodies
> to "keep the natives quiet."

Mayor Hatcher of Gary makes a similar observation in his contribution to *The Black Man in American Politics:*

> A colonial power cannot exploit its colony without the support of the natives . . . In like fashion, blacks in this country could not be so colonized were it not for the soul brothers who sell their soul. Mr. Charlie needs his gitlows [flunkies]. In Gary, as elsewhere, there is no shortage. For a few dollars and a bottle of beer they run errands for the power structure that despises them for it.

These flunkies and petty ward heelers are agents of the entrenched political system, Hatcher suggests, and if they are not totally subservient or corrupted as yet, they are self-seeking, and every action they undertake is filtered through ego and molded by ambition. They are not easily detectable in their outward appearance, Mayor Hatcher warns. "They come in all hues and colors and from all walks of life—some are garbed in gray flannel suits; others, to escape detection, are adorned with afro hairdos and wear brand new dashikis."

In the realm of politics all activity has a large element of individual and class interest, with a potential for reactionary as well as liberal social results. The petty ward heeler is but one small cog in a much larger enterprise which now involves middle-class blacks in the political process. The demand for the new black politics boosted black-middle-class political power. It opened up opportunities on both sides of the segregated political arena, either in token positions in enclaves of white power or in black areas as agents for the party machine. The new black hierophants have benefited from both the integrationist slogans for civil rights, fair shares and full equality, and from the separatist call for racial unity, community control, and racial self-interest. Both paths have led to things that black elites want: more money, more power, social status, and homes in prestigious city and suburban neighborhoods. Moreover, some beneficiaries of the new black politics seek to protect their newfound bases of power and influence, often despite segregation. Their pursuit of the Holy Grail of "coalitions" and "alliances" frequently makes them associate with forces of hypocrisy masquerading as law and order. "Negotiations" with unscrupulous white counterparts enables them to "get a piece of the action" while carrying out a supervisory role in the ghetto. This, in effect, as in neo-colonial Africa, restores a discredited hegemony over captive black constituencies in which black elected officials and their middle-class allies serve as intermediaries between powerful and privileged whites and their exploited fellow blacks.

Violent upheaval in the past decade has brought some social changes, but not rapidly enough to meet the accelerating demands and needs of the black poor. Today few would argue that the black middle class has not grown and prospered, but the paltry gains of lower-paid groups trigger new grievances in the squalid labyrinthine slums of cities. The new black politics has not erased the grim realities of daily life—the rats and roaches, the low pay and high rents, and the racial discrimination which are the common lot. And on the horizon is a new phenomenon with as yet unknown consequences for black communities and their relations with whites in urban society. American cities, with all their problems, are in the throes of a great transition from white to black central-city populations.

Black settlements in American cities are segregated enclaves in which, ultimately, the only competitors for housing are members of a single, stigmatized race. Every major city has its core areas of heavy black population. Many of them begin at the edge of the central business district and radiate outward along major roads. Core black areas suffer from the twin evils of place-poverty and people-poverty. They are environmentally deprived human settlements, located near noisy, noxious facilities, and tied to declining employment areas. The residents are an urban tenantry with no stake in a segregated and decaying housing market. In health conditions blacks lag forty years behind whites. Maternal and infant mortality rates are three times that of whites. Blacks at twenty-five years of age have a life expectancy of six years less than whites of the same age. There are high rates of homicide and drug and alcohol abuse. Black suicide rates among fifteen- to twenty-four-year-olds have doubled since 1960; the rates among females have tripled. Blacks in comparison to whites are more than four times as likely to be poor by official standards, only two thirds as likely to be in college, and more than twice as likely to be unemployed. Black unemployment rates are high and at depression levels of 20 to 30 percent in the worst black areas: Cleveland's Hough area, Phoenix's Salt River Bed, Oakland's Bayside, St. Louis's Northside, Chicago's Woodlawn district, and New York's Bedford-Stuyvesant area.

Blacks are irrevocably city dwellers after a half century of massive rural to urban and South to North migration. During the decade of the sixties, black urbanization outstripped that of white. Now there is a greater proportion of black Americans than white Americans living in cities, 81 percent and 72 percent respectively. Until 1910, 90 percent of all blacks were rural Southerners—mainly tenant farmers and sharecroppers—and there were fewer than a million blacks living in all cities in the North and West. By 1970, the proportion of all blacks in the nation living in the South had dropped to 52 percent and black populations had grown rapidly in major cities; New York and Chicago each had more than one million black residents. In sixty years successive waves of Southern black migrants went North and West, and within the South, blacks moved from rural to urban centers. Significantly, between 1960 and 1970 almost a million and a half blacks left the South for the already overcrowded ghettos and marginal neighborhoods of the urban North. The South lost nearly one eighth of its entire black population. Half of these migrants settled in urban areas of the industrial Northeast region, the rest in the big cities of the Central states and the West Coast. Their entry into cities in such large numbers marked the final stages of the black man's transition from the plantation to the ghetto. Now, for the first time, the majority of black Americans are a metropolitan, central-city people. Recent census data indicate that three quarters live in metropolitan areas and about three fifths in central cities. Furthermore, four out of every ten black Americans live in twenty-six cities with black populations of 100,000 or more. For them, big cities are the end of the line.

Black communities within these cities have grown ominously

larger, and depressingly poorer. While the suburbs have had huge increases in the white metropolitan population, low incomes and segregation hold blacks in the central city. Year by year the pressure of population builds up. High natural increases are maintained because of the youthfulness of the black population, high birth rates, lowered infant death rates, and increased life expectancy. And there are no signs of slackening in the concentration of blacks in the central cities of major metropolises. There are several reasons for this which merit some further discussion here.

Black urban population growth in the North is no longer dependent on migration from the South. Despite the high rates of South to North migration during the first half century—which show signs of diminishing as new opportunities open up outside of agriculture—well over half the blacks living in the North today were born there and have never seen the South. The population specialists Karl and Alma Taeuber point this out quite clearly in their contribution to *The Black American Reference Book*. It is doubtful that Northern-born blacks will return to the rural and small-town South; more likely, their migration patterns will be what demographers term "intra-metropolitan," i.e., those who move will head for other metropolitan areas.

Southern-born blacks resident in the North are more likely to return South, but so far have done so in relatively small numbers. Some perspectives on this topic are given in the U.S. Department of Commerce, Bureau of Census, *Current Population Reports, The Social and Economic Status of the Black Population in the United States* (1973). Census figures for 1970 indicated that 3.2 million of the 13 million blacks, five years old and over, born in the South, were living in other parts of the country. At the same time there were fewer than 200,000 blacks born outside the South living in the South. And, more crucial for our discussion, the majority of black persons who moved to the South between 1965 and 1970 (113,000 out of 171,000) were returning to their region of birth. Migration to the South by Northern-born blacks and by Southern-born blacks returning home does not appear to be significant and there is little reason to suppose that this general picture has radically changed since then or will do so in the immediate future.

It is predictable, therefore, that most Northern black residents, regardless of place of birth, will remain more or less where and as they are. Certainly the pace of urban renewal in central cities, though disruptive, and attempts by planners and developers to entice middle-income whites back to the city have not reduced the trend toward increasing black concentration or created large-scale, racially mixed, black-white residential areas. Black suburbanization is insignificant and merely represents a very modest spilling over of central-city residents into the outlying areas. When these factors are viewed together, it is doubtful that current trends toward majority black central-city areas will be reversed.

Already three major cities have black majorities: Washington, D.C., 71.1 percent; Newark, 54 percent, and Atlanta, 51.3 percent. Blacks in six other cities are 40–50 percent of the population: Baltimore, New Orleans, Detroit, Birmingham, Richmond, and St. Louis. And it is estimated that by 1984 there will be black or "non-white" majorities in New York, Chicago, Philadelphia, and many smaller cities. If continuing trends of white exodus and black central-area concentration persist, it is predicted that by the year 2000, at least a dozen great urban areas will be "black cities" with majorities of black or non-white populations whose needs cannot be met without a massive injection of financial resources and basic changes in planning and investment policies.

There is much evidence of variation in the living standards and opportunities of black communities in different cities. In Los Angeles and Washington, D.C., for example, a combination of high levels of high-school and college graduates and well-paid jobs in manufacturing or government employment provides relatively high-income levels and a large proportion of blacks in professional, technical, and managerial posts. Moreover, black communities in major cities vary in their historical development. Detroit is the city of black industrial trade unionism and militancy in the automotive manufacturing industries. Chicago blacks inherit from Oscar De-Priest and William L. Dawson a long background of participation in urban and national politics. Washington, D.C., until recently a special case of black municipal disenfranchisement, and Atlanta are traditional seats of higher education and a stable black bourgeoisie.

Yet, in many ways, despite their individual differences, America's new "black cities" are very much alike. Five social evils stalk the mean ghetto streets—Want, Squalor, Disease, Ignorance, and Idleness. These streets are the same from one end of America to the other, and very few can fully escape. As LeRoi Jones, a poet of the ghetto, says in his book *Home: Social Essays:*

> Sometimes, walking along, among ruined shacks and lives, of the worst Harlem slum, there is a feeling that just around the corner you'll find yourself in South Chicago or South Philadelphia, maybe even Newark's Third Ward. In these places, life and its possibility has been distorted almost identically. And the distortion is as old as its sources: the fear, frustration, and hatred that Negroes have always been heir to in America. It is just that in the cities, which were once the black man's twentieth century "Jordan," promise is a dying bitch with rotting eyes. And the stink of her dying is a deadly killing fume.

Blacks, in contrast to whites in America, see government as the major agent for change in their life conditions. Black strategists—moderates as well as militants—generally welcome the growth and consolidation of black areas, black majority urban populations, and black-controlled city halls. They see them as arenas of political development, based on community participation, through which blacks can gain material advancement, a heightened sense of dignity and self-respect, and greater bargaining strength in a pluralistic society.

But there is a strong current of anxiety about inheriting central cities that are huge reservations of powerless forgotten people living in deprived environments, old and squalid housing abused for generations, amortized and abandoned by whites. Nevertheless, impassioned arguments are put forth to "hold on to our urban territories, they are the only base we have." This is the message of strategists like Bobby Seale, Black Panther leader and a recent mayoral candidate in Oakland, of Gary's Mayor Hatcher, and of U.S. Representative Charles Diggs of Detroit.

The editorial pages of the California-based radical intellectual journal *Black Scholar*, April 1970, warned:

In the 19th century, we were encouraged to migrate from our land base in the South, which was the source of economic power. In the 20th century, we can anticipate similar attempts to disenfranchise blacks and deprive us of our logical land base—the major industrial cities of the country.

We must move to the formation of the black city state. If a city has a majority of blacks, we must control it. We must levy taxes, homestead land and expropriate, as and when necessary, to secure a lasting economic base.

A man with no land is a man with no power. We must have power over our cities if we are to liberate ourselves—or even survive.

But these goals may not be achieved immediately, or even in the near future.

The answer to the problem lies first of all in the nature of the urban inheritance bequeathed to blacks. A rising tide of black discontent lapped at the pillars of urban governance during the 1965–75 golden age of black politics and swept 135 black mayors into office in large and small, rural and urban communities. Eighty-two of them were in the South, particularly in small rural places of fewer than one thousand persons. At the other end of the spectrum, black mayors also served eleven cities with populations of 100,000 or more. Another twenty held offices in cities with populations between 25,000 and 100,000, of which six were in the South and fourteen outside that region.

At the outset it should be recognized that the problems and prospects for the future of black-led towns and cities are sharply different. Small towns have been neglected and require special aid for rural development, says A. J. Cooper of Prichard, Alabama, chairman of the Southern Conference of Black Mayors; and there is also a need to use the income derived from natural resources to combat the crippling effects of widespread rural poverty. More attention is focused, however, on the problems of black-led medium and large cities with populations of 25,000 or more—the size of city in which 80 percent of Americans live. Such cities are among the poorest and most overcrowded in the nation and suffer from a wasting disease, the "dying city syndrome."

At first sight, medium and large cities with black mayors appear to be productive and, in some cases, attractive. Gary is the home of U.S. Steel. Detroit is famous as "Motown," the head-quarters of automotive manufacturing. Major educational institutions are located in Los Angeles; Berkeley; Atlanta; College Park, Maryland; Boulder, Colorado; Chapel Hill, North Carolina; and New Brunswick, New Jersey. Washington, D.C., is a tourist's delight and the focal point of a key national industry—government. In every one of them, however, there are the unmistakable symptoms of the urban crisis—decay, high density, poverty, housing problems, fiscal insolvency, and white exodus. Moreover, black mayors are severely constrained in their ability to exercise decisive controlling power and influence; and there are several important reasons why this is so, as Dr. Herrington J. Bryce has pointed out in a study published in 1974. In most of these cities blacks are a distinct minority. The majority voting populations are white and easily stampeded by rumors of black excesses in city hall and on the streets. Furthermore, the checks and balances set by city charters and prevailing forms of urban governance—the city commission and council-manager systems—all limit the mayor's veto and statutory powers over budgets, appointments, and other crucial aspects of city management. The hard, cold facts are, therefore, that black mayors in medium and large cities are elected by a white public to serve its needs. The mayors are in no position to redress existing grievances in favor of minority blacks, many of whom make up a disproportionate share of the needy. In sum, the power of the black mayor to change existing inequities rests, regardless of his presumed race-oriented goals, on little more than the persuasiveness of his own personality and the good will and respect he can muster from time to time among his fellow legislators and the public.

The situation takes on a more dramatic focus when one looks at the most prestigious of the big-city mayors. Richard Hatcher of Gary was first in 1967. Carl Stokes, who served two two-year terms in Cleveland, Ohio, in 1967 and 1969, was second. Kenneth Gibson was elected mayor of Newark in 1970, and 1973 produced a bumper crop as Thomas Bradley of Los Angeles, Maynard Jackson of Atlanta, and Coleman Young of Detroit entered city hall. In 1974 Walter Washington was elected mayor of the nation's capital. Furthermore, New York's Deputy Mayor Paul Gibson and Manhattan's Borough President Percy Sutton have moved into key positions. If current trends persist, there may be five more black mayors in office before the turn of the century in Baltimore, St. Louis, Chicago, New York, and Philadelphia. But big-city mayors face overwhelming problems on every front. Creating an effective party machinery to get apathetic black voters to the polls is one. Combating racially discriminatory gerrymandering is another. And black mayors are particularly hard-pressed as they seek to placate business interests and suburban whites and rejuvenate ailing cities with large poor and black central-city populations.

Detroit's Twelfth Street, heart of the 1967 riot and the local business area, has collapsed. In this automotive city, where blacks make up some 44 percent of the population, Mayor Coleman Young has his hands full dealing with a declining tax base, increasingly obsolescent factories, and the unsympathetic attitude of white ethnics and trade unions toward black entry into new jobs and new areas. Despite his earlier claims of undying support from the black masses, Mayor Young's authority depends ultimately on maintaining the good will of middle-class whites and city financial interests and support from black political elites such as Congressmen Charles Diggs and John Conyers.

The old commercial corridors in the black communities of Washington, D.C., were badly hit after the assassination of Dr. Martin Luther King, Jr. In 1974 the city held its first elections for a mayor and city council after regaining home rule from Congress, and Walter Washington was elected to a four-year term. Before that, he had been appointed mayor. Eleven of the thirteen members of the new city council are black, as is Walter Fauntroy, who is the city's delegate to Congress. The new black political establishment now firmly in control of the nation's capital faces a Herculean task of opening up new pathways of hope in a city with a sordid history of racial injustice and neglect.

Atlanta's blacks are 51 percent of the city's population and about 45 percent of its registered voters. Now that the boom period of economic growth has abated, Mayor Maynard Jackson will have formidable difficulties in reconciling the needs and requirements of suburban whites with those of central-city blacks, who still lag far behind in housing, health, and education. Support for Jackson's temperate urban policies comes from Georgia state senator Julian Bond and from Andrew Young, adviser to the late Dr. King, confidant of President Carter, and recently appointed ambassador to the United Nations. On the city level, however, Mayor Jackson will require greater support from the white populace in general and from black officeholders in appointed and elected offices.

Newark claims the first black mayor of a major Northeastern urban area. Alabama-born Mayor Gibson was trained as a transportation and structural engineer and takes direct interest in the work of the city planning commission. But he has discovered life, as the old Negro adage says, "ain't no crystal stair." Newark's traditional assets of central location and access to rail and river transportation have been devalued by the advent of giant superhighways and electronic communication. The Newark Airport expansion program may bring more fiscal headaches than it solves, according to some observers, and seems destined to contribute few gains to black and low-income workers. The city's 54 percent black and 10 percent Puerto Rican groups, mainly central-area residents, bear the brunt of urban decay and suffer a variety of burdens. Newark has the greatest percentage of slum housing, the highest crime rate per capita, the heaviest tax burdens, and the highest incidence of venereal disease and infant mortality of any large American city. Newark is a very sick city, and local pundits say that wherever America's cities are headed, Newark is likely to get there first.

Mayor Gibson has his hands full in a city where race relations are bad and the threat of racial violence is ever-present. His appointment of a black chief of police to deal with crime and the integration of the 1,400-man police force brought considerable resistance from white ethnic groups. Whereas only a quarter of the police are black, and 7 percent are Puerto Rican, the majority are whites of European immigrant backgrounds and live in the suburbs far from any concern with the plight of central-city blacks. Gibson's emphasis on shared power has gained him a modicum of good will among middle-class whites and wealthy businessmen but has increasingly alienated him from the black community whose strident demands for help he has been powerless to meet. In addition, he has to contend with the opposition of Imamu Amiri Baraka, who was instrumental in his election.

When black mayors assume office, they encounter vociferous public demands for better housing and social services. They also face rising costs, shrinking tax bases, and major cutbacks in federal urban-aid funds. Fiscal bankruptcy is an ever-present fact of municipal life, but in the rundown central cities it reaches crisis proportions. Budgetary cuts and freezes introduced by the Nixon Administration and maintained under President Ford halted or drastically diverted the flow of federal funds to cities, with severe effects, according to the authoritative publication of the National League of Cities, *The Federal Budget and the Cities.* Hardest hit are grants for economic development, public facilities and amenities, low-income and moderate-income housing, emergency employment measures, and social services.

In the light of these fiscal problems, the economic powerlessness of the black leader and the black community is all too apparent. As Mayor Hatcher observed shortly after taking office: "There is much talk about black control of the ghetto. What does that mean? I am mayor of a city of roughly 90,000 black people but we do not control the possibilities of jobs for them, of money for their schools, or state-funded social services. These things are in the hands of the United States Steel Corporation and the County Department of Welfare of the State of Indiana. Will the poor in Gary's worst slums be helped because the pawnshop owner is black, not white?" Without new sources of municipal finance, and more government aid, black mayors face a dismal future and a rising tide of unrest among their poor and black constituents if "political freedom" is not accompanied by economic improvement.

New black mayors must also cope with a growing public interest, particularly among white taxpayers and businessmen, in "metro-government"—the trend toward larger units of government on a metropolitan-wide basis to broaden the urban tax base and enable the efficient delivery of public services. Metro-government takes two basic forms. One creates regional and metropolitan-wide, multi-jurisdictional planning, development, and coordinating commissions outside the control of the electorate and the mayor. The other amalgamates the city with the wealthier suburbs and surrounding territories by annexation and city-county consolidation, with consequent structural changes in the organization, function, and power of the constituent jurisdictions.

Both forms of metro-government diminish the power of black political leaders. They can expect only token appointments to the commissions, and within the enlarged governmental units the black population percentage—and hence its power—will decrease considerably. In Northern cities like Newark and Detroit, where metro-government of the first type is most likely to be operative (mainly because Northern Democratic Party leaders and politicians are against city-county consolidation), black mayors will have to win concessions from multi-jurisdictional commissions responsible for spending federal funds for urban public services. In Southern cities, like Atlanta, where metro-government of the second type is most likely to be operative (mainly because of explicit anti-black attitudes), the threat of annexation and city-county consolidation of white suburbs will force black leaders to forgo pressing for widespread black control in favor of bargaining for gradual incremental changes and trade-offs. It is quite likely that in the hurly-burly of race politics the trend toward metro-government, in one form or the other, will grow in those metropolitan areas where the proportion of blacks in the central city is growing rapidly, and especially where it is approaching 40 to 50 percent.

Another set of problems facing black mayors relates to revenue sharing—a federal program sharing some $30 billion with states and localities. General revenue-sharing funds are distributed according to formulae based on population, tax contributions, and relative per capita income. Unrestricted use of funds is granted in broadly defined priority areas: public safety, transportation, environmental protection, and social services. In addition, special revenue-sharing funds are currently proposed for urban community development, law enforcement, and manpower training.

Revenue sharing was initiated by the Nixon Administration as the chief instrument of the President's concept of "new federalism," which called for the redistribution of authority among federal, state, and local governments. It broadly involved the shift of control of many federal programs back to states and localities in an effort to trim the power of the federal bureaucracy and restore the vitality of lower tiers of government. However, it is now widely held that revenue sharing has seriously undermined the position of underprivileged groups. A major bone of contention is the suspected undercount of the black population in the 1970 census, which shortchanges cities with high proportions of blacks in the distribution of general revenue-sharing money.

Black strategists fear that revenue sharing has had negative effects for the poor black and minority groups. It gives more power to state, county, and metropolitan authorities to influence decisions on the use of federal money and hence has had the effect of lessening the power of central-city populations and black mayors. There are few guidelines and controls on expenditures; conceivably, recreation funds could be spent on providing tennis courts and bridle paths in middle-class areas rather than vital amenities in poorer areas. Metropolitan-wide commissions receiving funds are too far removed from local interests and have not been required to submit their spending plans to government for approval. Finally, there are no iron-clad civil-rights guarantees with provision for effective community participation in the decision-making processes.

It is now clear that several challenges face black mayors and urban political strategists. There is the need to place more blacks in government, obtain more resources, and improve municipal services for black communities, especially school systems and the transportation links between homes, jobs, and shopping centers. Furthermore, land-use policies must be changed so that blacks can break out of the slums. If blacks are to stay in central cities, they need not be doomed to live perpetually as impoverished tenants in decaying tenements and vandalized public-housing projects. New programs of urban homesteading can offer families the opportunity to gain the requisite title and federal aid to rehabilitate vacant and abandoned dwellings. There is also the challenging need of capitalizing on the decentralization of federally supported housing and job programs; this means drawing on the strength of black elected officials at the county, state, and national levels.

Over the past decade black political awareness and sophistication have increased substantially. Leaders are learning how to create tactics to woo white and black voters; these include persuasion, bargaining, crusading, reform, and even revolutionary rhetoric. What is sorely needed is a new set of strategies to meet the challenges of urban governance: "danger-limiting" strategies to prevent structural changes considered dangerous, and "advantage-maximizing" strategies to increase political and economic strength when change is inevitable. New planning perspectives are also required; there must be a more systematic search for solutions to the plight of urban blacks and this requires the formation of comprehensive plans on which to base discussions about alternative futures for black communities in the next century.

Planning alternative futures for black communities necessitates a variety of new supportive organizations providing professional and technical assistance. Until recently there were only two overworked and understaffed agencies funded jointly by the Ford Foundation dealing with policy issues affecting black leaders and elected officials. In New York, the Metropolitan Applied Research Center (MARC) has served as an important catalyst for policy research. It began in the mid-sixties as a consortium of social scientists headed by Professors Kenneth Clark and Hylan Lewis and later Professor Charles V. Hamilton of Columbia University, and was dedicated to research and action to secure the rights of black and underprivileged groups using "every rational and ethical method of influencing public policy." In Washington, an associate group created in May 1970, the Joint Center for Political Studies, provides assistance to the nation's black elected officials. Funds from the Rockefeller and Ford Foundations help the JCPS sponsor campus-based seminars, conduct black political-participation surveys, and publish a monthly newsletter, *FOCUS*, and an annual *National Roster of Black Elected Officials*. JCPS also hosts non-partisan conclaves, for example, the 1975 Third National Institute for Black Elected Officials, to initiate strategies for effective use of the political system to improve the condition of blacks. Less-well-known efforts to inform political action have also been launched in Chicago and Atlanta. The Black Legislative Clearinghouse in Chicago, organized by Illinois State Senator Richard Newhouse, was founded to aid state legislators. The Southern Elections Fund in Atlanta, chaired by Georgia State Senator Julian Bond, supports mayoral campaigns in small Southern towns with black majorities. Despite its small annual budget, estimated to be $70,000, largely financed by white contributors, the fund was instrumental in the campaigns of more than four hundred black candidates, including the successful elections of A. J. Cooper in Prichard, Alabama, Clarence Lightner in Raleigh, North Carolina, and Bennie G. Thompson in Bolton, Mississippi.

What is more problematical, however, as far as planning alternative futures is concerned, is the paucity of qualified black city managers, urban designers, and urban and regional planners. Structures of urban governance rely quite heavily on the skills and services of professional city managers and administrators. This is especially true in the two systems most typical of cities having black mayors, namely, the commission and council-manager forms of government, in which the mayor is only the titular head of the city. According to recent estimates by a minority executive placement agency in Washington, there are only seven blacks among the 2,600 city managers in America, and the lone black chief administrator serves in Newark, New Jersey. The percentage of blacks serving as assistant city managers and department heads is equally dismal—about 1 percent.

Black architects, some four hundred out of an estimated twenty thousand United States architects currently in practice, have made a distinguished contribution to the field but, like their white counterparts, have been reluctant to give up their beaux arts tradition for a new advocacy role. The hope is that as new black architects are trained in the growing number of professional courses in black colleges, they will become involved in the search for solutions to urban problems. New and enlarged programs are required, however, in practical work and theory ranging from projects in community design and advocacy planning to renovating church basements and building low-cost housing estates.

The need for qualified black planners is, perhaps, greatest of all. Their precise number, though small, is not known. Planning is a relatively ill-defined discipline in America and has not yet proved as attractive to blacks as architecture, in which blacks are about 2 percent of the profession. Given the need, every city should have a center of black planning studies educating specialists in land management, fiscal administration, and social and environmental planning. (Some interesting steps in this direction are being undertaken at Pittsburgh's Carnegie-Mellon University School of Urban and Public Affairs, which has a 40 percent black enrollment, and the Center for Urban Affairs of the predominantly black Morgan State College in Baltimore, where students pursue planning and policy analysis studies in a community service context.) Special training must include the monitoring of the effects of planning proposals and large-scale urban projects. For example, in Houston, said to be "one of the healthiest cities in America" in terms of the job market, blacks were left out of the recent economic boom. The "Houston Plan" for blacks promised them more employment in the construction industry but lacks enforcement powers, and a $13 million Model Cities program has not come to grips with basic problems of housing and poverty. In Baltimore, the dockside improvement plan will have long-term blighting effects and repercussive social and economic impact on the black community, as will the land annexation and redevelopment activities of academic institutions, notably Johns Hopkins University and the University of Maryland's Baltimore campus. Similar results are expected in Newark following the completion of its central-area-redevelopment and airport-modification schemes. On the other hand, in Atlanta, according to planners and local political figures, the mass-transit plan of the city authority will disrupt black communities and fail to link them with city job centers. The same is true of the Washington, D.C., mass-transit plan.

Planning will also require much more research, knowledge, and information about the urban development process. What political and economic forces shape development initiatives? What options are there for restructuring the development process and for introducing community management and control so that the results of planning can be delivered quickly and efficiently? How can we translate a new goal of value creation for community benefit into concrete programs of social, economic, and cultural emancipation? Without better-informed planning approaches and the creation of better means of decision-making, there is little doubt that the plight of urban black communities, and more particularly of the new black cities, will be the same or worse than it is today, i.e., large numbers of poorer people, ill-serviced and without adequate jobs and amenities.

In sum, when whites move out of the central city, they do not forfeit power to the blacks they leave behind. They do not accept the reality of widespread black urban leadership in the seventies and eighties as they historically accepted Irish, Italian, and Jewish leadership. New systems of control are created which reduce the power of black leadership in city hall. As a result, the rise of black-controlled and even black-majority central cities could turn out to be a hollow prize. Many options will be closed to black politicians as they deal with essentially hostile forces in industry and government to gain resources. Severely limited choices will have to be made between advocating community control from a weak financial base or programs operated by distant federal controls. Between encouraging more jobs in the black community and dispersal of black workers, and hence black voters, into the expanding surburban employment centers. Between building a political base around a declining inner city and seeking the best trade-offs possible within a wider metropolitan system controlled by suburban whites and regional commissions.

Black cities are the black man's last hope, for better or worse. The future of black cities, and of race, class, and power relations within them, will not be uniform. Many black leaders will simply become showpieces—like the highly visible black receptionist in plush Madison Avenue offices. It would be a profound tragedy if, in keeping with ultra-nationalist and white-racist designs, the new black cities of America remain poor-black reservations controlled and manipulated by powerful external forces, led by conservative blacks in top-level posts, governed by a black middle class fattened on a black capitalist mystique, policed by enforcers of white control and by paramilitary youth gangs who also supervise illicit activities, and mollified by cultural organizations which create an aura of satisfaction while planners and architects make living conditions a bit more tolerable.

Fresh ideas and actions are needed to forestall this possibility and to plan for the material advancement of poor and slum-locked blacks. Most experts would agree that the rise of black politics, mayors, and urban concentrations can have significant consequences for urban governance. The challenge that lies ahead is how to change inherited structures to make them more responsive to present and future needs, and to prove that with black political leadership urban society can bring about social, political, economic, and environmental improvement in the lives of ordinary citizens.

Selected Bibliography

I have found most of the works mentioned in this bibliographical essay useful as background reading and in the writing of this book. Many of them are secondary works readily available to the general reader and the college student; however, no attempt has been made to include all the materials on which the book is based.

General Works

A recently published general reference work of note is Mabel M. Smythe, ed., *The Black American Reference Book* (Englewood Cliffs, New Jersey: Prentice-Hall, 1976); it includes excellent summary articles and comprehensive bibliographical notes, and updates information contained in an earlier work by the late John P. Davis, ed., *The American Negro Reference Book* (Englewood Cliffs, New Jersey: Prentice-Hall, 1966).

Three important sociological works of relevance are Gunnar Myrdal, *An American Dilemma* (New York: Harper & Brothers, 1944); Oliver Cox, *Caste, Class and Race* (New York: Doubleday, 1948); and Talcott Parsons and Kenneth B. Clark, eds., *The Negro American* (Boston: Houghton Mifflin, 1966).

Historical documentaries I have made use of include two works by John Hope Franklin, *From Slavery to Freedom*, 4th ed. (New York: Knopf, 1974); *An Illustrated History of Black Americans* (New York: Time-Life Books, 1970); and two works by Herbert Aptheker, *A Documentary History of the Negro People in the United States* (New York: The Citadel Press, 1967) and *Afro-American History: The Modern Era* (New York: The Citadel Press, 1973). An excellent source of scholarly observation and historical and contemporary documents are the works associated with August Meier. These include August Meier, Elliott Rudwick, and Francis L. Broderick, eds., *Black Protest Thought in the Twentieth Century* (Indianapolis and New York: Bobbs-Merrill, 1971); John H. Bracey, Jr., August Meier, and Elliott Rudwick, eds., *Black Nationalism in America* (Indianapolis and New York: Bobbs-Merrill, 1970); August Meier and Elliott Rudwick, *From Plantation to Ghetto*, 3rd ed. (New York: Hill and Wang, 1976); and August Meier and Elliott Rudwick, eds., *The Making of Black America*: Vol. 1, *The Origins of Black Americans*, and Vol. 2, *The Black Community in Modern America* (New York: Atheneum, 1969).

Chapter 1

A number of important works which shed light on the complexities of the black experience in Africa and the New World are Elliott P. Skinner, ed., *Peoples and Cultures of Africa: An Anthropological Reader* (Garden City, New York: Published for the American Museum of Natural History by Doubleday, 1973); C. L. R. James, "The Atlantic Slave Trade and Slavery: Some Interpretations of Their Significance in the Development of the United States and the Western World," in John A. Williams and Charles F. Harris, eds., *Amistad 1* (New York: Random House, 1970); Adelaide C. Hill and Martin Kilson, eds., *Apropos of Africa: Afro-American Leaders and the Romance of Africa* (Garden City, New York: Doubleday Anchor Books, 1971); and Roger Bastide, *African Civilisations in the New World* (London: C. Hurst and Co., 1971).

Some useful books dealing with the formation of the character of American society are Max Lerner, *America as a Civilization* (New York: Simon & Schuster, 1957); Seymour M. Lipset, *The First New Nation: The United States in Historical and Comparative Perspective* (New York: Basic Books, 1963); Richard Hofstadter, *America at 1750: A Social Portrait* (New York: Vintage, 1973); Daniel J. Boorstin, *The Americans*, Vol. I, *The Colonial Experience*, and Vol. 2, *The National Experience* (London: Pelican Books, 1965); and Arthur M. Schlesinger, Sr., *Birth of the Nation: A Por-*

trait of the American People on the Eve of Independence (New York: Knopf, 1968).

The themes of integration and separatism have a long and well-recorded history, as amply illustrated in the General Works already cited; some additional perspectives on these themes in different epochs may be found in Sterling A. Brown, ed., *The Negro Caravan* (New York: Arno Press and *The New York Times*, 1970); W. E. B. Du Bois, *Black Reconstruction in America* (New York: Meridian Books, 1964); Benjamin Quarles, *Black Abolitionists* (New York: Oxford University Press, 1969); Eugene D. Genovese, *In Red and Black: Marxian Explorations in Southern and Afro-American History* (New York: Vintage Books, Random House, 1968); Kenneth B. Clark, *Dark Ghetto: Dilemmas of Social Power* (New York: Harper Torch Books, Harper & Row, 1965); James A. Moss, ed., *The Black Man in America: Integration and Separation* (New York: Dell Publishing Co., 1971); Amy Jacques Garvey, *Garvey and Garveyism* (New York: Collier Books, 1970); C. Eric Lincoln, *The Black Muslims in America* (Boston: Beacon Press, 1961); E. U. Essien-Udom, *Black Nationalism* (University of Chicago Press, 1962); Robert Williams, *Negroes with Guns* (New York: Marzani and Munsell, 1962); Martin Luther King, Jr., *Where Do We Go from Here: Chaos or Community?* (New York: Bantam Books, 1968); and Alphonso Pinkney, *Red, Black and Green: Black Nationalism in the United States* (Cambridge and New York: Cambridge University Press, 1976).

Chapter 2

In writing this chapter on Malcolm X, I have consulted relevant biographies and life surveys: *The Autobiography of Malcolm X*, with the assistance of Alex Haley (New York: Grove Press, 1964); Peter Goldman, *The Death and Life of Malcolm X* (New York: Harper & Row, 1973); Louis E. Lomax, *To Kill a Black Man* (Los Angeles, California: Holloway House Publishers, 1968); and James Baldwin, *One Day When I Was Lost* (London: Corgi Books, 1974).

In addition, I have relied mainly on Malcolm's spoken words as recorded on tapes and records and as they appear in various collections of selected speeches and commentaries. These include George Breitman, *The Last Year of Malcolm X: The Evolution of a Revolutionary* (New York: Schocken Books, 1968); *Myths about Malcolm X: Two Views* by Reverend Albert Cleage and George Breitman (New York: Pathfinder Press, 1971), a reprint from *International Socialist Review*, September–October 1967, pamphlet; *The Assassination of Malcolm X:* 1. Unanswered Questions—George Breitman, 2. The Trial—Henry Porter, pamphlet (New York: Merit Publishers, 1969); *Malcolm X: The Man and His Ideas,* a speech by George Breitman, pamphlet (New York: Pathfinder Press, 1971); *Malcolm X: Two Speeches* (New York: Pioneer Publishers, 1965); *Malcolm X on Afro-American History,* expanded and illustrated edition, pamphlet (New York: Pathfinder Press, 1970); *Malcolm X: By Any Means Necessary,* speeches, interviews, and a letter by Malcolm X, edited by George Breitman (New York: Pathfinder Press, 1970); and *Malcolm X Speaks,* selected speeches and statements, edited with prefatory notes by George Breitman (New York: Merit Publishers, 1965).

I have also found extremely useful *Malcolm X: The Man and His Times,* edited, with an introduction and commentary, by John Henrik Clarke (New York: Collier Books, 1969); *The Speeches of Malcolm X at Harvard,* edited, with an introductory essay, by Archie Epps (New York: Morrow, 1968); *Malcolm X: The End of White World Supremacy,* four speeches, edited and with an introduction by Benjamin Goodman (New York: Merlin House, distributed by Monthly Review Press, 1971); Louis E. Lomax, *When the Word Is Given: A Report on Elijah Muhammad, Malcolm X, and the Black Muslim World* (Cleveland, Ohio: World, 1963); *The Negro Protest:* James Baldwin, Malcolm X, and Martin Luther King, Jr., talk with Kenneth B. Clark (Boston: Beacon Press, 1963); and Robert Penn Warren, *Who Speaks for the Negro?* (New York: Random House, 1965).

Chapter 3

Among the best bibliographical sources relating to the period of the sixties is "The Black Revolt of the 1960's," in August Meier and Elliott Rudwick, *From Plantation to Ghetto,* 3rd edition (New York: Hill and Wang, 1976). Excellent material of a background nature may also be found in Lewis M. Killian and Charles Grigg, *Racial Crisis in America* (Englewood Cliffs, New Jersey: Prentice-Hall, 1964); Patricia W. Romero, ed., *In Black America 1968: The Year of Awakening* (Washington, D.C.: The Association for the Study of Negro Life and History, International Library of Negro Life and History, 1969); and John Hope Franklin and Isidore Starr, eds., *The Negro in Twentieth Century America: A Reader on the Struggle for Civil Rights* (New York: Vintage Books, 1967).

Insights to the opposing views of civil-rights integrationists and Black Power militants may be discovered in Floyd B. Barbour, ed., *The Black Power Revolt: A Collection of Essays* (Boston: Porter Sargent Publishers,

1968); Lerone Bennett, *What Manner of Man: A Biography of Martin Luther King* (Chicago: Johnson Publishing Co., 1964); Bayard Rustin, *Down the Line: The Collected Writings of Bayard Rustin* (Chicago: Quadrangle Books, 1971); Stokely Carmichael, *Stokely Speaks* (New York: Random House, 1971); Julius Lester, *Look Out, Whitey, Black Power's Gon' Get Your Mama* (New York: Dial Press, 1968) and his *Revolutionary Notes* (New York: Grove Press, 1969); Stokely Carmichael and Charles V. Hamilton, *Black Power: The Politics of Liberation in America* (London: Pelican Books, 1967); James Farmer, *Freedom When?* (New York: Random House, 1966); James Forman, *The Making of Black Revolutionaries* (New York: Macmillan, 1972); Len Holt, *The Summer That Didn't End* (New York: Morrow, 1965); and Joanne Grant, ed., *Black Protest: History, Documents and Analyses, 1619 to the Present* (Greenwich, Conn.: Fawcett Publications Inc., 1968). Two important appraisals of student activist groups are given in August Meier and Elliott Rudwick, *CORE: A Study in the Civil Rights Movement, 1942–1968* (New York: Oxford University Press, 1973) and Howard Zinn, *SNCC—The New Abolitionists* (Boston: Beacon Press, 1964).

The causes and dimensions of conflict and violence are discussed in, among others, R. H. Connery, ed., *Urban Riots: Violence and Social Change*, Proceedings of the Academy of Political Science, Columbia University, New York, 1968; *Report of the National Advisory Commission on Civil Disorders* (New York: Bantam Books, 1968); *Violence in America: Historical and Comparative Perspectives*, a Report to the National Commission on the Causes and Prevention of Violence (New York: Signet Books, 1969); and *The Politics of Protest*, a Report Submitted by Jerome H. Skolnick, Director, Task Force on Violent Aspects of Protest and Confrontation of the National Commission on the Causes and Prevention of Violence (New York: Simon & Schuster, Clarion Books, 1969).

Chapter 4

A literature associated with the concept of revolutionary black nationalism is still to be developed, and in its absence one must make reference to the printed statements in various forms, from street handouts and prison letters to hastily compiled autobiographies, of the best-known militant spokesmen. These include Bobby Seale, *Seize the Time: The Story of the Black Panther Party and Huey Newton* (New York: Harcourt Brace Jovanovich, 1973); Huey P. Newton, *Revolutionary Suicide* (New York: Harcourt Brace Jovanovich, 1973); and *To Die for the People: The Writings of Huey*

P. Newton (New York: Vintage Books, 1972); Philip S. Foner, ed., *The Black Panthers Speak* (New York: Lippincott, 1970); Imamu Baraka (LeRoi Jones), *African Congress: A Documentary of the First Modern Pan-African Congress* (New York: Morrow, 1972); H. Rap Brown, *Die Nigger Die* (New York: Dial Press, 1969); Eldridge Cleaver, *Soul on Ice* (New York: Mc-Graw-Hill, 1968) and *Post-Prison Writings and Speeches*, edited and with an introduction by Robert Scheer (London: Panther Books, 1971); and Angela Davis, *An Autobiography* (New York: Random House, 1974).

Of special relevance to the prisoners' movement are the works of George Jackson, *Soledad Brother, The Prison Letters of George Jackson* (New York: Bantam Books, 1970) and *Blood in My Eye* (New York: Random House, 1972); Angela Davis, *If They Come in the Morning* (New York: Third Press, 1971); *Attica: Official Report of the New York State Special Commission* (New York: Bantam Books, 1972); *Who Took the Weight? Black Voices from Norfolk Prison, an Anthology of Poems, Essays, Stories and Plays*, with an introduction by Elma Lewis (Boston: Little, Brown, 1972); and Etheridge Knight and other inmates of the Indiana State Prison, *Black Voices from Prison* (New York: Pathfinder Press, 1970).

Chapter 5

Recent black contributions to the cultural arts are accorded a comprehensive review in Mabel M. Smythe, ed., *The Black American Reference Book*. Some examples of the ways in which black writers, poets, and dramatists grapple with problems of redefining black cultural identity are Clarence Major, ed., *The New Black Poetry* (New York: International Publishers, 1969); A. X. Nicholas, ed., *The Poetry of Soul* (New York: Bantam Books, 1971); *You Better Believe It: Black Verse in English from Africa, the West Indies and the United States*, selected and annotated by Paul Breman (London: Penguin Books, 1973); Addison Gayle, ed., *Black Expression* (New York: Weybright and Talley, 1969) and *The Black Aesthetic* (New York: Doubleday, 1972); Ralph Ellison, *Shadow and Act* (New York: Random House, 1964); Mercer Cook and Stephen E. Henderson, *The Militant Black Writer in Africa and the United States* (Madison: University of Wisconsin Press, 1969); Abraham Chapman, ed., *Black Voices: An Anthology of Afro-American Literature* (New York: Mentor Books, 1968) and *New Black Voices* (New York: Mentor Books, 1972); Ed Bullins, *Five Plays by Ed Bullins* (New York: Bobbs-Merrill, 1968); Dudley Randall and Margaret Burroughs, *For Malcolm* (Detroit: Broadside Press, 1967); Ben Caldwell et al., *A Black Quartet: Four New Black Plays*, with an introduction by Clayton Riley (New York: New American Library, 1970); and James Baldwin and Nikki Giovanni, A *Dialogue* (Philadelphia and New York: Lippincott, 1973).

Among the many observations of black culture, high and low, male and female, sacred and secular, I found the following works quite useful: Charles V. Hamilton, *The Black Preacher in America* (New York: Morrow, 1972); E. Franklin Frazier, *The Negro Church in America* (New York: Schocken Books, 1963); Robert G. Weisbord and Arthur Stein, *Bittersweet Encounter: The Afro-American and the American Jew* (New York: Schocken Books, 1972); Clarence Major, *Black Slang: A Dictionary of Afro-American Talk* (New York: International Publishers, 1970); Toni Cade, ed., *The Black Woman: An Anthology* (New York: Signet Books, 1970); Gerda Lerner, ed., *Black Woman in White America: A Documentary History* (New York: Vintage Books, 1973); Harold Cruse, *The Crisis of the Negro Intellectual* (New York: Morrow, 1967) and *Rebellion or Revolution* (New York: Morrow, 1968); William H. Grier and Price M. Cobbs, *Black Rage* (New York: Basic Books, 1968); Herbert Hendin, *Black Suicide* (New York: Basic Books, 1969); Nathan Hare, *The Black Anglo-Saxons* (New York and London: Collier Books, 1970); Imamu Baraka (LeRoi Jones), *Blues People* (New York: Morrow, 1963); Armstead L. Robinson et al., eds., *Black Studies in the University: A Symposium* (New Haven: Yale University Press, 1969); Albert Cleage, Jr., *The Black Messiah* (New York: Sheed and Ward, 1968) and *Black Christian Nationalism* (New York: Morrow, 1972); and James H. Cone, A *Black Theology of Liberation* (Philadelphia: Lippincott, 1970) and *Black Theology and Black Power* (New York: Seabury Press, 1969).

Chapter 6

A range of issues relating to black economic development can be gleaned from William F. Haddad and G. Douglas Pugh, eds., *Black Economic Development* (Englewood Cliffs, New Jersey: Prentice-Hall for the American Assembly, Columbia University, 1969); Robert L. Allen, *Black Awakening in Capitalist America: An Analytic History* (New York: Doubleday Anchor, 1970); *The Black Middle Class*, special issue, *Ebony* magazine, Chicago, August 1973; E. Franklin Frazier, *Black Bourgeoisie: The Rise of a New Middle Class* (New York: The Free Press, 1957); Theodore L. Cross, *Black Capitalism: Strategy for Business in the Ghetto* (New York: Atheneum, 1970); Eli Ginsberg, ed., *Business Leadership and the Negro Crisis* (New York: McGraw-Hill, 1968); John F. Kain, ed., *Race and Pov-*

erty: The Economics of Discrimination (Englewood Cliffs, New Jersey: Prentice-Hall, 1969); Julius Jacobson, ed., *The Negro and the American Labor Movement* (New York: Doubleday Anchor, 1968); *The Neglected Black Majority: Essays on the Attitudes and Concerns of Some Forgotten Americans*, with an introduction by Bayard Rustin (New York: A. Philip Randolph Educational Fund, May 1971); and John H. Bracey, Jr., August Meier, and Elliott Rudwick, eds., *Black Nationalism in America* (Indianapolis and New York: Bobbs-Merrill, 1970).

Some extremely helpful research findings on black business and professions, and relevant statistics and summaries of economic and social data may be found in the journal *Black Enterprise*, New York, 1971 to the present; *The Review of Black Political Economy*, published by the Black Economic Research Center, New York, Vols. I–V, 1970–74; Michael J. Flax, *A Study in Comparative Urban Indicators: Conditions in 18 Large Metropolitan Areas* (Washington, D.C.: The Urban Institute, April 1972); *Characteristics of Negro Immigrants to Selected Metropolitan Areas: 1970*, Supplementary Report, U.S. Department of Commerce, 1970 Census of Population PC (S1)–47, June 1973, U.S. Government Printing Office, Washington, D.C.; Current Population Reports, *The Social and Economic Status of the Black Population in the U.S. 1971*: Special Studies, Series P–23, No. 42, U.S. Department of Commerce, Bureau of Census, July 1972, U.S. Government Printing Office, Washington, D.C.; and Current Population Reports, *The Social and Economic Status of the Black Population in the U.S., 1972*: Special Studies, Series P–23, No. 46, U.S. Department of Commerce, Bureau of Census, July 1973, U.S. Government Printing Office, Washington, D.C.

Chapter 7

Since the sixties, books by and about political figures have become a major publishing growth area. Some illustrative works are Nathan Wright, ed., *What Black Politicians Are Saying* (New York: Hawthorn Books, Inc., 1972); Mervyn Dymally, ed., *The Black Politician: His Struggle for Power* (Belmont, California: Doxbury Press, 1971); Shirley Chisholm, *The Good Fight* (New York: Harper & Row, 1973) and *Unbought and Unbossed* (Boston: Houghton Mifflin, 1970); Julian Bond, *A Time to Speak, a Time to Act: The Movement in Politics* (New York: Simon & Schuster, 1972); Dick Gregory, *No More Lies: The Myth and Reality of American History* (New York: Harper & Row, 1971) and *Dick Gregory's Political Primer* (New

York: Harper & Row, 1972). The dilemmas of party political leaders are clearly outlined in a basic work by James Q. Wilson, *Negro Politics: The Search for Leadership* (New York: The Free Press, paperback, 1965) and on a grander scale the effects of white American politics on black people are discussed in Samuel F. Yette, *The Choice: The Issue of Black Survival in America* (New York: Berkeley Medallion Books, 1971).

The publications of the Metropolitan Applied Research Center and the Joint Center for Political Studies have taken a prominent place in the literature devoted to policy and technical aid to black politicians; in particular I found useful *The Black Man in American Politics: Three Views, Kenneth B. Clark, Julian Bond, Richard G. Hatcher* (New York: A publication of the Metropolitan Applied Research Center, Inc., for the Institute for Black Elected Officials, December 1969); the *National Roster of Black Elected Officials*, 1975 edition (Washington, D.C.; Joint Center for Political Studies, 1975); Kenneth S. Colburn, *Southern Mayors: Local Problems and Federal Responses* (Washington, D.C.: Joint Center for Political Studies, 1974); and articles in the center's monthly newsletter, *FOCUS*, especially the contributions of Herrington J. Bryce, "Problems of Governing American Cities: The Case of Medium and Large Cities with Black Mayors" (August 1974), and "Black Mayors of Medium and Large Cities: How Much Statutory Power Do They Have?" (October 1974), and Morton H. Sklar, "Revenue Sharing: What Share for Minorities?" (March 1975).

Urban geography and city planning in the context of black urban affairs are the subjects of Harold M. Rose, "The Spatial Development of Black Residential Subsytems," *Economic Geography*, Vol. 48, No. 1 (January 1972) and his article "The Origin and Pattern of Development of Urban Black Social Areas," in *The Journal of Geography*, Vol. LXVIII, No. 6 (September 1969); Walter W. Stafford and Joyce Ladner, "Comprehensive Planning and Racism," *Journal of the American Institute of Planners*, Vol. XXXV, No. 2 (March 1969); and Joyce Ladner and Walter W. Stafford, "Black Repression in the Cities," *Black Scholar* (April 1970).

Varying issues associated with black urban life are dealt with in Hollis R. Lynch, *The Black Urban Condition* (New York: Thomas Y. Crowell, 1973); August Meier and Elliott Rudwick, *From Plantation to Ghetto* (New York: Hill and Wang, 3rd ed., 1976); Kenneth B. Clark, "The Negro and the Urban Crisis," in Kermit Gordon, ed., *Agenda for the Nation* (New York: Doubleday, 1968); Nathan Glazer and Daniel P. Moynihan, *Beyond the Melting Pot: The Negroes, Puerto Ricans, Jews, Italians, and Irish of New York City*, 2d ed. (Cambridge, Mass.: M.I.T. Press, 1970); Kenneth B. Clark, *Dark Ghetto: Dilemmas of Social Power* (New York:

Harper Torch Books, Harper & Row, 1967); *Black Cities: Colonies or City States?*, special issue, *Black Scholar* (April 1970); and LeRoi Jones, *Home: Social Essays* (New York: Morrow, 1966).

Finally, two main obstacles to the new black politics, that is, the ethnic backlash and the economic pinch on federal aid to cities, are clearly evident in P. C. Sexton and B. Sexton, *Blue Collars and Hard Hats: The Working Class and the Future of American Politics* (New York: Vintage Books, 1971) and The National League of Cities, *The Federal Budget and the Cities* (Washington, D.C., February 1973).

Index